FIRE IN THE VALLEY

FIRE IN THE VALLEY
The Making of the Personal Computer

Paul Freiberger
Michael Swaine

Osborne/McGraw-Hill
Berkeley, California

Published by

Osborne/McGraw-Hill
2600 Tenth Street
Berkeley, California 94710
U.S.A.

For information on translations and book
distributors outside of the U.S.A., please write to
Osborne/McGraw-Hill at the above address.

FIRE IN THE VALLEY

234567890 DODO 8987654

ISBN 0-88134-121-5

Mary Borchers, *Acquisitions Editor*
Judy Ziajka, *Project Sponsor*
Denise Penrose, *Technical Editor*
Ted Gartner, *Copy Editor*
Jan Benes, *Text Design*
Claudia Steenberg-Majewski, *Cover Design*

Cybernet is a registered trademark of Control Data Corporation; Microsoft BASIC is a registered trademark of Microsoft Corporation; Dazzler is a registered trademark of Cromemco, Inc.; PET is a registered trademark of Commodore Business Machines, Inc.; Apple is a registered trademark of Apple Computer, Inc.; Breakout is a trademark of Atari, Inc.; CP/M is a registered trademark of Digital Research; VisiCalc is a registered trademark of VisiCorp; Peachtree Software is a trademark of Management Science America, Inc., (MSA); WordStar and SuperSort are registered trademarks of MicroPro International Corporation; TRS-80, TRS Model II, and TRS Model III are trademarks of Radio Shack, a Division of the Tandy Corporation; Pocket Computer and Color Computer are registered trademarks of Radio Shack, a Division of the Tandy Corporation; EasyWriter is a trademark of Information Unlimited Software, Inc.; TI-99/4 is a registered trademark of Texas Instruments, Inc.; Lisa and Macintosh are trademarks of Apple Computer, Inc.; Osborne 1 is a registered trademark of the Osborne Computer Corporation; SuperCalc is a registered trademark of Sorcim Corporation; SoftCard is a trademark of Microsoft Corporation; IBM is a registered trademark of International Business Machines Corporation.

To our parents:

Ida and Norman Freiberger
Barbara and Earl Swaine

Contents

About the Authors

Paul Freiberger was born in New York City in 1953. He studied at the State University of New York at Binghamton, Middlebury College, and the University of Florence, earning a B.A. in history and an M.A. in Italian. He plays the clarinet and is a devotee of opera and Italian cuisine. He and his Macintosh computer currently reside in Palo Alto, California.

Michael Swaine was born in Minnesota in 1945 and grew up in Indiana, earning a B.A. in psychology and an M.S. in computer science from Indiana University. He enjoys reading, and writing, fiction and mathematical puzzles. Swaine is the creator of Mr. Usasi, the mathematical puzzle detective. He resides in Palo Alto, California.

Preface

This is the story of the development of the personal computer. We have sought to capture a sense of the period during which the events took place and to depict the people who had the vision to make the personal computer revolution happen. Our research grew into hundreds of hours of interviews with most of the principals, as each interview led to others and drew us deeper into the story. Many of the people we interviewed graciously supplied us with documents, records, letters, and photographs. The result is, in more ways than one, their story. Among others, we are grateful to the following individuals for sharing their experiences with us and thus with you:

Scott Adams, David Ahl, Alice Ahlgren, Bob Albrecht, Paul Allen, Bill Baker, Steve Ballmer, Rob Barnaby, John Barry, Alan Baum, John Bell, Ray Borrill, Dan Bricklin, Keith Britton, David Bunnell, Douglas Carlston, Hal Chamberlain, Mark Chamberlain, Alan Cooper, Ben Cooper, John Craig, Eddie Curry, Steve Dompier, John Draper, John Dvorak, Chris Espinosa, Gordon Eubanks, Ed Faber, Lee Felsenstein, Bill Fernandez, Todd Fisher, Richard Frank, Bob Frankston, Paul Franson, Nancy Freitas, Don French, Gordon French, Howard Fulmer, Dan Fylstra, Mark Garetz, Harry Garland, Bill Gates, Bill Godbout, Chuck Grant, Wayne Green, Dick Heiser, Carl Helmers, Kent Hensheid, Ted Hoff, Thom Hogan, Rod Holt, Randy Hyde, Peter Jennings, Steve Jobs, Gary Kildall, Joe Killian, Dan Kottke, Tom Lafleur, Andrea Lewis, Dave Liddle, Bill Lohse, Dorothy McEwen, Regis McKenna, Mike Markkula, Bob Marsh, Roger Melen, Edward Metro, Jill Miller, Dick Miller, Forrest Mims, Fred Moore, Lyle

Morill, George Morrow, Jeanne Morrow, Robert Noyce, Terry Opdendyk, Adam Osborne, Chuck Peddle, Harvard Pennington, Fred "Chip" Poode, Jeff Raikes, Ed Roberts, Phil Roybal, Seymour Rubinstein, Chris Rutkowski, Art Salsberg, Wendell Sanders, Ed Sawicki, Joel Schwartz, Jon Shirley, John Shoch, Michael Shrayer, Bill Siler, Les Solomon, Alan Stein, Barney Stone, Don Tarbell, George Tate, Paul Terrell, Glen Theodore, John Torode, Jack Tramiel, Bruce Van Natta, Jim Warren, Larry Weiss, Randy Wigginton, Margaret Wozniak, Steve Wozniak, and Greg Yob.

We wrote this book using personal computers designed by Lee Felsenstein, Steve Wozniak, and Steve Jobs, and software designed by Gary Kildall and Rob Barnaby.

Paul Freiberger
Michael Swaine
Palo Alto, 1984

Acknowledgments

Many of the people involved in the development of the personal computer have not received the credit they deserve. Their story is an important one. Learning it and telling it has been exciting and challenging.

Naturally, any errors or omissions are our responsibility alone. But we could not have told this story without the help of talented and understanding friends and colleagues. Special thanks to: Eva Langfeldt and John Barry for reading our initial proposal; David Needle for his research assistance on the East Coast; Thom Hogan for providing useful comments and suggestions; Dan McNeill for editing and finding the right word so many times; Cindy Martin for proofreading; Nelda Cassuto for editing, indexing, and for delicious zabaglione; Levi Thomas for her photographic expertise; our editors at Osborne/McGraw-Hill, Judy Ziajka, Denise Penrose, and Ted Gartner.

Introduction

In the late 1960s a group of Seattle teenagers met each afternoon outside Lakeside High, the private suburban high school they attended, and biked to the offices of a local company. Although the company's employees were going home for the evening and the firm was officially closing, the boys were just getting started. They thought of themselves as an unofficial night shift. Every night they worked till long after dark, pounding the keys of the company's DEC (Digital Equipment Corporation) computer, while dining on carry-out pizza and soft drinks.

The leaders of the group were an unusual pair. More than any of the others, they were fascinated by computers; in fact, this fascination had earned them the label "computer nuts" among their classmates. Paul Allen, a soft-spoken 15-year-old, would have paid for the chance to work on the machines. His friend Bill Gates, 13 years old and looking even younger, was proud of his abilities in mathematics and was hooked on programming.

Gates, Allen, and the others had been hired—"allowed" might be a better word, since they worked for the fun of it, without pay—to find errors in the computer's programming. Computer Center Corporation (the boys called it C Cubed) was happy to have them around. According to the terms of C Cubed's contract with DEC, as long as C Cubed could show DEC that DEC's programs had bugs (errors that caused the programs to malfunction or "crash"), C Cubed didn't have to pay DEC for using the computer. The kids were postponing the day when C Cubed had to pay its bill to DEC.

The DEC programs were new and complex, and there was nothing surprising in the fact that they were not entirely error-free. DEC's arrangement with C Cubed was a common technique for tracking down the subtlest bugs in such complex programs, and the kids found plenty of bugs in the next six months, with young Bill Gates finding more than his share. The *Problem Report Book*, as the boys labeled the journal of their discoveries, grew to 300 pages. Finally DEC called a halt, telling C Cubed, as Gates later recalled it, "Look, these guys are going to find bugs forever."

Allen and Gates stayed on for some months at C Cubed after the other boys left, and eventually drew pay for their work. The computer they worked on was a marvel of modern engineering. DEC had pioneered the concept of the minicomputer, which changed the computer from a wall of circuitry affordable by only the federal government and the largest companies into a box the size of a refrigerator, a machine that medium-sized offices, factories, and academic departments could afford. But the minicomputer was just a step on the path of miniaturization that would lead to the personal computer. Allen and Gates, loving their work at C Cubed, found themselves dreaming of the day when they would own their own computers. "It's going to happen," Paul Allen used to tell his friend.

It happened. Today the personal computer is an established consumer product sold like a stereo system. Its sleek plastic case may be slender enough to slip into a briefcase. Flashy graphics and joysticks make it a programmable personal video game arcade. Its information storage is encyclopedic, its capabilities Protean. The personal computer — or microcomputer — can act as typewriter, calculator, accounting system, financial spreadsheet, telecommunications instrument, library, paint and easel, tutor, and toy. Personal computers, nonexistent as recently as 1974, are now in use in the office, in the home, in the laboratory, in the school, on airplanes, and at the beach. Retail outlets for these universal machines have in a few years become as common as camera shops. Almost overnight, a revolution has taken place: what was once a fearsome "electronic brain" tended by a white-coated computer priesthood is now a consumer product.

The personal computer field is now almost synonymous with "high tech," yet the machines did not develop in the well-equipped, antiseptic labs that phrase calls to mind. The personal computer and the personal computer industry were created by hobbyists such as Gates and Allen, working after hours in garages, warehouses, basements, and bedrooms. These "computer nuts" fired the personal computer revolution out of their own fascination with the technology. Their story is as unusual as any in modern business. It is the story of overnight millionaires bewildered by their success, populist engineers soldering in their garages machines that would change our lives, manufacturers afflicted with a spirit of fierce consumerism, consumers who accepted faulty merchandise for the fun of fixing it themselves, and a spirit of sharing of hard-won technical information — a spirit rare in any industry, but essential for the proliferation of the personal computer.

The fire of the personal computer revolution broke out in many places in the mid-1970s, but nowhere did the fire spread as it did in Silicon Valley, the center of high tech development in California. This is the history of that revolution in the Valley and elsewhere.

Timeline

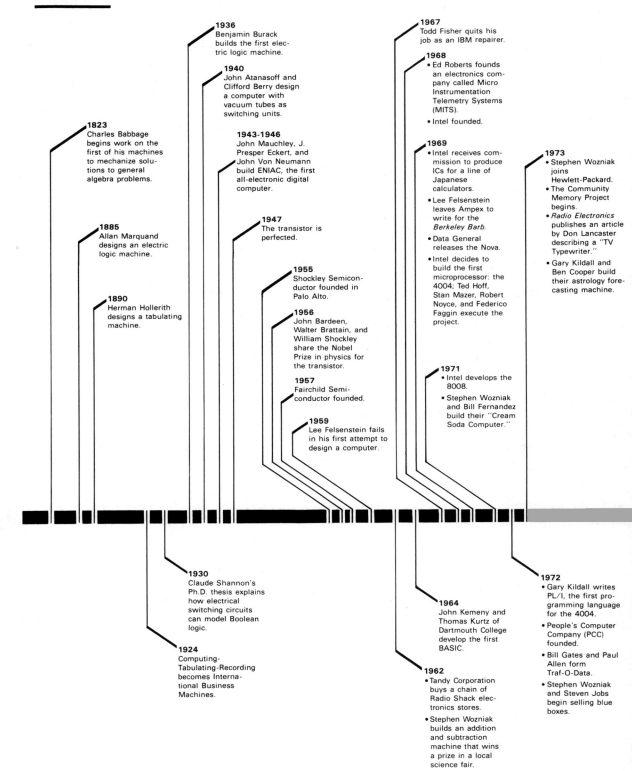

1823
Charles Babbage begins work on the first of his machines to mechanize solutions to general algebra problems.

1885
Allan Marquand designs an electric logic machine.

1890
Herman Hollerith designs a tabulating machine.

1936
Benjamin Burack builds the first electric logic machine.

1940
John Atanasoff and Clifford Berry design a computer with vacuum tubes as switching units.

1943-1946
John Mauchley, J. Presper Eckert, and John Von Neumann build ENIAC, the first all-electronic digital computer.

1947
The transistor is perfected.

1955
Shockley Semiconductor founded in Palo Alto.

1956
John Bardeen, Walter Brattain, and William Shockley share the Nobel Prize in physics for the transistor.

1957
Fairchild Semiconductor founded.

1959
Lee Felsenstein fails in his first attempt to design a computer.

1967
Todd Fisher quits his job as an IBM repairer.

1968
• Ed Roberts founds an electronics company called Micro Instrumentation Telemetry Systems (MITS).
• Intel founded.

1969
• Intel receives commission to produce ICs for a line of Japanese calculators.
• Lee Felsenstein leaves Ampex to write for the *Berkeley Barb*.
• Data General releases the Nova.
• Intel decides to build the first microprocessor: the 4004; Ted Hoff, Stan Mazer, Robert Noyce, and Federico Faggin execute the project.

1971
• Intel develops the 8008.
• Stephen Wozniak and Bill Fernandez build their "Cream Soda Computer."

1973
• Stephen Wozniak joins Hewlett-Packard.
• The Community Memory Project begins.
• *Radio Electronics* publishes an article by Don Lancaster describing a "TV Typewriter."
• Gary Kildall and Ben Cooper build their astrology forecasting machine.

1930
Claude Shannon's Ph.D. thesis explains how electrical switching circuits can model Boolean logic.

1924
Computing-Tabulating-Recording becomes International Business Machines.

1964
John Kemeny and Thomas Kurtz of Dartmouth College develop the first BASIC.

1962
• Tandy Corporation buys a chain of Radio Shack electronics stores.
• Stephen Wozniak builds an addition and subtraction machine that wins a prize in a local science fair.

1972
• Gary Kildall writes PL/I, the first programming language for the 4004.
• People's Computer Company (PCC) founded.
• Bill Gates and Paul Allen form Traf-O-Data.
• Stephen Wozniak and Steven Jobs begin selling blue boxes.

1975
- MicroSoft (formerly Traf-O-Data) writes the first BASIC for the Altair.
- *Popular Electronics* publishes an article describing the MITS Altair.
- Bob Marsh and Lee Felsenstein rent garage space in Berkeley.
- Cromemco founded.
- Homebrew Computer Club holds its first meeting.
- Amateur Computer Group of New Jersey founded.
- Processor Technology formed.
- Southern California Computer Society holds its first meeting.
- Dick Heiser opens the first retail personal computer outlet, The Computer Store, in Los Angeles.
- First issue of *Byte* magazine published.
- Paul Terrell opens the first Byte Shop in Mountain View, California.

1977
- Jonathan Rotenberg founds Boston Computer Society.
- David Bunnell begins publishing *Personal Computing*.
- Seymour Rubinstein joins IMSAI as software product marketing manager.
- The first ComputerLand franchise store opens in Morristown, New Jersey under the name ComputerShack.
- Apple Computer opens its first offices in Cupertino.
- Community Memory incorporates.
- The first West Coast Computer Faire is held.
- Apple introduces the Apple II.
- Commodore introduces the PET computer.
- Ed Roberts sells MITS to Pertec.
- Tandy/Radio Shack announces its first TRS-80 microcomputer.
- Adventure International founded.

1978
- Apple introduces and begins shipping disk drives for the Apple II.
- "Black Wednesday" firings at IMSAI.
- Apple initiates Lisa research and development project.

1979
- IMSAI files for bankruptcy.
- Steven Jobs visits Xerox PARC.
- Processor Technology closes.
- Tandy/Radio Shack announces the TRS-80 Model II.
- MicroPro releases WordStar.
- IMSAI closes its doors.
- Personal Software introduces VisiCalc.

1980
- Hewlett-Packard releases the HP-85.
- The Apple III is announced.
- Microsoft signs a consulting agreement with IBM to produce an operating system.

1981
- Osborne Computer Corporation incorporates and a short time later, introduces the Osborne 1, the first portable computer.
- Steve Wozniak suffers a plane crash.
- Xerox releases the 8010 Star and the 820 computers.
- IBM announces its Personal Computer.

1982
- Apple Computer announces Lisa.
- DEC announces a line of personal computers.

1984
- Apple Computer announces the Macintosh.

1974
- Ted Nelson's *Computer Lib* published.
- Intel invents the 8080.
- Xerox releases the Alto.
- John Torode and Gary Kildall begin selling a microcomputer and disk operating system.
- *Radio Electronics* publishes an article calling the Mark 8 "your personal minicomputer."

1976
- Ed Faber joins IMSAI as director of sales. IMSAI begins shipping its first computers.
- Bill Gates's "Open Letter to Hobbyists" lamenting software piracy published.
- George Morrow's MicroStuf founded.
- The first issue of *Dr. Dobbs* published.
- Data Domain founded.
- World Altair Computer Conference held.

- Gary Kildall founds Intergalactic Digital Research (later Digital Research).
- Trenton (New Jersey) Computer Festival held.
- Kentucky Fried Computers founded.
- Midwest Area Computer Club conference held.
- Steve Leininger and Don French begin work on Radio Shack's first microcomputer.

- Processor Technology's Sol appears on the cover of *Popular Electronics*.
- Stephen Wozniak demonstrates the Apple I at Homebrew Computer Club.
- Personal Computing Festival held in Atlantic City.
- S100 bus named.
- ComputerLand incorporates.
- Mike Markkula visits Steven Jobs's garage.

1983
- IBM announces the PCjr.
- Osborne Computer Corporation files Chapter 11.

- The first sale of CP/M.
- Michael Shrayer creates Electric Pencil.

Tinder for The Fire

Chapter 1

I wish to God these calculations had been executed by steam.

Charles Babbage

Steam

The personal computer sprang up in the mid-1970s, but its roots run deeper, beyond the giant electronic brains of the 1950s, to the "thinking" machines of 19th century fiction.

Could a machine actually think? This was a tantalizing and frightening question for the intellectuals of the 19th century. Two famous observers of the changes being wrought by science, Lord Byron and Percy Bysshe Shelley, sat out one rainy summer in Switzerland discussing artificial life and artificial thought, pondering whether "the component parts of a creature might be manufactured, brought together, and endued with vital warmth." Mary Wollstonecraft Shelley, a party to the discussions, mentally took notes of the conversation and expanded the theme of artificial life in her novel *Frankenstein*. Mary Shelley's book was a genuinely frightening allegory to readers in the age of steam.

The early part of the 19th century was an age of mechanization, and the symbol of mechanical power was the steam engine. The steam engine had first been put on wheels in that century, and in 1825 the first railway was opened for public use. Steam was the symbol of power and represented the mystique that electricity and atomic power would have for later generations. When in 1833 mathematician, astronomer, and inventor Charles Babbage worked out the first design for a steam-driven machine that he claimed would mechanize thought, many people looked upon him as a real-life Victor Frankenstein.

Although the limited precision of machine tools of that time prevented him from carrying out his design, Babbage was no idle dreamer; he worked on his Analytical Engine, drawing on the ideas of mathematicians like George Boole until his death in 1871. Babbage intended that the machine free people from the more boring aspects of thinking, just as some of the new machines of that era were freeing people from physical drudgery.

Babbage had a colleague, patroness, and scientific chronicler, Augusta Ada Byron, daughter of Lord Byron, pupil of algebraist Augustus De Morgan, and later Countess Lovelace. A writer herself and a fine mathematician, she thought it wise to reassure people that the Analytical Engine did not think for itself but could do only "what people knew how to order it to perform." What Ada Lovelace did not say, because she did not know it, was that the Analytical Engine was very close to being a true computer in the modern sense of the word. What people knew how to order it to perform was to be accomplished by means of coded instructions that would today be called software.

The Analytical Engine Babbage planned was to be a huge, loud, outrageously expensive machine, capable of storing 1000 numbers of 50 decimal digits each. Today this would be spoken of in terms of the *memory size* of the machine (memory is the word for a computer's internal storage). The Analytical Engine had a larger memory than the first true computers and early microcomputers of the 1970s had. It was to be capable of one addition operation — not logical operation — per second. The Engine was to be powered by steam. But neither the money to build the machine nor for that matter the precise technology to make the fine gears the Engine would require in large numbers was available. The machine, brilliantly and minutely designed over many years of Babbage's life, was beyond the technology of the time and was never built.

If the machining tools of the 1830s had possessed more finesse and Byron's daughter had been a wealthier woman, there might have been an enormous steam engine computer belching logical clouds over Dickens's London, balancing the books of some real-life Scrooge, or contemplating a chess move. But electricity was the force that was required to make the machine Babbage wanted.

In the 1860s, the American logician Charles Sanders Pierce began lecturing on the work of George Boole. In doing so he brought symbolic logic to the United States and radically modified and extended Boole's algebra in the process. Pierce probably knew more about Boolean algebra than anyone else in the mid-19th century, and by the 1880s he realized that Boolean algebra could be used to model electrical switching circuits. This realization meant that electrical calculating machines and logic machines could, in principle, be built. One of his students, Allan Marquand, actually designed an electric logic machine in 1885.

The "switching circuit" (or "switching unit" or "switching organ" or "relay organ" — there are many names for it) Pierce proposed to use to model Boolean algebra is one of the fundamental elements of a computer. Switching organs can appear in a wide variety of technological guises, including electrical circuits, but their logical function remains the same. Corresponding in some ways to the neuron in the brain, a switching unit is any device that responds to a specified stimulus or set of stimuli with an energetically independent response. The energy of the response — whether electrical, mechanical, or chemical — is not supplied by the stimulus but by an independent source. The stimulus merely directs the energy of the response, much like a valve or a switchman at a railway siding.

The substitution of electrical circuitry for mechanical parts allowed, among other benefits, a reduction in computer size. In fact, the first electric logic machine ever constructed was a portable device designed and built by Benjamin Burack to be carried in a briefcase. Burack's logic machine, built in 1936, was built to test the elementary deductive schemata called syllogisms. "All men are mortal," and "Socrates is a man," Burack could code into the machine. The logic machine would accept the conclusion, "Socrates is mortal." Improper deductions ("All men are Socrates," "Socrates is a woman") closed circuits and caused labeled lights to glow indicating the kind of logical error committed.

Burack's device was certainly a limited-purpose machine with limited capabilities. But practical special-purpose devices primarily dealt with numbers, not logic. Much earlier, Hermann Hollerith had designed a tabulating machine used effectively in the census of 1890. Hollerith's company was later absorbed by what came to be called the International Business Machines Corporation, and IBM was, by the late 1920s, making money putting special-purpose calculating machines in businesses and thereby automating routine numerical thought.

Spurred by Claude Shannon's PhD thesis at MIT explaining how electrical switching circuits could be used to model Boolean logic, IBM executives in the 1930s agreed to finance a large computing machine based on electromechanical relays. Although they later regretted it, IBM executives gave Howard Aiken, a Harvard professor, $500,000 to develop Mark 1, a calculating device much in the spirit of Babbage's Analytical Engine.

Babbage, though, had designed a purely mechanical machine. Numbers were to be stored in registers formed of toothed wheels, and carrying in addition was done via cams and ratchets. The Mark 1 was an electromechanical machine with electrical relays serving as the switching units and with numbers stored in banks of these relays. Calculation was a noisy affair; the electrical relays clacked open and shut incessantly. When the Mark 1 was completed in 1944, it was widely hailed as the electronic brain of science fiction fame. But IBM executives wailed when, as they saw it, Aiken failed to acknowledge IBM's contribution at the unveiling. And IBM had other reasons to regret its investment. Even before work began on the Mark 1, technological developments elsewhere had made it obsolete.

Electricity was making way for electronics. As others had earlier put electrical relays in the place of Babbage's steam-driven wheels and cogs, John Atanasoff, a professor of mathematics and physics at Iowa State College, saw how electronics could replace the relays. Shortly before the American entry into World War II, Atanasoff, with the help of Clifford Berry, designed the ABC, the Atanasoff-Berry Computer, a computer whose switching units were to be vacuum tubes rather than relays. This switch was an important technological advance. Vacuum tube machines could, in principle, do calculations considerably faster and more efficiently than relay machines.

The ABC, like Babbage's Analytical Engine, was never completed, probably because Atanasoff got less than $7000 in grant money to build it. Atanasoff and Berry did assemble a simple prototype, a mass of wires and tubes that resembled a primitive desk calculator. But by using tubes as switching elements, Atanasoff advanced the development of the computer. The efficiency of tubes would make the computer a practical possibility.

By the first third of the 20th century the advent of computing machines was obvious. What also seemed obvious was that they would be huge, expensive, and special-purpose devices. It took decades to belie the first two of those assumptions, but the last was already doomed.

Until the 1930s, machines had always been built to perform a specific task; British mathematician Alan Turing envisioned a machine designed for no other purpose than to read coded instructions *describing* a specific task and to follow the instructions to complete its own design. Within approximately a decade, Turing's radical theory became reality. The instructions became programs, and his concept, in the hands of another mathematician, John Von Neumann, became the general-purpose computer.

In 1943, at the Moore School of Engineering in Philadelphia, John Mauchly and J. Presper Eckert proposed and began supervising the building of ENIAC, which was to be the first all-electronic digital computer. ENIAC, with the exception of the peripheral machinery needed to get information in and out, was a pure vacuum tube machine, apparently based in part on ideas Mauchly got from a visit to Atanasoff. Mauchley and Eckert attracted to the project a number of bright mathematicians, including one brilliant mathematician named John Von Neumann.

Von Neumann got involved with the Moore School work and made various — and variously reported — contributions to ENIAC, but he also offered an outline for a more sophisticated machine called EDVAC. Von Neumann swung the emphasis at the Moore School from technology toward logic. He saw EDVAC as more than a calculating device: it could perform logical as well as arithmetic operations, it operated on coded symbols, and its instructions for operating on — and for interpreting — the symbols could themselves be symbols coded into the machine and operated on. This was the last fundamental insight in the logical development of the modern computer. By specifying that EDVAC should be programmable by instructions themselves fed in as data, Von Neumann created the specifications for the general-purpose computer. His EDVAC realized Turing's and Boole's abstract ideas electronically.

After the war, Von Neumann proposed a method for turning ENIAC into a programmable computer like EDVAC, and Adele Goldstine wrote the 55-operation language that made the machine easier to operate. No one ever used ENIAC in its original mode of operation again. When ENIAC was finished in early 1946, it ran 1000 times as fast as its electromechanical counterparts. ENIAC was a roomful of clanking teletype machines, whirring tape drives, and walls of electronic circuitry. It had 20,000 switching units, weighed 30 tons, and dissipated 150,000 watts of energy. With all this power ENIAC could handle 20 numbers of 10 decimal digits each. But even before construction was completed, ENIAC was put to significant use: during 1945, as completion was nearing, ENIAC was used to do calculations for Los Alamos.

A new industry emerged from World War II. Building computers became a business, and by the very nature of the machines, it was big business. The Remington Typewriter Company became, with engineers John Mauchly and J. Presper Eckert fresh from their ENIAC triumph, Sperry Univac, and for a few years "Univac" meant computer just as "Kleenex" meant tissue.

But Sperry Univac had some formidable competition. IBM executives recovered from the shock of the Mark 1 and began building general-purpose computers. The two companies developed distinctive styles; IBM acquired a blue pinstripe image, while the halls of Sperry Univac were filled, according to one observer, with young academics in sneakers. But whether because of image or managerial know-how, before long IBM had taken the industry away from Sperry Univac. Soon most computers were IBM machines, and the company's share of the market continued to grow.

And the market continued to grow too. Other companies developed, and they were generally under the guidance of engineers who left IBM or Sperry Univac. Control Data Corporation in Minneapolis spun off from IBM, and soon there were Honeywell and Burroughs, General Electric, RCA, and NCR. Collectively, these companies were to own the large computer market a decade or so later, but with IBM so far ahead of the others in revenues, they were often referred to as Snow White (IBM) and the Seven Dwarfs.

But IBM and the others were manufacturing "dinosaurs." A new kind of computer emerged in the 1960s. This machine was smaller and cheaper, and was named, in imitation of the popular miniskirt, the minicomputer. Among the most significant companies producing smaller computers were Digital Equipment Corporation (DEC) in the Boston area and Hewlett-Packard (HP) in Palo Alto, California.

The computers these companies were building were all general-purpose machines in the Turing-Von Neumann sense, and the computers were getting more compact, more efficient, and more powerful. Soon, however, a technological breakthrough would allow startling advances in computer power, efficiency, and miniaturization.

&

*Inventing the transistor meant the fulfill-
ment of a dream; almost the perpetuum
mobile.*

Ernest Braun and Stuart MacDonald,
Revolution in Miniature, 1978

The Breakthrough

In the 1940s, the switching units in computers were mechanical relays, opening
and closing, clattering like freight trains. In the 1950s, vacuum tubes took the
place of mechanical relays. But tubes were a technological dead end. They
could only be made so small, and since they generated heat, they could only be
placed so close to one another. As a result, tubes afflicted the early computers
with a kind of technological elephantiasis. But by 1960, physicists working
with solid-state elements had introduced an entirely different mechanism into
the field.

The device that consigned the vacuum tube and magnetic core to the back-
alley bin was the transistor, a tiny, seemingly inert slice of crystal with interesting electrical properties. The transistor was recognized almost immediately
as a revolutionary development. Many scientists feel that the transistor is the
only significant *scientific* advance embodied in the computers that are so omni-
present today. John Bardeen, Walter Brattain, and William Shockley shared the
Nobel Prize in physics in 1956 for their work on the innovation.

The transistor had more significance than the mere obsolescence of another
bit of technology. This device, the result of a series of developments in the
applications of quantum physics, changed the computer from a "giant electronic brain" in the exclusive domain of engineers and scientists to a commod-
ity like a television set. The transistor was the technological breakthrough that
brought forth the minicomputers of the 1960s and made possible the personal
computer revolution of the 1970s.

Actually, Bardeen and Brattain made the breakthrough that has been called
"the major invention of the century" six years earlier, in 1947, two days before
Christmas. But understanding the significance of the device that came into
existence in Murray Hill, New Jersey, that winter requires looking even farther
back in time.

In the 1940s, Bardeen and Shockley had both been working in an apparently
unrelated field. Quantum physics had made certain odd predictions about the
electrical behavior of crystals, and some physicists were intrigued by the distinctive behavior that crystals of elements such as germanium and silicon displayed in an electrical field. Since the crystals could not be classified electrically
as insulators or as conductors, they were called semiconductors.

Semiconductors had one property that fascinated electrical engineers. A semiconductor crystal could be made to act as a conductor for electrical current passing through it in one direction, but not in the other. Engineers had put this discovery to practical uses. Tiny slivers of such crystals were used to rectify electrical current, that is, to turn alternating current into direct current. Early radios, called crystal sets, were the first commercial products to use these crystal rectifiers.

The crystal rectifier was a curious device. With no moving parts, it was incapable of doing more than merely rectifying a current. A different device soon replaced it almost entirely. This item was Lee DeForest's triode, the vacuum tube that made radios glow. The triode was much more versatile than the crystal rectifier. It could amplify current passing through it and use a weak secondary current to alter a strong current passing from one of its poles to another. This ability to change one current by means of another, effectively a signal, was essential to an EDVAC-type computer design. At the time, though, some researchers felt the triode's main importance lay in telephone switching circuits.

Shockley was working for Bell Labs and was interested, as were other researchers, in a particular area of semiconductor research: the effect of impurities in the semiconductor crystals. These impurities, trace amounts of some other substance, could provide the extra electrons needed to carry current. Shockley convinced Bell Labs to let him put together a team to study the effect. He was convinced he could create a solid-state amplifier.

His team consisted of experimentalist Walter Brattain and, in 1945, theoretician John Bardeen. For some time the group's efforts got nowhere. Similar research was underway at Purdue University, and the Bell group closely observed the work there.

Bardeen finally solved the puzzle. An inhibiting effect on the surface of the crystal, he said, was interfering with the flow of current. Brattain conducted the experiment that proved Bardeen right, and on December 23, 1947, the transistor was born.

The transistor did everything the vacuum tube did, and it did it better. Semiconductor devices have a number of properties that make them preferable to tubes. They are smaller, they don't generate as much heat, and they don't burn out. Most important, the functions performed by several semiconductor devices can be incorporated into a single semiconductor sliver.

Next, researchers set out to create semiconductor devices that could perform more complex tasks. Such devices integrated a number of transistors—or tiny features about as complex as transistors—into a more complex circuit and were therefore called integrated circuits, or ICs. Since physically they were only tiny chips of silicon, they also came to be called chips.

Creating the chips was a complicated and expensive process and generated an entire industry. The first semiconductor corporations to begin producing chips commercially were the existing electronics companies. One very early start-up company, however, was Shockley Semiconductor, which Shockley founded in 1955 in his home town, Palo Alto, California. Shockley's firm employed many of the best semiconductor people in the world at the time.

Those people didn't all stay with the company. Shockley Semiconductor spawned Fairchild Semiconductor, and Fairchild spawned a number of other companies. A decade after Fairchild was formed, virtually every semiconductor company in existence could boast a large number of former Fairchild employees. Even the big electronics companies that entered the semiconductor industry in the 1960s, such as Motorola, employed ex-Fairchild engineers. And with some large exceptions — like Motorola, Texas Instruments, and RCA — most of the semiconductor companies were located within a few miles of Shockley's operation in Palo Alto, in the Santa Clara Valley. Since by this time nearly all semiconductors were made of silicon, the area came to be known as Silicon Valley.

The semiconductor industry grew with amazing speed, and the size and price of its products shrank at the same pace. Competition was fierce. At first there was little demand for highly complex ICs outside of the military and aerospace industries. Certain kinds of ICs were in common use in large, so-called mainframe computers and minicomputers, especially as memory chips — semiconductor devices that could retain data as long as power was applied to them. Other chips did not retain the data flowing through them, but changed it in assigned ways. There were chips that performed arithmetic operations and logic operations. The densest were the memory chips with hundreds of transistors apiece. But in the early 1970s, the runaway demand for electronic calculators provided semiconductor manufacturers with a market for a new and considerably more complex kind of chip.

*The microprocessor has brought electronics
into a new era. It is altering the structure of
our society.*

Robert Noyce and Marcian Hoff, Jr.,
"History of Microprocessor
Development at Intel"
IEEE Micro, 1981

Critical Mass

In early 1969, Intel Development Corporation, a Silicon Valley semiconductor manufacturer, received a commission from ETI, a Japanese calculator company, to produce chips — ICs — for a line of calculators. Intel had the credentials: it was a Fairchild spinoff, and its president, Robert Noyce, had helped invent the integrated circuit. Although Intel had opened its doors for business only a few months earlier, the company was growing as fast as the industry. An engineer named Marcian "Ted" Hoff had joined Intel as its twelfth employee, and when, within a year, he began working on the ETI job, the company already employed 200 people.

Hoff was fresh from academia. After earning a PhD, he continued as a researcher at Stanford University's Electrical Engineering department, where his work on the design of semiconductor memory led to several patents and to the job at Intel. Noyce felt Intel should produce semiconductor memory chips and nothing else, and he hired Hoff to dream up applications for these chips. But when ETI proposed the calculator chips, Noyce reconsidered. Maybe a custom job while the company was building up its memory business wouldn't hurt, he thought. Hoff was chosen to meet the Japanese engineers who came to discuss what ETI wanted.

The first meeting was brief, since Hoff left for a vacation in Tahiti the evening of the day the engineers arrived. The trip apparently gave him time for contemplation because he returned from paradise with a mission. It bothered him that the ETI calculator would cost as much as a minicomputer and would be almost as complex. Minicomputers had become relatively inexpensive, and research laboratories all over the country were buying them. It was not uncommon to find two or three minicomputers in a psychology or physics department of a university. Hoff had worked with DEC's new PDP-8 computer, one of the smallest and cheapest of the lot, and found that it had a very simple internal organization. Hoff realized that the PDP-8, a computer, could do everything the planned ETI calculator was to do and more. Yet the PDP-8 was not much more expensive than the ETI calculator would be.

To Ted Hoff this was more than a puzzle — it was an affront to sense. Hoff went around Intel asking why people should pay the price of a computer for a

fraction of the capacity. The question revealed his academic bias and his na-
ivete about marketing. *He* would rather have a computer than a calculator. The
marketing people patiently explained that it was a matter of packaging. If
someone only wanted to do calculations, there was no need to have to fire up
the computer and run a "calculator" program to make the machine emulate a
calculator. And people, even scientists, were put off, awed by computers. A
calculator was just a calculator, from the moment you turned it on. A computer
was an instrument from the Twilight Zone.

Hoff followed the reasoning all right, but he knew building a special-purpose
device when a general-purpose one was just as easy to construct was still
wasteful. Besides, he thought, generalizing the project made it more interesting. He proposed to the Japanese engineers a revised design, one loosely based
on the PDP-8.

The analogy to the PDP-8 computer was only approximate. Hoff was propos-
ing a set of chips, not a computer. But one of these chips would be the most
important in several ways. First, it would be dense. Chips then had a maximum
of perhaps 1000 features—the equivalent of 1000 transistors—but this chip
would have at least double that number of features. In addition, this chip
would, like any IC, accept input signals and produce output signals. But while
these signals would represent numbers in a simple arithmetic chip and logical
values (true or false) in a logic chip, the signals entering and leaving Hoff's chip
would be more complex. The input signals would form a set of instructions for
the IC, and the output signals might return data or control other chips or
devices.

As a consequence of this sophistication, the chip could extract data from its
memory and interpret the data as an instruction. In this way a whole set of
instructions could be stored in memory, and the chip would read the instructions and act upon them. This would enable the chip to run programs. The
customers were asking for a silicon Analytical Engine; Hoff set out to design a
silicon EDVAC, a true general-purpose computing device on a sliver of silicon.
Hoff's design resembled a very simple computer although it did not incorporate
some computer essentials like memory and facilities for human input and output. The term that evolved to describe such devices was "microprocessor," and
microprocessors were general-purpose devices specifically because of this programmability. By using the stored-program concept of Turing and Von Neumann and storing appropriate instructions permanently in memory, the calculator makers could make the Intel microprocessor act like any kind of calculator
they wished. That, anyway, was Hoff's idea. He was sure it was possible. But
the Japanese engineers weren't interested. Frustrated, Hoff went to Noyce,
who encouraged him to proceed anyway. When Stan Mazer left Fairchild to
come to Intel, Hoff and Mazer completed the design for the chip.

At that point they had not actually produced a chip. A semiconductor design
specialist would still have to transform the design into a two-dimensional pattern of lines, and this pattern would have to be etched into a chip of silicon
crystal. These later stages in a chip's development were expensive, so Intel did

not intend to go beyond the logic-design stage without talking further with the customers.

In October, executives of ETI flew in from Japan to inspect the Intel project. The Japanese engineers offered their ideas and Hoff presented his and Mazer's innovation. As a result, ETI decided to accept the Intel design and signed an exclusive contract for the chips. Hoff was relieved. Work began on the actual layout of the circuit the following spring under the direction of Federico Faggin, also recently hired from Fairchild. Hoff and Mazer had done the functional or logical design of the chip; they specified, in some detail, what it should do. Faggin converted that logical design into a two-dimensional pattern of features that actually *would* do what Hoff had hoped. They called it the 4004, which was approximately the number of transistors the device replaced and a measure of its complexity.

On one hand, a microprocessor was nothing more than an extension of the arithmetic and logic IC chips that semiconductor manufacturers had been making for years. It merely incorporates more of these functions onto one chip. On the other hand, there are so many functions, and they complement each other so closely, that their use involves learning a simple language. The instruction set of a microprocessor constitutes a programming language.

Today's microprocessor is the equivalent of a roomful of circuitry in 1950. The 4004 chip that Hoff designed in 1969 was a crude first step toward something that Hoff, Noyce, and the Intel management could scarcely anticipate. The 8008 chip that Intel produced two years later was the second step.

The 8008 microprocessor was developed for a company then called CTC—Computer Terminal Corporation—and later called DataPoint. CTC had a technically sophisticated terminal and wanted some chips for it. Hoff again suggested a larger-scale integration of the product. He proposed a one-chip implementation of the control circuitry, replacing its essential internal electronics with a single integrated circuit. Hoff and Faggin were interested in the project partly because ETI had an exclusive contract for the 4004. Hoff had been hired to come up with applications for Intel products, yet his 4004 was not reaching the open market. Faggin, working in the lab with electronic test equipment, had seen the 4004 as an ideal controller for testers. Since ETI had the exclusive rights for the 4004, Hoff felt that maybe this new terminal chip could be marketed and used in testers instead. Intel took on the job of designing and starting work on an 8-bit microprocessor—one that could transfer and operate on eight binary digits at once. The 4004 operated on only four binary digits at a time. This represented a significant limitation since, for instance, the 4004 could not even handle a piece of data the size of a single character—the letter A for example—in one operation. The 8008 could encode it all at once. Nevertheless, CTC's executives lost interest in the project because Intel wasn't making progress as fast as they had hoped. Intel found it had invested a great deal of time and effort in two highly complex and expensive products, the 4004 and 8008, with no general market for either of them.

As competition intensified in the calculator business, ETI asked to renegotiate the price on the 4004 downward. "For God's sake," Hoff urged Noyce, "get us the right to sell these chips to other people." Noyce did. But possession of the right, it turned out, did not guarantee that Intel would exercise it. Intel's marketing department was cool to the idea of releasing the chips to the general engineering public. Intel had been formed to produce memory chips, which were easy to put to use and were sold in volume like razor blades. Microprocessors presented enormous customer support problems for the young company. Hoff countered with ideas for applications. For instance, one could build an elevator controller around a chip. Moreover, the processor offered cost-reduction to an electronic design engineer, and the engineer would thus make the effort to design it into products. Hoff knew *he* would.

Hoff's persistence finally paid off, and Intel hired advertising man Regis McKenna to promote the product in a fall 1971 issue of *Electronic News*. "Announcing a new era in integrated electronics: a microprogrammable computer on a chip," the ad read. A computer on a chip? Technically the claim was puff, but when visitors read the product specifications for the 4004 at an electronics show that fall, they were impressed by the chip's programmability. And in an important sense McKenna's ad was correct: the 4004 incorporated the essential control and decision logic of a computer. Meanwhile, Texas Instruments had picked up the CTC contract and had also delivered a microprocessor. There were now three different microprocessors in existence.

Intel's marketing department had been right about the amount of support the microprocessors demanded. One kind of support was instructions for the user: the operations the chips performed, the "language" they recognized, the voltages they used, the heat they dissipated, and a host of other things. Someone had to write the manuals, and at Intel the job was given to an engineer named Adam Osborne, who would later play an important part in making computers personal.

Another kind of essential support was software. The chips, as general-purpose processors, needed programs, the instructions that would tell them what to do. The disadvantage of a general-purpose computer or processor is that it does nothing without programs. To create them, Intel first put together an entire computer around each of its chips. These computers were not commercial hardware products but development systems — tools to help write programs for the processor. They were also, although no one used the term at that time, microcomputers.

One of the first to begin developing these programs was Gary Kildall, a professor at the Naval Postgraduate School down the coast from Silicon Valley in Pacific Grove, California. Like Osborne, Kildall would be important in the development of the personal computer, and already in late 1972, Kildall had written a simple language for the 4004. Basically it was only a program that translated cryptic commands into the more cryptic 1s and 0s that formed the internal instruction set of the microprocessor. Although written for the 4004, the program actually ran on a large IBM 360 computer. With this program one could type commands on an IBM keyboard and generate a file of 4004 instructions that could then be sent to a 4004, if one were somehow connected to the IBM machine.

But connecting the 4004 to anything at all was no trivial task. The microprocessor had to be plugged into a specially designed circuit board with connections to other chips and to devices like Teletype machines. The development systems existed for that job, and so Kildall was drawn to the microcomputer lab at Intel, where the development systems were kept. Eventually, he contracted to write a language for Intel and produced a microcomputer version of a large, complicated computer language called PL/I. A computer language is a set of commands the computer can recognize. The computer can, however, only really respond to a fixed set of commands incorporated into its circuitry or etched into its chips. Writing a new language means creating a program that will translate the kinds of commands a user can understand into the machine's commands. PL/I was an odd choice. The microprocessors were tiny not only physically, but also logically. They got by with a minimum of logical equipment, and they were therefore hard to program. It was difficult to design any language for them, let alone a complicated one. A friend and co-worker of Kildall's later explained the choice, saying that Gary Kildall wrote PL/I *because* it was difficult. Like many of the most important programmers and designers, before and since, Kildall was in it primarily for intellectual fun.

The most significant software Kildall developed at that time was much simpler.

Intel's early microcomputers used paper tape to store information. It was essential to have a program that would allow the computer to control the paper tape reader or punch automatically, accepting the data electronically as they streamed in from the tape and storing them in memory registers, or locating the data in memory and feeding them out to the paper tape punch. The computer also had to be able to manipulate data in memory, keeping track of which registers were free and which were not at any given moment.

Programmers do not want to have to think about such routine tasks every time they write a program, and large computers automatically take care of these tasks by the use of programs called operating systems. To programmers writing in a mainframe language like PL/I, the operating system is a given. It is a part of the way the machine works, a feature of the environment. But Kildall was working in a more primordial environment.

At Intel Kildall wrote parts of an operating system that was very simple and compact, since it had to operate on a microprocessor. Eventually this operating system evolved into something Kildall called CP/M, and it made his fortune. But when he asked Intel executives if they had any objections to his marketing it on his own, they shrugged and told him to go ahead. They weren't going to sell it themselves.

Intel had already ventured beyond its charter in building microprocessors, and although the company was not about to retreat from that enterprise, there was solid resistance to moving even farther afield. Talk had come up about getting into end products, designing machines around the microprocessors, even about using a microprocessor as the main component in a small computer.

Microprocessor-controlled computers, however, seemed to have a marginal sales potential at best. Noyce felt that microprocessors would find their chief market in watches. The Intel executives discussed other possible applications, mostly "embedded systems" such as microprocessor-controlled ovens, stereos, and automobiles. But these were all products for someone else. There was strong opposition at Intel to making any product that could be viewed as competing against its own customers who sold such equipment.

And there was something else. Intel was an exciting place to work in 1972. Its executives felt that they were in the center of things, that microprocessors were going to soar. To Mike Markkula, the marketing manager for memory chips, as to Kildall and others, it seemed obvious that the innovative designers of microprocessors should be working at the semiconductor companies. They decided to stick to putting logic on slivers of silicon and to leave the building (and programming) of computers made from the chips to the mainframe and minicomputer companies. When the minicomputer companies didn't take up the challenge, Markkula, Kildall, and Osborne thought better of their decision and within a decade would each create a multimillion-dollar personal computer or personal computer software company.

&

We [Digital Equipment Corporation] could have come out with a personal computer in January 1975. If we had taken that proto-type, most of which was proven stuff, the PDP-8A could have been developed and put in production in that seven- or eight-month period.

David Ahl

Breakout

By 1970 there were two distinct kinds of computers and two kinds of compan-ies selling them. The room-sized mainframe computers were built by IBM and by Control Data Corporation, Honeywell, and the other "dwarfs." These machines were designed by a generation of engineers, cost a sizable fraction of a million dollars, and were often built one at a time as requested by customers.

Then there were the smaller minicomputers built by such companies as DEC and Hewlett-Packard. These machines were built in larger quantities and sold to scientific laboratories and businesses. They were only relatively cheap and small. The typical minicomputer cost tens of thousands of dollars rather than hundreds of thousands and might take up the space of a bookcase instead of a room.

The minicomputers used semiconductor devices to reduce the size of the machine. The mainframes also used semiconductor components, but they generally used them to increase density and thus create even more powerful machines. Semiconductor tools like the Intel 4004 were beginning to be used to control peripheral devices like printers and tape drives, but they could also be used to shrink the computer and make it cheaper.

The mainframe computer and minicomputer companies had the money, the expertise, and the unequaled opportunity to place computers in everyone's hands. It did not take a visionary to look down the path of miniaturization and see at the end a personal computer, one that would fit on a desktop or in a briefcase. In the late 1960s and early 1970s, these companies seemed the only logical candidates to bring out such a computer. And it was an obvious devel-opment. Since the time of Burack's syllogism machine, people had been build-ing desktop- or briefcase-sized machines that performed computer-like func-tions. Engineers in computer companies and designers at semiconductor companies knew that the trend for components to get cheaper, faster, smaller, and more powerful every year was one they could count on. The indicators pointed inescapably to the development, most likely by a minicomputer com-pany, of a small, personal computer. It was only logical.

But it didn't happen. Without exception, the existing computer companies passed up the chance to bring computers into the home and onto the desk. The next generation of computers, the microcomputer, was created entirely by individual entrepreneurs working outside the established corporations.

The reason was not that the notion of a personal computer had never occurred to the decision-makers at the major computer companies. At some of them, eager engineers offered detailed proposals and even working prototypes. In certain cases, projects to develop personal computers actually commenced. But the proposals were all rejected, the prototypes shelved, and the projects allowed to die. The mainframe companies seemed to think that if a market for low-cost, personal computers existed, the minicomputer companies would exploit it. But at the minicomputer companies, that just didn't happen.

At Hewlett-Packard, a company that grew up in the Silicon Valley and was producing everything from mainframe computers to pocket calculators, senior engineers studied and spurned a design offered by one of their employees, an engineer-without-degree named Stephen Wozniak. In their rejection, the HP engineers acknowledged that Wozniak's computer worked and could be built cheaply, but they told him it was not a product for HP. Wozniak eventually gave up on HP and built his computers in a start-up garage enterprise named Apple.

Likewise, Robert Albrecht, working for Control Data Corporation in Minneapolis in the early 1960s, quit in frustration over the company's unwillingness to look into a personal computer market. He was interested in computers as an educational aid. After leaving CDC, he moved to the San Francisco Bay Area and established himself as a kind of computer guru, publishing what could be called the first personal computer publication and disseminating information about how individuals could learn about and use computers.

The prime example of an established computer company that failed to explore the new technology was Digital Equipment Corporation. With annual sales close to a billion dollars by 1974, DEC was the first and the biggest of the minicomputer companies. DEC made some of the smallest computers then available. The PDP-8 — which had inspired Ted Hoff to design the 4004 — was the closest thing to a personal computer one could find. One version of the PDP-8 was small enough that sales representatives could carry it in the trunks of their cars and set it up at the customer's site. Broadly, it was a real portable computer. DEC could have created the personal computer. The story of its rejection of the idea gives some indication of the mentality in computer corporate boardrooms in the early 1970s.

DEC employee David Ahl had reason to remember that story. For him, it began when he was taken on as a marketing consultant in 1969. He had picked up degrees in electrical engineering and business administration and had not quite finished his PhD in educational psychology. Ahl came to DEC to develop its educational products line, the first product line at DEC to be defined in terms of potential users rather than hardware. When, responding to the recession in 1973, DEC cut back on educational products, Ahl protested and was fired.

He was rehired in a division of the company dedicated to developing new products, that is, new hardware. He soon became entirely caught up in the building of a small computer, smaller than any yet built. Ahl's group didn't know what to call the machine, but if it had survived, it would have been a personal computer.

Ahl's interests had already grown somewhat incompatible with DEC's hardnosed style. DEC viewed computers as an industrial product. "Like pig iron. DEC was interested in pushing out iron," Ahl later opined.

In the educational division Ahl had written an educational newsletter that frequently published computer games. After his departmental shift, he talked the company into publishing a book he had put together, *BASIC Computer Games*. He was starting to see the computer as an individual educational tool, and games seemed natural to that perspective.

Although DEC was not set up to sell computers to individuals, Ahl had learned something of the personal market for computers while working in educational products. Occasionally the division would receive a request from a doctor or an engineer who wanted a computer. DEC's machines were cheap enough to sell to these people. But the company didn't know how to handle these requests. There was a vast difference between selling a computer to an organization, which could hire engineers and programmers and buy support from the company, and selling to individuals. DEC was not ready to take on individuals.

The new product was intended to open the market. Although its price tag would keep it out of most homes, Ahl saw schools as the wedge. The machines could be sold in large quantities to schools, yet used individually by students. And Ahl thought Heath, a company specializing in electronics hobby equipment, would be willing to build a kit version for DEC, which would lower the price still further.

The new computer was built into a DEC terminal, where circuit boards thick with semiconductor devices were shoehorned around the base of the tube. To the designers it seemed that every square inch of the terminal case had electronics in it. The computer was heavy, but no larger than a television set. Ahl had not designed it, but he felt as protective of this computer as if it were his child.

He presented the plan to market personal computers at a meeting of DEC's Operations Committee. Kenneth Olsen, the president of the company and a figure regarded throughout the industry as one of its wisest executives, was there along with some vice-presidents and a few outside investors. As Ahl later recalled, the board was polite but not enthusiastic about the project, though the engineers seemed interested. After some tension, Kenneth Olsen finally said that he could see no reason for anyone to want a computer in the home. Ahl winced.

Although the board had not actually rejected the plan, Ahl saw that without Olsen's support it would fail. He was frustrated. He had been getting frequent calls from executive search firms known as headhunters, offering him jobs. The next time a headhunter called, he accepted. Ahl, like Wozniak and Albrecht and many others, had walked out the door and into a revolution.

I swore off computers for about a year and a half — the end of the ninth grade and all of the tenth. I tried to be normal, the best I could.

Bill Gates

Hackers

Had the personal computer revolution waited for the mainframe computer and minicomputer companies to act, it might still lie in the future. But there were those who would not just wait patiently for it to happen, those whose impatience led them to take their own steps toward creating the revolution. Some of these revolutionaries were very young.

While David Ahl was slowly losing patience with DEC, Paul Allen and his school friends at Seattle's private Lakeside High worked at C Cubed finding bugs in the work of DEC system programmers. They learned fast and began to get cocky; soon they were adding touches of their own to make the programs run faster, and Bill Gates was criticizing individual DEC programmers: "Hey, so-and-so made the same mistake again."

Perhaps Gates got too cocky. Certainly he was exhilarated by the sense of power he derived from controlling the giant computers. He started experimenting with computer security systems. On time-sharing computer systems, such as the DEC TOPS-10 system Gates knew about, many users shared the machine and effectively used it simultaneously. Hence, safeguards were built into such systems to prevent one user from invading another's data files or "crashing" the program — that is, causing it to fail and terminate — or worse yet, crashing the operating system, bringing the whole computer system to a halt.

Gates learned how to invade that system and later other systems. He became a "hacker," an expert in the underground art of subverting computer system security. His baby face and bubbly manner masked a very clever and determined young man who could, by typing just 14 characters on a terminal, bring an entire TOPS-10 operating system to its knees. He grew into a master of electronic mischief.

Hacking brought Gates fame in certain circles, but it also brought him grief. After learning how easily he could crash the DEC operating system, he cast about for bigger challenges. The DEC system had no human operator and could be breached without anyone noticing and sounding an alarm. On other systems, human operators constantly monitored activity. For example, CDC had a nationwide network of computers called Cybernet, which CDC claimed was entirely reliable at all times. The claim, for Gates, amounted to a dare.

A CDC computer at the University of Washington had connections to Cybernet. Gates set to work studying the CDC machines and software; he studied the specifications for the network as though he were cramming for an exam. "There are these peripheral processors," he explained to Paul Allen. "The way you fool the system is you get control of one of those peripheral processors and then you use that to get control of the mainframe. You're slowly invading the system." It was like invading the hive dressed as a worker bee. The operator observed the activity of the peripheral processor, but only electronically, in the form of messages on the terminal. Gates controlled all the messages the peripheral processor sent out. He hoped to maintain a veneer of normality for the operator to observe as he cracked the system wide open.

The scheme worked. Gates got control of a peripheral processor, electronically insinuated himself into the main computer, bypassed the human operator without arousing suspicion, and planted the same "special" program in all the component computers of the system. His tinkering caused "them all to crash at the same time," Gates later said, laughing. Gates was amused, but CDC was not, and he had not covered his tracks as well as he had thought. CDC caught him and sternly expressed its disapproval. Gates swore off computers for more than a year.

But hacking was the high art of the technological subculture. All the best talent was hacking. When Gates wanted to establish his credentials a few years later, he didn't display some clever program he had written. He just said, "I crashed the Burroughs; I crashed the CDC." Then they knew he was good.

When Intel's 8008 microprocessor came out, Paul Allen was ready to build something with it. He was also able to lure Gates back into computing. Allen got a manual and told Gates, "We should write a BASIC." BASIC was a simple high-level programming language that had become popular on minicomputers over the past decade. Allen proposed to write a BASIC interpreter—a translator that would convert statements from BASIC input into sequences of 8008 instructions—so that anyone could control the microprocessor by programming in the BASIC language. It was an appealing idea since controlling the chip directly via its instruction set was, Allen could tell, a painfully laborious process. Gates was skeptical. The 8008 was the first 8-bit microprocessor, and it had severe limitations. "It was built for calculators," Gates told Allen.

But Gates came up with the money anyway. They spent $360 on what Gates thinks was the first 8008 sold through a distributor, got a third enthusiast, Paul Gilbert, to help with the hardware design, and built themselves a machine.

By this time Gates and Allen were contemplating not BASIC, but a machine to generate summary statistics on traffic flow from a rubber tube strung across a highway. Allen wrote the development software, which allowed them to simulate the operation of their machine on a large computer so that Gates could write the software they actually needed. It took almost a year to get this project running. They called their company Traf-O-Data—a name that Allen is quick to point out was Gates's idea — and began approaching city engineers.

Traf-O-Data was not a brilliant success. Perhaps some of the engineers balked at buying from kids. Gates was then sixteen and looked younger. At the same time the state of Washington began to offer free traffic-processing services to all county and city traffic controllers, and Allen and Gates found themselves competing against a free service.

After this venture collapsed, Allen left for college. But TRW, a huge corporation that produced software products in Vancouver, Washington, had heard about Gates and Allen's work for C Cubed and offered them jobs in a software development group. At something like $30,000 a year, the job was too good to ignore. Allen came back from college, Gates got a leave of absence from high school, and they went to work.

For a year and a half they lived a computer kid's dream life. They learned a great deal, more than they had learned at C Cubed or working as Traf-O-Data. Programmers can be protective of their hard-earned knowledge, but Gates knew how to use his youth to loosen up the older TRW experts. He was, as he put it, "non-threatening." After all, he was just a kid. Gates and Allen also discovered the financial benefits that such work could bring: Gates bought a speedboat and the two often went waterskiing on nearby lakes.

But there were rewards in programming that appealed to Gates and Allen far more than slowly fattening bank accounts. They had worked late nights at C Cubed for no financial gain, and they pushed themselves at TRW harder than anyone asked them to. Something in the clean edge of the logic and the fairness of the game of programming had bitten them.

The project they worked on at TRW eventually fizzled out, but it had been a profitable experience for the two hackers. Later, Gates went off to Harvard and Allen took a job with Honeywell. It wasn't until Christmas of 1974 that the bug bit them again, but when it did, the bite proved incurable.

&

The Voyage to Altair

Chapter 2

You can't deny that Ed Roberts started the industry.

Mark Chamberlain

Ed Roberts? You gotta give him credit for doing the first one. But give the guy that published him as much credit: Les Solomon.

Chuck Peddle

Uncle Sol's Boys

By the early 1970s, signs of frustration were beginning to appear in the hobby electronics magazines, publications such as *Popular Electronics* and *Radio Electronics,* which were read by engineers and electronics hobbyists who worked regularly with computers and knew what they wanted and did not want in a computer. Most of all, these enthusiasts wanted more control over the machine. They didn't like waiting in line to use the tool of their trade or hobby; they wanted to be able to use it at home. Hobbyists wanted immediate access to the files they created on the computer, even if they were off on a business trip. They wanted to play games on it without someone telling them to get to work. In short, what these enthusiasts felt they needed was their own personal computers.

A major step toward the manifestation of this dream occurred in September 1973, when *Radio Electronics* magazine printed an article by Don Lancaster describing a "TV Typewriter." Lancaster, one of the more prolific contributors to electronics magazines, later published his idea in book form. He was nothing less than visionary: "Obviously, it's a computer terminal for time-sharing services, schools, and experimental uses. It's a ham radio teletype terminal. Coupled to the right services [which didn't exist then], it can also display news, stock quotations, time, and weather. It's a communications aide for the deaf. It's a teaching machine, particularly good for helping preschoolers learn the alphabet and words. It also keeps them busy for hours as an educational toy." Lancaster's TV Typewriter, though, was only a terminal, an input/output device to link the hobbyist with a mainframe computer. What the hobbyist wanted was a personal computer.

Even as Lancaster's article came out, Technical Editor Leslie (Les) Solomon of *Popular Electronics* was on the lookout for a computer story for his magazine. Both Solomon and Editorial Director Arthur Salsberg wanted to publish a piece on building a computer at home. Neither had the technical expertise to assess the practicality of such a venture — no one had — but they felt in their bones that it should work. They did not realize that their competitor, *Radio Electronics,* was preparing to publish an article on such a machine.

If a home-built computer design were possible, Solomon felt that it would come from one of his boys — the young, technically sharp *Popular Electronics* contributors like Stanford graduate students Harry Garland and Roger Melen, like Don Lancaster, who, along with some of the others, also wrote for *Radio Electronics,* and like Forrest Mims and Ed Roberts down in Albuquerque.

Solomon wanted something good. Designs were in fact coming in, but they were not from the stars, and he and Salsberg found them unimpressive. Solomon characterized them as "a rat's nest of wires," and Salsberg agreed: "They were terrible designs, they were tinker toys, they were kludges."

But Solomon encouraged his boys to send him their best, and they took him seriously. A colorful and ebullient editor with a wry New York wit, Les Solomon had come to be known to his boys as "Uncle Sol." He was close to them, carried on long telephone conversations with them, and visited their labs or workshops whenever he could. Solomon told them extraordinary stories, not always strictly factual, and entertained them with stunts such as levitating stone tables. Part of the fascination for some lay in determining how much of Uncle Sol was pure put-on.

Much like an uncle or a father, he often gave them advice. For example, when Garland and Melen submitted one of their designs, Solomon realized that they needed a distributor and put them in touch with Ed Roberts, president of an Albuquerque-based company called MITS.

Solomon himself had met Roberts some time earlier. While vacationing with his wife in Albuquerque he stopped to see *Popular Electronics* contributor Forest Mims. Mims enjoyed "Uncle Sol," who had a gift for tall tales and a fascination with gadgets, and wanted him to meet his business partner, Ed Roberts. Mims told Solomon that Roberts was "weirder than you," and took him to Roberts's house. Roberts and Solomon liked each other immediately, and this meeting proved to be significant.

Roberts was also a gadget freak. He had played with electronics since his childhood in Miami and had even built a crude relay computer when he was in his teens. Although he had wanted to become a doctor, Roberts joined the Air Force in order to receive electronics training. In 1968, while stationed in Albuquerque, he, Mims, and two other Air Force officers started a small electronics company. They began it in Roberts's garage by selling radio transmitters for model airplanes through the mail. They called it Micro Instrumentation Telemetry Systems, or MITS.

Roberts soon had MITS involved in other projects. For a time, MITS was building and selling a digital oscilloscope for engineers, but Roberts wanted to take on something more daring, closer to the cutting edge. His three partners objected to some of his wilder ideas, but by 1969 he had bought them out and suddenly found himself alone at the helm. Roberts was accustomed to giving orders in the Air Force; he was a big, imposing man who brooked no nonsense from employees. And he ran a tight operation at MITS. In every sense MITS was Roberts's company.

By 1969 MITS had moved out of the garage and into a former restaurant whose name, "The Enchanted Sandwich Shop," still hung over the door. Roberts had begun manufacturing calculators.

In the early 1970s, calculators were in vogue. They were easier to manufacture because of the advent of the integrated circuit and large-scale integration (LSI), the technology that put the equivalent of 100 transistors on a single chip. This same technology had made Intel's 4004 and 8008 processor chips possible. LSI made calculators much simpler to build, and Roberts decreed that MITS would produce programmable calculators in kit form. The kit was an ideal product for the hobby electronics magazines, and there Roberts publicized it. For some time the programmables sold well among enthusiasts. As the general consumer calculator market began to blossom toward the middle of the decade, Roberts invested the bulk of MITS's capital and effort in commercial handheld calculators.

The decision turned out to be disastrously ill-timed.

Two movements in the application of semiconductor technology reached critical stages in 1974 and created the climate in which the microcomputer was born. One was the trend of the semiconductor companies to produce and market applications of their own technology, especially calculators. The other was the refinement of the early, crude microprocessor chips. The first wiped Roberts out. The second saved him.

In the early 1970s, the semiconductor houses, racked by fierce technological and price wars, noticed that some of their customers were making much healthier profits than they were. For example, Commodore, a Canadian electronics company, had moved into Silicon Valley from Toronto and started selling calculators assembled around a Texas Instruments (TI) chip. Commodore was raking in money from a product whose technological achievement was substantially TI's. The demand for calculators seemed endless, and great profits were being made in meeting it. By 1972, TI had also entered the calculator business, and other semiconductor manufacturers soon followed suit. "They just came in and ripped everybody to shreds," according to semiconductor designer Chuck Peddle. TI's attack on the industry was characteristically aggressive: it burst upon the market, undercutting everyone's prices.

When the semiconductor manufacturers entered the calculator market in force, products became smaller and more powerful, prices dropped dramatically, and profits shrank almost as fast. Blighted further by a recession, 1974 was not a hallelujah year for the calculator industry. Peddle, then working on microprocessor design at Motorola, recalled: "The market went to hell that year. Supply started catching up with demand. Everybody that year lost money in the calculator business." Calculators went from careful purchases to sidewalk giveaways. The average price for a consumer calculator in 1974 was $26.25, down from around $150 the year before.

One of the stricken firms was MITS. In January of 1974, MITS was selling a simple 8-function calculator kit for $99.95, and it couldn't bring the price any lower. TI was offering a comparable, fully-assembled calculator for less than half of MITS's price. The tiny firm couldn't swim in these waters. Roberts lay awake nights trying to decide where he had gone wrong.

The other pivotal development in semiconductors was the completion, in April 1974, of a successor to the 8008. Intel had indeed created the brain of a computer in the 8008. But the 8008 was, in Art Salsberg's words, "a kludge and a monster." Everything was there, but not in the right places. It handled vital operations in slow, roundabout ways and demanded a contorted, awkward form of work. Engineers at Intel had long argued about whether the 8008 could actually function commercially as the brain of a viable computer. In a sense, the argument was the answer, and they went ahead to invent its successor, the 8080.

&

Why don't you call it Altair? That's where
the Enterprise *is going tonight.*

Lauren Solomon

Going for Broke

Ed Roberts made a decision of his own that spring: to build a kit computer. He had been toying with the idea for some time, but by early 1974 the chips were down. MITS's calculator business had blown away like desert dust, leaving the company heavily in debt. Faced with the possibility of going broke, Roberts decided to go for broke. He would build a product essentially without precedent or defined market—a product most people considered fanciful at best. In fact, the threat of bankruptcy may have been irrelevant to this decision. Roberts always cared much more about technological challenges than business risks and might have gone ahead with the kit computer under any circumstances.

Roberts looked into Intel's chips—the early 4004, the 8008, and an intermediate product called the 4040—and rejected the 4004 and 4040 as too crude. He was considering building a machine around the 8008 until a programmer told him that he had tried to implement the BASIC programming language on this chip and had found it excruciating to work with. The 8008 carried out the BASIC instructions too slowly to be useful. Roberts thus decided on the new Intel 8080. By this time Motorola also had a microprocessor, called the 6800, and Texas Instruments and other companies had similar products, but Roberts judged that, technologically, the 8080 was the best candidate. It had a second, perhaps even more important advantage. Intel normally charged $360 for an 8080. Roberts was sure he could get the chips cheaper, a lot cheaper.

He did—at $75 apiece. It was an excellent deal. However, the contract required him to buy in volume, and each computer needed only one processor. But that was all right, he opined. After the calculator fiasco, which Roberts called "something you don't want to go through twice in a lifetime," Roberts would have to sell a lot of computers or a lot of *something* to salvage his affairs. He was looking for volume.

Whether planned or not, Roberts's price was the best argument he had with the best ally he could get. *Popular Electronics* was narrowing its search for a computer to promote. "We got in a bunch of computers," Art Salsberg recalled. "We wound up with two models and decided it was going to be a choice of one or the other. One was a promise. The promise was, I can get the chips at a lower price and make this whole thing feasible. That was Ed Roberts. The other one was a microcomputer trainer by Jerry Ogdin."

Ogdin's computer actually existed. Salsberg and Solomon had seen it. They were inclined to support the tangible machine, even though it was built around the 8008, "an about-to-be-phased-out chip," and wait for Roberts or someone to come up with an 8080 device. "It looked like it was a go with the microcomputer trainer," according to Salsberg. And then *Radio Electronics* came out with the Mark-8.

When the July 1974 issue of *RE* hit the newsstands with its article on building the Mark-8, an Intel 8008-based computer, it caused a lot of excitement among the hobbyists, if not a lot of orders. The article had its effect at *Popular Electronics* too. The Mark-8 may have been fatally limited by the crude 8008 microprocessor, but its appearance in *RE* made *Popular Electronics* realize that it needed something better. Salsberg saw the article and said, "That kills the trainer." Solomon agreed. Ogdin's trainer was "very similar to the 8008 machine that *Radio Electronics* had." *Popular Electronics* had to have an 8080 machine.

So Solomon few to Albuquerque to talk to Roberts to work out the details. Salsberg had wanted the computer packaged like a serious commercial product, not a rat's nest, and therefore Roberts spent many nights in Albuquerque hashing out the exact components of a desktop computer that could sell for under $500. (The Mark-8 sold for about twice that price.) In the end, Roberts promised to deliver the first machine to *PE* as soon as it was built, and Solomon said he would publish a series of articles about it.

When Solomon and Salsberg picked Roberts, they staked the reputation of their magazine on a promise and a hunch. No one at MITS had *ever* built a computer. Roberts had only two engineers on his staff, and one of them had his degree in aeronautical engineering. Roberts had no prototype, no detailed proposal. But Uncle Sol was convinced Roberts could pull it off.

Roberts was less sure about *Popular Electronics*. However much he liked and respected Les Solomon, he mistrusted Solomon's cheerful assurances. And the more he realized the importance of a cover story in *Popular Electronics,* the more worried he became. His company's future was in the hands of a man who levitated tables.

Over the summer, Roberts had sketched out the machine he wanted. As his ideas took shape, he passed them along to his engineering team, Jim Bybe and Bill Yates. Yates, a quiet and serious man, worked long hours on the layout of the main circuit board for the machine, planning how each electrical signal would get from one point to another in the computer.

Roberts wanted the computer to be expandable like the minicomputers. In addition to the main circuit board, the user should be able to install other circuit boards for particular functions, such as controlling an input/output device or providing extra memory. Roberts wanted the boards to plug easily into the computer, a capacity that required not just a socket, but specific, defined data paths. If different elements of the computer were to reside on physically distinct circuit boards, the boards had to be made to communicate. Communication in turn required certain conventions. One board had to send information when and where it was expected by another. Almost by default, a *bus* structure for the computer evolved.

A bus is a channel for data or instructions in a computer. Normally, it is a parallel channel with several different signals passing simultaneously. The MITS computer had 100 separate paths, and each had to have an agreed-upon purpose. Sometimes physical or electrical constraints may determine particular layouts. For instance, electrical cross-talk — interference between closely placed wires — makes it unwise to place channels for certain kinds of signals too close together. But Roberts allowed Yates no time for such niceties of design, since the creditors had already begun to bay. Wherever the data channels fell, they stayed. If the bus design were a painting, it could have been entitled "Expedience."

While Yates laid out the boards, another MITS employee, technical writer David Bunnell, was casting about for a name for the computer. His favorite candidate was "Little Brother," but he wasn't altogether comfortable with this fraternal tag. Bunnell wasn't really comfortable with the whole computer idea, as Roberts recalls. But he controlled whatever skepticism he may have felt, since Roberts had little patience with dissent. Bunnell had been with MITS since 1972. He and Roberts had co-written articles for *Popular Electronics,* and their series of tutorials on digital electronics was running in the magazine at the same time they worked long hours in the workshop on their computer.

However, the computer seemed destined to die in the workshop. MITS owed around $300,000, and in mid-September, with Les Solomon reminding him that the article's deadline was imminent, Roberts made a grim trek to the bank. He needed another loan and fully expected the bank to turn him down. Moreover, with his current credit rating and his depleted assets, he could not believe anyone would lend him the necessary $65,000. His efforts would falter, then stop.

The officers of the bank listened patiently. He was going to build a kit computer, yes. And what exactly was that? Ah. And who, did he think, would buy such a product? Electronics hobbyists, sight unseen, from ads in magazines? Ah. And how many of these kit computers did he think he could sell to these electronics hobbyists through advertisements in magazines in the next year? "Eight hundred," Roberts told them, straight-faced.

"No, not eight hundred," they corrected him. Roberts was fantasizing. Still, the bank officers saw no profit in bankrupting companies. If he could sell 200 of the things it would help MITS to repay the bank a little. They would advance him the $65,000.

Roberts was surprised. He was glad he hadn't mentioned the informal market survey he had conducted. Trying to get some sense of how the machine would be received, Roberts had described it to engineers he knew and asked if they would buy it. None would. He was a little disappointed. But although he never considered himself a good businessman, he thought he knew when to ignore market research. Roberts took his $65,000 and he, Yates, and Bybe worked feverishly to complete the prototype to send to *Popular Electronics.* They made it pretty; it was going to appear on the cover.

While Roberts and Yates scrambled to finish the computer and the article, they realized they still didn't have a name for their machine. Since they thought Solomon would put a *Popular Electronics* name on it if they didn't beat him to it, they called it the PE-8. It may have been Roberts's last small hedge against *PE*'s scuttling the project.

According to Les Solomon, his 12-year-old daughter Lauren finally came up with the name that stuck. As she was watching *Star Trek,* her father walked into the room and told her, "I need a name for a computer. What's the name of the computer on the *Enterprise?*" Lauren thought a moment and said, "Computer." Her father obviously didn't think *that* was much of a name, so Lauren suggested, "Why don't you call it Altair? That's where the *Enterprise* is going tonight."

Altair. He called Roberts to try the name out on him. "I don't give a damn what you call it," Roberts answered. "If we don't sell two hundred, we're finished." Solomon reassured him that selling 200 was possible, and that things were going well. Solomon wasn't just being polite, soothing the raw nerves of a man flayed in the calculator crash. The Altair, he was confident, had the potential to far outstrip the Mark-8. The Mark-8 was an experimenter's toy, a way for the engineering hobbyist to learn about computers firsthand. But the Altair was a real computer. Its bus structure would make it possible to expand the capabilities of the machine by plugging in new circuit boards. It was capable, at least potentially and in miniature, of everything the large mainframe computers could do.

Solomon was convinced of that much and he told Roberts so. But he didn't voice his concern that the message might not get across. *PE* had to offer its readers more than just instructions on building the device. To prove that the Altair was a serious computer, *PE* had to offer one solid application, one demonstrable practical purpose to which the Altair could be put right away. What that might be Solomon had no idea.

The deadline came for Roberts to deliver the prototype computer to Solomon. Roberts told him to watch for it. It would be coming by Railway Express. Solomon waited. No computer arrived. Roberts reassured him: it was sent, it should be arriving any day now. Solomon was getting nervous. Roberts flew to New York to demonstrate the machine, telling Solomon that it would surely arrive before he did.

It didn't. Railway Express had apparently lost their computer. This was a catastrophe. *PE* was committed to a cover story and had no computer to put on the cover. Roberts felt that his nights awake, worry buzzing in his brain like static, had now been justified. His engineers couldn't possibly assemble another computer in time to meet the deadline. They were beaten.

Unless, of course, they faked it. Yates could slap together a box, poke little lights through the holes in the front, and ship it to New York. Les Solomon didn't like the idea. Art Salsberg didn't like it either. Ed Roberts was embarrassed. But when the January 1975 issue of *Popular Electronics* went to press, it featured a flashy cover photo of an empty metal box masquerading as a computer.

By December, Solomon actually had an Altair computer. At first he set it up in his office, but the noise from the Teletype machine he was using as an I/O device made him instantly unpopular in the *Popular Electronics* offices. So he took the system home and set it up in his basement. It was there that Roger Melen first saw it.

The day after Roberts and Yates's piece on the Altair arrived, another article came across Solomon's desk and caught his attention. Harry Garland and Roger Melen, the two Stanford graduate students Solomon had earlier put in touch with Ed Roberts, had sent in a description of a digital camera they had designed. The Cyclops, as Garland and Melen called it, reduced a visual image to a rectangular grid of light and dark squares and provided a low-cost visual system for a digital computer. In December of 1974, coincidentally just before the *PE* Altair issue came out, Roger Melen decided to fly to New York. His trip ultimately led him to Les Solomon's basement.

Melen reminded Uncle Sol of Roberts in a way. Both were big men, well over six feet and heavy, and both were inveterate engineer/hobbyists. Roberts was older though, and tougher, Air Force-trained. Melen was a quiet, gentle man, the product of one of the top engineering schools in the world. Still the two would see eye-to-eye, Les thought, chuckling to himself at the joke.

He led Melen through his basement to a strange piece of equipment.

"What's that?" Melen asked.

"That, sir," Solomon told him, "is a computer."

When Les told him what the Altair was and how much it cost, Melen politely demurred — Solomon must be mistaken, because Melen knew for a fact that the microprocessor chip alone cost as much as he claimed this whole computer did.

Solomon hid a smile and assured him that the price was correct. Roberts was actually going to sell this computer for $397. Enjoying Melen's reaction, Solomon picked up the phone, called Roberts in Albuquerque, and checked the price as Melen stood there. Yep. $397.

Melen was stunned. As he and most hobbyists well knew, Intel was then charging $360 for the 8080 alone. He left New York that day, but instead of flying directly back to San Francisco, he took a side trip to New Mexico.

Melen landed that evening in Albuquerque, where Roberts greeted him enthusiastically at the airport and drove him back to MITS. There Melen got another surprise: MITS was far from being the large company he had assumed. Located in a shopping center, wedged in between a massage parlor and a laundromat, MITS looked as odd to Melen as it must have looked to the suburban shoppers who walked past its doors that winter. "It was obviously the skeleton of what used to be a company, because they had lots of equipment around," Melen later recalled. "But they only had, I think, ten employees at that time. They had been very successful in producing calculators, but that was a fad that had passed. He [Roberts] saw this as his big chance for success—his second shot to pull him out of his predicament."

Melen saw a mutual opportunity, and he proposed attaching his Cyclops camera to the Altair. Roberts was interested. After a brief tour of MITS, the two big men sat down to work. Melen studied the Altair schematics, gathering all the information he thought he would need to design an interface between the two devices. He and Roberts talked about computers in general and the Altair-Cyclops interface in particular until dawn, when Melen hurried back to the airport to catch an eight o'clock flight to San Francisco.

Soon after, Solomon wrote to Garland and Melen suggesting a television adapter for Cyclops, but they replied that it would be prohibitively expensive. Instead, they described their plan to link their device to the Altair for use as a security camera. Solomon was gleeful. The security camera was the practical application he had sought. He incorporated the idea into their article on the Cyclops.

Uncle Sol's enthusiasm was less tempered than Ed Roberts's. The brainstorming session with Melen was not to be Roberts's last sleepless night. Despite Les Solomon's cheery encouragement, Roberts felt that PE could scrap the project even on the eve of publication. If it did, MITS was through. Already hundreds of thousands of dollars in debt, Roberts had borrowed heavily to finance this computer venture. He had purchased enough parts to build several hundred machines and he still had to pay for advertising. At $397 for one machine, he would need to sell hundreds just to break even. He began to wonder if he had made a terrible mistake.

&

PROJECT BREAKTHROUGH! World's First Minicomputer Kit to Rival Commercial Models...ALTAIR 8800

Popular Electronics cover,
January 1975

Two thousand people sent checks to an unknown company.

Les Solomon

It absolutely fired the imagination of everyone who was even remotely technically oriented, who wanted, sometime, to have a computer.

George Morrow

It was an absolute, runaway, overnight, insane success.

Harry Garland

All Hell Breaks Loose

Ed Roberts was still worried about his investment as the first orders came in. But within a week, what was clear was that whatever problems MITS would face in the immediate future, bank foreclosure would not be among them. Within two weeks, Roberts's tiny staff had opened hundreds of envelopes and read, with giddy excitement, orders for all the computers they had ever hoped to sell. Within a month, MITS had gone from one of the bank's biggest debtors to its fiscal hero. MITS's balance went in a few weeks from $400,000 in the red to $250,000 in the black. Just opening the orders seemed to take up everybody's time.

No one had realized how primed the market was. The January issue of *Popular Electronics* signaled to thousands of electronics hobbyists, programmers, and others that the era of the personal computer had finally arrived. Even those who didn't send in checks took the appearance of the Altair article as a sign that they could now have their own computers. The Altair seemed like the fruits of the technological revolution delivered straight into the hands of the people. They went crazy.

Roberts had gambled his company's life on the existence of *some* market for the machines, but the magnitude of the response amazed him. His experience in selling $99 kit calculators had been of little value in predicting the number of buyers of a $397 computer. In addition to the price difference, a calculator had a clear and obvious function. Everyone knew what it did. Despite Salsberg's artfully vague promise in *Popular Electronics* of "manifold uses we cannot even think of at this time," the basic Altair was a very limited device, and it was not at all obvious to what "manifold uses" a customer would put it. Yet Roberts's phone was ringing almost nonstop. People were buying promised potential.

With company ads promising delivery in 60 days, Roberts decided that he had to establish priorities or they would never make any deliveries. He issued a no-frills edict: initial production would encompass only the bare machine. All "bells and whistles"—such as extra memory, the promised clock board, the interface boards to allow the computer to be connected to a Teletype—would have to wait. MITS would ship the box and CPU board with 256 bytes of memory and the front panel and nothing else until the backlog was cleared. As delivered, the Altair was no more powerful than the Mark-8. Only its possibilities were greater. A few orders were filled early. Garland and Melen, working on Cyclops in the second bedroom of Melen's Mountain View, California, apartment, were MITS's first computer customers. They received Altair No. 0002 in January (the first Altair, lost in shipment to New York, was unnumbered, and Les Solomon got number 0001), and they immediately set to work on the interface board that would allow the computer to control the camera.

But Garland and Melen were not typical customers. The normal order went out only after it bumped to the head of the queue. This process took time. Despite MITS's promise of 60-day delivery, orders were not filled in any quantity until the summer of 1975. One hobbyist, Michael Shrayer, later to write a most important software program, described his experience with MITS: "I sent away my $397. It took forever. Many phone calls later, the computer finally came. At that time I had a big empty box with a CPU card and 256 bytes of memory. No terminal, no keyboard, nothing. To put anything in it, one had to play with the switches on the front panel and put in minor programs. A lot of peripherals were being promised but not delivered."

"Minor programs" was generous. Programs had to be written in machine language and entered by flipping switches, one flip of a switch for every binary digit. And once entered, the programs could do little but make the lights on the front of the box blink. One of the first programs written for the Altair was a game. It caused the lights to blink in a pattern, which the player was supposed to mimic by flipping switches.

The buyer faced another problem after delivery. The Altair was sold as a kit, and assembly took many hours. The chance that the computer would eventually work depended on the skill of the hobbyist and the quality of the parts: two shaky legs. Most of the first machines didn't work.

Steve Dompier, a young building contractor in Berkeley, California, found that some of MITS's advertised equipment didn't even exist. He recalled sending his check for $4000 with a terse request for "one of everything." When half his money came back with an apologetic note from a beleaguered MITS secretary saying that they "didn't have all that stuff yet," Dompier boarded a plane for Albuquerque.

Flying from San Francisco to Albuquerque over a delay in an order for hobby equipment might seem overzealous to some, but not to Dompier. "I wanted to see if they were really there. I rented a car and drove past the place about five times. I was looking for a big building with a front lawn with the letters *MITS* on it. It turned out it was in a tiny building next to a laundromat in a shopping center. There were two or three rooms. All they had was a box full of parts." He picked up some of those parts and flew back to San Francisco.

Dompier reported on MITS on April 16, 1975, to the next meeting of the Homebrew Computer Club, a pioneering microcomputer club that started in Menlo Park, California. He drew an attentive audience. MITS, he told his listeners, had 4000 orders and couldn't even begin to fill them. The 4000 orders, more than anything else, sparked people's interest. What they had been waiting for had happened. The door had been kicked open.

The Altair. Maybe all it could do was blink its lights, but for these people it was enough that it existed. They would take it from there.

"They made the business happen," semiconductor designer Chuck Peddle said of these early hobbyists. "They bought computers when they didn't work, when there was no software for them. They created a market, and then they turned around and wrote the programs that brought other people in."

The early purchasers of the Altair *had* to write programs. MITS initially supplied no significant software at all. A typical response of a computer hobbyist to the *Popular Electronics* article was (1) to send for an Altair, and when it arrived (and had been successfully assembled), (2) to begin writing software for it.

Two programmers in Boston decided to skip step 1.

Paul Allen was still working for Honeywell in Boston. Bill Gates was a freshman at Harvard, where he had customized a curriculum that allowed him to take graduate mathematics courses. On weekends they would get together to brainstorm about microcomputers. "We were trying to figure out some things we could do," Allen recalled. "We wanted to do *something*." They sent out offers on their old Traf-O-Data stationery to write PL/I compilers for $20,000. They considered selling Traf-O-Data machines to a company in Brazil. In the middle of a Boston winter, they were spinning their wheels.

Then, walking through Harvard Square one day, Allen noticed the *Popular Electronics* cover. Like many other computer enthusiasts, he realized the Altair was a tremendous breakthrough. But he saw it as something more personal as well. Allen ran to tell Bill that he thought their big break had come. Bill agreed. "So we called this guy Ed Roberts," said Gates. "We had a fairly aggressive posture. We said, 'We have a BASIC. Do you want it?'"

Roberts was justly skeptical. He had heard from many programmers who claimed they could write software for his computer. He told Gates and Allen what he was telling everyone, that he would buy the first BASIC he saw actually running on an Altair.

But Gates and Allen followed through, and about six weeks later Allen flew to Albuquerque to show Roberts their BASIC. The demonstration was successful, even if the BASIC initially did little more than announce its presence. The Traf-O-Data company, newly renamed Micro-Soft (later to become Microsoft) had made its first sale as a microcomputer software house.

In March, Roberts offered Allen the position of director of software at MITS. Frustrated at Honeywell and eager to work in such a promising field, Allen accepted immediately and flew to Albuquerque with all the cash he and Gates could muster. MITS Software Director was not quite the illustrious post Allen imagined. As it turned out, he was the entire software department.

Every good idea was half-executed at MITS.

Bill Gates

Putting It Together

MITS's hobbyist customers had to be creative to use the Altair. By mid-1975, when MITS was delivering regularly, the assembled machine was simply a metal box containing a power supply unit bolted next to a large circuit board. This board was called the motherboard because it was the main piece of circuitry in the machine. It contained 100 lines of gold connecting 18 slots for other circuit boards.

The 18 slots represented the Altair's expandability and symbolized owners' frustration. Whatever they might have ordered, they received a machine with only two slots filled, one with a CPU board, and one with a board containing 256 bytes of memory. Also included was another board (which was to be attached to the motherboard by dozens of wires—a task requiring hours of tedious work by the owner) that was called the front-panel board and that controlled the lights and switches on the front of the box by means of which users communicated with the machine.

A CPU, a memory, and an I/O unit: the early Altair met the minimal definition of computer and no more. It lacked any permanent storage. Users could put information into the machine and manipulate it, but once they shut off the power—or set aside the current problem to look at the next—the information disappeared. Even temporary storage was extremely limited. Although the Altair had a memory board, its 256 bytes held no more than a paragraph's worth of information. And as an I/O system, the front panel was awkward and tedious. To enter information, users had to flip tiny switches, one per bit. To read output, they had to interpret flashing lights. Entering and verifying the paragraph's worth of information that the Altair held might take several minutes, even with practice. Until paper tape readers and Gates and Allen's BASIC became available, Altair owners had to speak to their machines in machine language.

Machine language meant the native language of the Altair's microprocessor, the Intel 8080. A machine language is the particular commands, in the form of numeric codes, that the central processor component or unit (CPU) of a computer will respond to. Each such code causes the CPU to execute one of its elementary functions, such as copying the contents of one specified memory location onto another or adding a value of one to a stored value. There are programmers who prefer to work in machine language or something similar because of the intimate, immediate control the language gives them over CPU operation. They are the true hackers. But all programmers agree that programming in a "higher-level" language is easier. Altair BASIC was such a higher-level language. Unfortunately, Altair BASIC itself took up 4096 bytes of memory—remarkably little for a high-level language, but sixteen times the amount that MITS provided.

By filling the Altair's 18 slots with 256-byte memory boards and entering Gates and Allen's BASIC—a matter of flipping the switches over 30,000 times without an error—users could theoretically get a high-level language running. But the amount of memory left for their own programs would be minuscule. Moreover, the BASIC would have to be reentered every time the machine was turned off. Two things were needed to make the BASIC, and in fact the Altair, useful: higher density memory boards and a method for entering programs quickly. MITS was at work on both of these. In fact, MITS was at work on a lot of things.

When Paul Allen arrived in Albuquerque, MITS's biggest hardware project was a 4K memory board, which Ed Roberts had designed and technician Pat Godding was trying to build. In computer jargon, K, from "kilo," represents 1024, the closest power of two to 1000. Thus, 4K is 4096. Since digital computers use a binary number system, in which every number is expressed as a sum of powers of two, exact powers of two are especially easy to work with. Hence, computer capacities, such as amount of memory or the largest integer representable, are generally powers of two.

Since this 4K memory board would make it possible to run Gates and Allen's BASIC on the machine, Allen was particularly concerned that it work reliably. It didn't. Or they didn't. The problem was not just the board itself, but also the performance of two or more boards together. "It was almost analog circuitry," Allen said. "Things had to be calibrated so exactly."

Bill Yates and the other MITS engineers came to dread Allen's visits to their work area. In order to test the enhancements he was adding to his BASIC, he had to try them out on a working Altair with working 4K memory boards. There were no working 4K memory boards. The boards had personality, though. Allen would bring in his latest modification and key it into the machine, whereupon all the lights would go on, the Altair's way of throwing up its hands. When technical changes failed to correct the 4K boards, engineers tried redundancy. At one point MITS was keeping seven Altairs running just to ensure that three would run reliably. "That 4K dynamic memory board was atrocious," Roberts later admitted.

Of course, Allen didn't have to key in all of BASIC every time he wanted to use it. The Altair being used in the workshop had some capabilities that MITS wasn't ready to release to customers yet. For instance, its programs and data could be stored on paper tape and later loaded back into memory. When Allen first demonstrated BASIC to Roberts, he had carried it in with him on paper tape. Later, paper tape would for a time be the major means of distributing the language. Bill Gates would later have reason to curse those paper tapes of his and Allen's because they provided the medium for widespread copying of their BASIC.

But paper tape had serious drawbacks as a storage medium for microcomputers. Paper tape readers and punches were expensive, considerably more expensive than the Altair computer itself. Paper tape was also not particularly fast or efficient.

MITS recognized the need for an inexpensive storage method and was considering using audio-cassette recorders. Many people already owned cassette tape recorders, and if the recorder could double as an Altair storage device, all the better. But like paper tape, cassettes were slow and clumsy. On the other hand, IBM had long used disk drives for this sort of storage, and disks, although also expensive, solved the main problems of tape storage. By storing information in tiny magnetized domains on the surface of specially coated, rapidly rotating plastic disks read by read/write heads capable of fast, precise positioning over any location on the disk, these devices made data storage and retrieval quick and easy.

Roberts thought MITS should put disk drives on the Altair. Paul Allen agreed. Later in 1975, when Bill Gates also moved to Albuquerque to work parttime on MITS programs, Allen asked him to write the software that would allow the Altair to communicate with a disk drive. But Gates was currently occupied with other tasks, and he put off writing the disk code.

There was no shortage of either hardware or software projects. MITS was working on interfaces to Teletypes, printers, and cassette recorders and linkage of a simple terminal to the Altair. The software work included programs to control these devices, BASIC versions and enhancements, and applications programs. In addition, all these items needed documentation. MITS further undertook such public relations projects as a user conference and a newsletter.

One unusual effort was the MITSmobile, also known as the Blue Goose. An outgrowth of Roberts's fondness for recreational vehicles, the Blue Goose was a promotional tool designed to spark interest in microcomputing. Gates described it as "one of those GM motor homes. We'd drive around the nation, and everywhere we'd go, we'd get somebody to start a computer club. I was on the thing. I was part of the song-and-dance for one of the tours." The Blue Goose, like many MITS innovations, inspired imitation, and Sphere, one of MITS's first competitors, soon set a Spheremobile roving about.

The Blue Goose was effective. One of the clubs it prompted was the Southern California Computer Society, which in turn created one of the influential early microcomputer magazines, *SCCS Interface*.

There were good reasons for starting computer clubs. The equipment in these early days often didn't work, and software was often unusable or nonexistent. Though buyers were usually engineering hobbyists, few of them had all the skills needed to understand a microcomputer. The clubs allowed a synergistic sharing of knowledge among the sophisticated but ignorant users of the machines. Without this interaction, this mutual aid, the industry would not have blossomed as it did.

MITS didn't depend on local initiative. By April, MITS had its own nationwide computer club with contests and a newsletter. David Bunnell started the publication *Computer Notes,* with Roberts writing an irregular column, "Ramblings." But within the year Bunnell turned the newsletter over to Andrea Lewis, who would later follow Gates and Allen in their own business venture. Throughout much of the newsletter's history, Gates and Allen wrote a sizable part of its contents.

The Altair club was meant for and offered free membership to Altair owners or those who could pass for owners before MITS was delivering. But other clubs were springing up that bore no particular allegiance to MITS. The Southern California Computer Society and the Homebrew Computer Club in Northern California, though filled with actual and prospective Altair owners, were also made up of technically sophisticated hobbyists who were soon contemplating building computers of their own. The Homebrew Club was especially interested in this challenge, and from its ranks a true competitor to one of MITS's most important products quickly emerged.

I think there was a feeling of Ed's that anyone even putting a competitor's board in our mainframe—as we laughingly called it—was [committing] blasphemy.

Mark Chamberlain

There was no competition until Processor Tech came out with the memory cards.

Ed Roberts

The Competition

MITS was a catalyst. Perhaps this role fell to it more by chance than by merit, but MITS inspired an industry. From Roberts's perspective, new competitors were poaching on territory he had claimed.

When MITS began delivering its 4K memory boards, customers noticed what Paul Allen had noticed: the boards didn't work. "I don't think I'd ever trust an Altair memory board as far as I could throw it," one MITS executive later admitted. Despite Roberts's later assessment of its design as "atrocious," at the time he brooked no complaints about it, as Bill Gates soon discovered. Gates was using a memory-test program he had written to check the boards as they were completed. "Every one that came off the line wouldn't work," Gates said. He told Roberts so, and the confrontation between the slender teenager and the burly Air Force veteran permanently damaged their relationship. Roberts considered Gates an 18-year-old smart aleck and ignored him. "I think that was a fundamental failing of Ed's," another MITS employee said. "If he said the memory boards worked, they worked."

But they didn't. And when Californian Bob Marsh, an out-of-work Homebrew Computer Club hobbyist, started a company called Processor Technology in April 1975 and began selling 4K boards that apparently did work, Roberts took it as a declaration of war. MITS was making little or no profit on the computers and needed the memory board sales that Processor Technology was cutting into.

Roberts used Gates and Allen's software as one of his weapons. The BASIC was a popular item; the MITS 4K board was not. So MITS resorted to a venerable marketing ploy. It tied the price of the BASIC to the purchase of the memory board and to other MITS hardware as well. Customers who bought MITS boards paid $150 for the BASIC. Those who didn't buy the boards paid $500 for the BASIC—more than the price of the machine. The effect on the market was dramatic. Hobbyists, seeing the 4K boards as worthless and the

BASIC as overpriced, made their own paper tape copies of the BASIC and distributed them for free. By the end of the year, most copies of BASIC in use on Altair computers had been pirated.

Processor Technology survived the BASIC price ploy and developed more Altair-compatible products. Other companies also began to produce boards that could be used in the Altair. A peculiar antagonism developed. Roberts railed at what he considered squatting in his territory. The board companies responded by "crashing" David Bunnell's First World Altair Computer Conference. When Roberts denounced these firms in his newsletter as "parasites," two Oakland, California, hobbyists christened their board company Parasitic Engineering.

The only company to win approval from MITS for its boards was Garland and Melen's Cromemco, named for Crothers Memorial Hall, their graduate dormitory at Stanford. Garland and Melen had gotten sidetracked from their plan to connect the Cyclops digital camera to the Altair. The interface board, intended to perform this feat, had taken on a life of its own and become a video interface board for displaying text and pictures generated by the Altair in color on a television monitor. The Dazzler, as they called the board, neatly solved the Altair's I/O problem. Roberts saw it as noncompetitive (MITS had nothing like it), and gave it a prominent place in Altair computers at the conference. The First World Altair Computer Conference, held in Albuquerque in March 1976, was the first in a series of microcomputer conventions. Hundreds of people attended this conference, but it was strictly a MITS Altair affair. All dozen or so speakers and presenters were there at MITS's invitation, and one of them showed a backgammon game he had written for the Altair. Cromemco was the only hardware company invited. Garland and Melen were there in person, a show unto themselves — burly Melen, a match for Roberts in size but far more reticent, the diminutive Garland bubbling with enthusiasm. There were also a number of uninvited companies whose representatives walked the floor, passing out circulars, inviting viewers to see competitive equipment in hotel rooms upstairs. Bob Marsh's Processor Technology was there.

The presence of these show-crashers did not sit well with MITS management. Lee Felsenstein, who had savaged the Altair in a hobbyist publication before working for Proc Tech, whose memory board that threatened Roberts's profits, thought Roberts was cool toward him. Bunnell was visibly perturbed by the gate-crashers.

If the majority of these board companies were competing against MITS's components, others were appearing that challenged MITS's core product, its computer. Don Lancaster's Southwest Technical Products, and Sphere, a Utah company, were both working on computers built around Motorola's recently released MC6800 processor.

Roberts had proposed building a 6800 machine too. But some of his employees, including Paul Allen, opposed this new venture, fearing that the company would spread itself too thin. "No, Ed," Allen objected, "we'll have to rewrite all our software for the 6800. We'll have two instruction sets to support. That just doubles our headaches." Nevertheless MITS did develop a 6800, starting work on it late in 1975. Named the Altair 680b and priced attractively at $293, this computer was substantially different from the original Altair 8800. Components from the 8800 could not be used in the 680b, nor could the original Altair BASIC. New engineers were found to work with the new design, and new line employees were hired. The attempt to keep up with the orders for the 8800 and the determination to rush out the 680b had swelled the ranks of MITS employees from 12 to over 100. When the new computer magazine *Byte* unveiled Southwest Tech's 6800 in November, the announcement was soon followed by MITS's announcement of the 680b.

One of the new employees was Mark Chamberlain, a quiet University of New Mexico student with a gift for understatement and a taste for assembly language programming. Chamberlain had worked on a Digital Equipment Corporation PDP-8 computer, probably the closest thing to a microcomputer in most universities at the time. "I had done a lot of assembly code...and got so turned on to it that they just couldn't keep me out." When a professor mentioned that a small company named MITS was looking for programmers, Chamberlain went to talk to its software director, Paul Allen.

Allen wasn't sure where MITS was going and wanted Chamberlain to know the risks involved. He had accepted these risks but wasn't about to inflict them on the unwary. He hired Chamberlain but told him, "If it doesn't work out, well, it doesn't work out." Chamberlain appreciated this logic and commenced writing software for the 680b. The 680b "was not enormously successful," Chamberlain recalled dryly. In fact, it encountered serious difficulty, and the low price heightened the problem. "Lots of them were ordered, but when I came on board at MITS, the whole project was already in trouble. They had to go through a complete redesign." In spite of the redesign, the 680b never really took off, but Chamberlain found plenty of work to do at MITS nonetheless. Roberts had other machines in mind, and each required new software.

Meanwhile, Allen and Gates were putting increased effort into their own company, Microsoft. Throughout 1975, Gates and Allen and Rick Wyland, hired to write 6800 BASIC, were doing more and more with the BASICs, including developing versions for other companies. The relationship between Microsoft and MITS was becoming less clear as the two companies grew.

The fact that Bill Gates had not yet written the disk code for the Altair 8800 didn't simplify matters, especially since Gates, on leave from Harvard, was considering returning to school. Paul Allen, in his role as MITS software director, nagged Gates about the code. According to Microsoft legend, in February of 1976 Gates checked into a motel with a pen and a stack of yellow legal pads. When he came out, he had finished the disk code.

By 1976 a change from dynamic memory to static memory (two ways of maintaining information in memory) seemed to have solved the vexing memory board problem, but MITS still had the task of troubleshooting the dynamic boards already in the field or buying them back. Also in early 1976 MITS, hoping to increase efficiency, revamped its quality-control procedures. MITS was already shipping the 680b and planned to ship the upgraded 8800 by mid-year. A disk operating system written around Gates's disk code was scheduled for release in July of 1976.

Mark Chamberlain was now running a library of user-submitted software, thereby setting a precedent for the industry. Anyone who had an Altair had probably written programs for it. Chamberlain was distributing such programs as widely as possible throughout the community of users since sharing of software vastly increased the value of the machine. He particularly sought software for the new 680b. But when Paul Allen announced pricing for 680b BASIC, customers saw an already familiar tactic. It cost nothing with the new 16K memory board, but $200 otherwise.

By mid-1976, the competition Roberts feared was becoming real. A new company named IMSAI imitated the Altair design and brought out its own computer, the IMSAI 8080. Polymorphic Systems introduced what looked like a serious competitor, the Poly-88. And Processor Technology caught the front cover of *Popular Electronics* with its Sol computer named after Les Solomon. Even loyal Cromemco was developing a CPU board, designed around the new Zilog Z80 microprocessor, as the successor to the Intel 8080 chip that was the heart of the original Altair computer. The Z80 was designed by Federico Faggin, who had left Intel to start his own semiconductor company after his work on the Intel 4004. This new microprocessor was catching a lot of attention among the high-tech cognoscenti.

None of the new microcomputer companies represented an immediate threat to MITS's market share for microcomputers. There MITS reigned uncontested. But all of their machines could, in principle, use the same circuit boards as the Altair. They all had the same 100-line bus structure. The bus was the key to compatibility, the key to plugging competitive boards into the Altair, as Roberts viewed things. He always referred to the bus as the Altair bus and wanted others to do the same. When some didn't comply, David Bunnell suggested they compromise with the "Roberts bus."

The bus-naming story highlights the curious mix of competitiveness and camaraderie in the nascent industry. The bus became a major point of contention between MITS and most of the rest of the microcomputing world. Roberts's position was simple: he and Yates had designed the bus just as they had designed the Altair. It was the Altair bus. His competitors preferred not to take his view. Advertisements began to give such awkward names as the "MITS-IMSAI-Processor Tech-Polymorphic bus." Garland and Melen fell to discussing what they thought of the bus name problem on a jet from San Francisco to Atlantic City, where PC 76, an early microcomputer conference, was held in August 1976. Garland and Melen were about to release a CPU board for this bus and were reluctant to refer to it by a lengthy list of their competitors. They agreed about two things: the name of the bus should not favor any company, and it should have an engineering ring, as would, for instance, one or more letters and a number. They considered "Standard 100" and then shortened it to S-100. That, they thought, sounded sufficiently official.

The goal then became to secure the approval of other hardware vendors. Melen remembered that "on this same airplane were the people from Processor Technology, specifically Bob Marsh and Lee Felsenstein. I had a can of beer in my hand, and in the course of our discussing the standard, the airplane hit a little bump, and I spilled beer on Bob. He agreed very quickly, to get rid of me and my beer can." The name "S-100" became essentially common coin, although MITS and *Popular Electronics* clung to "Altair bus" for some time. Seven years later Ed Roberts was still adamant: "The bus was used by MITS for two years before anybody else was producing a computer. It's the Altair bus. Calling the Altair bus the S-100 bus is like calling Mona Lisa 'Tom Boy.' I'm the only one in the world who's irritated by that, but I'm irritated."

In addition to the S-100 companies, MITS was seeing disturbing hints of competition from other, even more unsettling sources. MOS Technology, a semiconductor company, was doing well with Chuck Peddle's KIM-1, a low-cost hobbyist computer built around its own bargain-basement 6502 chip. This fact alone may have occasioned no immediate alarm, but two months later, in October 1976, Commodore bought MOS Technology. For the first time, a large, established company with extensive channels of distribution for electronics products would be selling a microcomputer.

An even more ominous threat was looming. Tandy Corporation, having "just got through killing off Lafayette [Electronics]," as Peddle put it, was casting about for a computer to sell in its hundreds of Radio Shack stores. "What Radio Shack wanted to do was to come up with a packaged machine," Peddle said, "because they knew their guys couldn't support, couldn't design, this kind of thing."

With semiconductor companies and electronics distributors getting into the act, the competition was gearing up.

&

Q: Did you think it was going to go under?
A: All the time, all the time.

Bill Gates
(from an interview)

The Fall

MITS had more to worry about than competition. The company had grown too big too fast. "We had too many irons in the fire," Roberts admitted later. "We had a lot more things going than a company the size of ours should have had going." The memory boards still in the field were not the only problem either. Quality control was not particularly effective, and customers were complaining. Often projects commenced despite the reservations of many MITS employees. Products failed.

"The high-speed paper tape reader is a good example," Mark Chamberlain recalled, "because I *know* we only sold three of those." The spark printer was another. MITS bought a printer from a manufacturer, rebuilt and repackaged it, and eventually had to charge "considerably more" than its supplier's retail price for the item. The MITS version didn't sell. Sometimes an entire major product line was thought a mistake. Allen objected strenuously to the 680b.

MITS's difficulties ran deep. "It really gets into a study of personalities," Mark Chamberlain said. "I don't know if it's possible to understand it without understanding all the aspects that were [a result of] people's personalities." One thing is clear. The channels of communication between upper-level employees and the president were not always open. "Ed isolated himself," Gates said. He "didn't have good rapport with other people in the company, didn't know how to deal with the growth." Roberts later acknowledged that a problem existed. "I was worried about so many things at the time that I felt like everything was a threat."

A number of changes occurred in MITS toward the end of 1976. By this time, Roberts had brought in his childhood friend Eddie Curry as executive vice-president and Bob Tindley from the bank that had financed him to help with management. But he was soon to lose an important employee. Paul Allen was restless. Microsoft was becoming a more serious enterprise, and Allen was eager to take control of his own destiny. Convinced that MITS's best days were long past, he and Bill Gates began working exclusively for Microsoft. Mark Chamberlain moved up to replace him as MITS's software director.

Chamberlain found that the job bore unexpected challenges. He quickly encountered upper-level dissension about what products to build and what projects to undertake. Chamberlain, his hardware counterpart Pat Godding, and others did not always agree with Roberts on critical decisions. Roberts, in holding so tightly to the reins of his company, may have been taking all the uncertainty and vulnerability of the fledgling industry upon himself rather than allowing others to share it. The burden was impossible. As Gates acknowl-edged: "Nobody really knew what was going on. There are so many things that would have been obvious to do if you'd had the vision back then. Nobody had the view of the market."

"He did have ideas," Chamberlain said of Roberts. "But we didn't fill out the product line; we didn't provide proper support. I think that the early pioneers who used the Altair in business were up against a hell of a lot of frustration."

So were Chamberlain and Godding. Convinced their ideas had value and equally sure that Roberts would not accept them, they went ahead on their projects without his approval or knowledge. One employee later called these the "secret projects." For example, once a high-level employee spoke with Roberts about a project that only needed a little more work and would, he was certain, generate sales immediately. Roberts put his foot down, saying that they absolutely would do no more work on the project. "And we did. He didn't know we were doing it."

Although MITS grossed $13 million in 1976, it was losing its edge. Its prod-ucts were not regarded as anywhere near the best, deliveries were slow, and service was poor. Most other microcomputer companies had similar problems at the time, but MITS's position led people to expect more. Furthermore, MITS had established an exclusive dealership program early on. Retailers who wished to be the only Altair dealers in their area could sell no other brands. But the knife of exclusivity cut both ways, and MITS began to have trouble getting dealers. Retailers and customers alike were dissatisfied. No one would have judged MITS to be near collapse, but competition was getting serious. Over 50 hardware companies had entered the market. At the first West Coast Computer Faire held in San Francisco in the spring of 1977, Chuck Peddle was showing Commodore's PET, a more serious machine than the MOS/Commo-dore KIM-1 and a formidable competitor; and Apple introduced its Apple II amid a fanfare that signaled a change in the market.

On May 22, 1977, Roberts sold MITS to Pertec, a company then specializing in disk and tape drives for minicomputers and mainframe computers. "It was a stock swap," Roberts said. "They bought MITS for essentially 6 million dol-lars." Whether Pertec got a bargain or a lemon depends on the degree to which Pertec management was responsible for MITS's ensuing slide into oblivion.

Roberts had talked to other companies, especially semiconductor companies, before selling to Pertec. Pertec had offered him not only personal stock in the company, but his own private research and development lab and the freedom to use it exactly as he pleased. The opportunity to work on new products and to tie his fortunes somehow to MITS undoubtedly meant something to Roberts. But basically he wanted to climb down off the nose cone. The calcula-tor bust still haunted him, and he knew a similar disaster could happen in personal computers. "Once you've been there," Roberts said, "staying awake every night wondering whether you're going to make payroll the following day...you're pretty gun-shy, and you're making decisions that aren't terribly logical."

The Pertec sale led to acrid controversy over ownership of the software. Gates and Allen had written the core of the BASIC before even meeting anyone from MITS, and Gates had only worked parttime, but "Pertec thought they were buying the software as part of the whole deal," Gates recalled. "And they weren't. We [Microsoft] owned the software. It was all under license." Gates remembered the head of Pertec telling him that if the software were not included in the transaction, Pertec would back out and as a result MITS would fold. "They sent this big-time lawyer out," he said. The matter went to arbitration, and the creators of the BASIC prevailed.

Ed Roberts felt he had been wronged; years later he still felt bitter and betrayed. According to Roberts, the agreement stipulated that Gates and Allen would receive royalties up to a maximum of $200,000. MITS had paid them this amount and therefore acquired ownership of the software. Roberts believed that the arbitrator misunderstood certain clear issues of fact, and that this misapprehension led directly to the ruling. "It was a fluke," Roberts maintained. "It was just wrong as rain."

Gates acknowledged that Roberts did not take the decision well. "His and my relationship really went to heck," he said. "Ed really got his feelings hurt." With their arbitration won and no ties to hold them to Albuquerque, Gates and Allen moved Microsoft to their native Bellevue, Washington.

Under Pertec, MITS came apart. Even before the acquisition, the company was losing its dominant role in the industry it had created. But MITS did not start sinking dramatically until Pertec management teams walked onto the scene.

Part of the reason seems to lie in Pertec's alienation of virtually all key MITS personnel. "They kept patting us on the head, saying we didn't understand the business," Roberts recalled. The MITS regulars simply didn't respond well to the Pertec management teams. The standard characterization was "two-bit managers in three-piece suits," so common an epithet that some just shortened it to "the suits." Pertec managed MITS as if it were a big business in an established industry. Before agreeing to buy MITS, Pertec executives asked Roberts to show them his five-year marketing forecast. MITS's planning had "consisted of where things would be on Friday," Roberts said. But to please his buyers, he and Eddie Curry invented projections that they thought would cause Pertec managers to break out the champagne. They told Pertec that sales would double each year and provided a pie-in-the-sky guess of how many machines the company would sell. Pertec bought the whole thing. During the following year managers came and went at Pertec in extraordinary numbers. "People based their careers on trying to live up to that [forecast]," said Curry.

Mark Chamberlain had no use for the Pertec style at MITS. "They sent in team after team. Each team came in to knock off the previous team. Any given team had about 60 to 90 days to turn the mess into something good. It wasn't enough time. It was just long enough for the people to come in and switch from a position of trying to understand the problem to becoming a part of the problem. After 60 to 90 days, you were definitely part of the problem. And they'd send in the next guy to fire you." Chamberlain left to go to work for Roberts in his lab. "I wanted out of that Pertec thing like right away," he said. "That thing was *crazy*." For a while Chamberlain worked with Roberts on a low-priced Z80-based computer but soon left.

Others also left. Bunnell had departed at the end of 1976 to start *Personal Computing*, an early microcomputer magazine. He published it from Albuquerque throughout 1977 with contributions from Gates and Allen. Andrea Lewis took over as editor of *Computer Notes* and changed it from a company-written newsletter to a slick magazine with outside contributions. Eventually she accepted an invitation from Paul Allen to come to Bellevue and take over Microsoft's documentation department. Chamberlain also joined Microsoft later on. Several engineering people left to work for a local electronics company. Even Ed Roberts, after five months, became fed up with Pertec. "I didn't think they understood the market. They told me I didn't." He bought a farm in Georgia, and declared he intended to become a gentleman farmer or go to medical school. Eventually, he did both with the same concentrated energy he had brought to MITS. Pertec gradually abandoned the MITS operation as a bad venture. According to Eddie Curry, who stayed on longer than any other MITS principal, Pertec continued making Altairs for about a year after the acquisition, but within two years MITS was gone.

It would be hard to overestimate the importance of MITS and the Altair. The company did more than create an industry. It introduced the first affordable computer, of course, but it also pioneered computer shows, computer retailing, computer company magazines, users' groups, software exchanges, and many hardware and software products. Without intending to, MITS made software piracy a widespread phenomenon. Started when microcomputers seemed wildly impractical, MITS pioneered a billion-dollar industry. But if MITS was, as Bunnell's ads proclaimed, number one, the scramble to be number two was won by one of the most unusual of the pioneering companies.

The Miracle Makers

Chapter 3

Everybody wants to be second.

Ted Nelson

After Altair

MITS may have been first, but it was not alone. During the two and one-half years between the *Popular Electronics* story and the sale to Pertec, an industry began to grow. The Altair announcement in January 1975 triggered both technological and social change. The hobbyists who read the *Popular Electronics* article may not have envisioned the subsequent proliferation of microcomputers, but they could and did recognize that they were witnesses to the start of a radical change in the pattern of access to computers. They had been waiting for it.

Programmers, technicians, and engineers who worked with large computers all knew the feeling of being "locked out of the machine room." When the digital computer first became widely available to scientists and engineers in medium-sized businesses in the 1960s, complex calculations were speeded up, but a "computer priesthood"—a set of engineers and technicians through which one had to work to reap the computer's benefits—also appeared. Computer time was expensive, and the resulting need to budget individuals' time led necessarily to a certain frustration for the users: tolerating interruptions at awkward times or submitting programs through a bureaucracy of intermediaries. The programmers felt the frustration of a skilled worker denied full access to tools, to the source of a livelihood, and as a result, programmers or engineers who did not dream of owning their own machines, even as early as 1975, were rare. This desire was the tinder and the *Popular Electronics* article the spark of a revolution.

The Altair breached the machine room door, and rivals emerged almost at once from garages all over the country. Roberts's price was hard to undercut, and if it had not been for the long delays in delivering the Altair, few competitors would have survived. Not many did anyway. But commercial success was almost irrelevant to the kindling of revolution. Those who failed did so openly with their schematics on the table. Mistakes were instructive and failures did not discourage more innovation. The revolution was running on its own internal drive, not the external pull of profits, and it did not take shape according to traditional economic laws.

MITS's competitors were hobbyist enterprises. None of the big corporations wanted to build microcomputers. And no one who was not totally and blindly fascinated by computers and electronics would have endured the tedious, detailed work required to design and build a computer by hand.

The idea of building a computer by hand sounded crazy to most people even in 1975. Such a task had become possible only in that decade, and the Altair had yet to prove itself a computer in more than a textbook-definition sense. But the hobbyist in 1975 knew it would.

Hobbyists were hooked on building computers. For instance, New Mexico fire spotter Don Lancaster had been teaching a generation of hobbyists the digital know-how they needed to understand computers through free-lance articles in electronics magazines. Lancaster became involved in the mid-1970s with a company called Southwest Technical Products. Southwest Tech made high-end audio components kits and in 1975 had released an Altair-like microcomputer using a new microprocessor from Motorola, the 6800. Many engineers, including Ed Roberts, thought the 6800 a better chip than the Altair's 8080, and Roberts kept a wary eye on Southwest Tech.

Lancaster wasn't secretive about his designs. Hardly anyone was then. A spirit of information-sharing dominated the field, a spirit generally unthinkable among business competitors. Magazines had helped create a nationwide community of hobbyists who regularly wrote to one another, argued at length and with passion, shared knowledge generously, and who as a result were prepared, technically and emotionally, to build their own computers. "They wanted it so bad they could taste it," said semiconductor designer Chuck Peddle.

At the University of California at Berkeley, computer science professor John Torode had examined the Intel 4004 and 8008 chips and decided that they were less than ideal for use as central processors in computers. Only when his old friend Gary Kildall, who was teaching computer science down the coast at Monterey and consulting at Intel, got him one of the first 8080 chips did he think seriously about a microcomputer. By mid-1974 Torode and Kildall had assembled a microcomputer and a disk operating system of sorts. But they were skeptical about the market for such a device and continued to refine the product strictly as a hobby; Kildall did the software, Torode the hardware. They sold two machines to a San Francisco Bay Area computer terminal company called Omron, but sold only a few others before the Altair announcement. They then pursued their interests independently; Torode built computers under the name Digital Systems and later Digital Microsystems, and Kildall wrote software as Intergalactic Digital Research (later Digital Research).

Although the San Francisco Bay Area was a hub of development, the phenomenon was nationwide. In Denver, "Dr. Bob" Suding turned his hobby into a business, Digital Group, which was soon respected by many hobbyist customers. Initially, the company produced plug-in circuit boards for the Altair and other emerging computers. Suding also pioneered an idea that was taken seriously five years later: a machine that could use different types of micro-processors interchangeably. The Altair was an 8080 machine and the South-west Tech computer a 6800, but either processor would work in Digital Group's computer. This innovation reflected the times. An interchangeable micro-processor was a boon to microcomputer designers (that is, hobbyists), but was of little use to ordinary consumers because of the absence of software for the new processors. The hobbyists were designing for themselves.

Even the appearance of the machines reflected the hobbyist orientation of their inventors. The typical computer resembled a piece of electronic test equipment — an ugly metal box with toggle switches, blinking lights, and wires running out the back, front, top, or sides. A kludge. No one gave much thought to the look of the machines since all designers were, whether they admitted it or not, creating the computer *they* wanted. When the Southern California-based company Vector Graphic rejected a designer's pink circuit boards with purple rheostats on the grounds that they clashed with Vector's green-and-orange computer, the designer was flabbergasted. Color coordina-tion was seldom a consideration in mid-1970s computer design.

One of the first companies to consciously consider aesthetic appeal and con-venience of desktop use was Sphere, a company started by Mike Wise in Boun-tiful, Utah. The Sphere computer was integrated; that is, the display monitor and keyboard were incorporated into the same case as the microprocessor. In this way the machine was a closed unit, with no mass of wires dangling out the sides.

The Sphere didn't last. A commercial product on the outside, inside it was all hobby machine, and the mechanism under the lid wasn't pretty even to a hob-byist's eye. It was too much the handmade item, crisscrossed by scores of hand-soldered wires. The Sphere was not engineered for production, nor was it particularly reliable. And it had, as one hobbyist of the time put it, "the world's slowest BASIC."

But there were others. Many of the corporate names reflected the informal-ity and lightheartedness of the hobbyist movement. Lee Felsenstein started a company called Loving Grace Cybernetics and later another called Golemics Incorporated. Itty Bitty Machine Company appeared in Chicago, Chicken Delight Computer Consultants cropped up in in New Jersey, and Kentucky Fried Computers began in Northern California.

Buyers and makers were not clearly differentiated in those early days. Using a microcomputer took so much dedication and expertise that it was hardly an exaggeration to say that any user could have become a manufacturer. There existed one amorphous subculture of technofreaks, hobbyists, and hackers, people untrained in business skills and more interested in exploring the poten-tial of the microcomputer than in making a fortune.

But there was at least one exception: IMSAI Manufacturing of San Leandro, California. IMSAI became Number Two and soon actually seized the lead in sales from MITS. Started by Bill Millard just months after the Altair announcement, IMSAI was distinctive in its origin and philosophy. Virtually all the other company presidents were hobbyists and knew each other through club meetings and newsletters. Millard instead was a former sales representative. He and his associates didn't know the hobbyists and didn't want to. They seldom went to the hobbyists' club meetings, where members would swap stories of their experiences with the new and unreliable machines, exchange rumors, and swap equipment, software, and insights. Millard and company didn't consider themselves part of that crowd.

From the very first, Millard and his team of hard-driving executives saw themselves as serious businesspeople in a field populated by blue-jeaned dilettantes. The IMSAI computer would be the desktop tool of the small business, Millard decreed. It would, among other things, replace the typewriter. In the eyes of IMSAI executives, the company was building commercial systems for business customers who wanted to do *real* things. It would not make toys for hobbyists.

In 1975, when IMSAI started making the IMSAI 8080 microcomputer, some hobbyists thought that Millard had begun trying to corner the business market a little early. The business community didn't know what microcomputers were. In fact, the serious hobbyists didn't yet know just what the machines could do. Microcomputers were still experimental and often didn't work right. So how did Millard and his associates determine that small businesses would buy the machines? "Guesswork," according to co-founder Bruce Van Natta. "We guessed that these things were really small business machines, even if the damn things did weigh 80 pounds and barely fit on a desk."

Technologically, the IMSAI computer was no breakthrough. It was essentially a copy of the Altair with some enhancements — notably a better power supply. The power supply of the Altair, which distributed the appropriate DC current and voltages to the various parts of the computer, was regarded by hobbyists as dismal. IMSAI, on the other hand, delivered "a power supply you couldn't lift," as Van Natta later put it. He was exaggerating, of course, though just a few years earlier everyone took it for granted that computers and their components were unliftably large. Although IMSAI later solved difficult technical problems, improving the Altair power supply and eliminating the handsoldered wires required in the Altair were perhaps the company's most significant hardware achievements.

IMSAI's most important contribution was not a technological feat but a marketing one. Millard took an uninspired design and a dubious market and built a company that became a power to be reckoned with in the nascent industry.

&

It was an unusual organization in that it really did believe in high-intensity, enthusiastic amateurs.

Bruce Van Natta

Amateurs and Professionals

Bill Millard was a magnet for his executives, and through them he set a singular tone for the company. His personality and goals became IMSAI's, so much so that his decision-making style steered IMSAI even when Millard wasn't around, as happened during some critical times in the company's history. Millard did not hire hobbyists, but he did hire enthusiastic amateurs.

Unlike Ed Roberts and many others, Millard was not fascinated by the hardware. For as long as he maintained an interest, Roberts was a true hobbyist, a computer junkie who really wanted to see what the thing could do. Like many microcomputer engineers after him, Roberts built the machine *he* wanted. If MITS managed to sell just a few hundred computers, enough to keep the company in its little shop next to the laundromat, Roberts wouldn't feel he had failed. He liked money, but for him a large part of the thrill was always *the machine itself*.

Bill Millard was different. He burned with a much more acquisitive fire. "He was a typical entrepreneur," according to one of his proteges, Bill Lohse, "except maybe a little more careless, a little more gutsy." Millard liked to take chances. He was a gambler.

He was also a salesman. Millard had sold for IBM and had done well. By the late 1960s, he was manager of data processing for the city and county of San Francisco. While dealing in this capacity with mainframe and minicomputer companies for five years in the early 1970s, Millard was identifying the players who would throw in with him in the biggest gamble of his life.

Millard was looking for a loyal and dedicated team to follow him onto the field. He wanted enthusiastic young men and women who didn't know too much about computers and who would take the risks he wanted to take. Every other computer company was run by engineers. Millard created a company run by sales people.

From a computer science dropout with a flair for selling to a former vitamin sales representative, Millard's people all displayed an intense desire to succeed and an unswerving confidence that they would. They were an odd bunch for that industry at that time. They wore suits and talked more about money than machines and more about goals and miracles than about money. And, almost without exception, they had "done the training."

"Doing the training" for Millard, as for many Californians at the time, meant going through Erhardt Sensitivity Training, or *est*, one of a spate of self-help movements that sprang up in the late 1960s. Millard had done the training and encouraged his family and friends to do it too; it became a condition of employment for upper-level executives at IMSAI. One *est* tenet had particular relevance for IMSAI: the viewing of failure or the admission of its possibility as evidence of a lack of desire to succeed. Thus, many *est* graduates were reluctant to admit that a task might be impossible or a goal unattainable. Millard liked that quality and actively sought it in the people with whom he wanted to work. He wanted those around him to have done the training. That was one reason he hired Joe Killian.

Initially, Millard had no intention of building a computer. He started IMS Associates to configure computer systems for businesses; that is, to determine what hardware and programs the companies needed to solve their data processing problems and put the two together. Millard had done exactly this sort of work for the city and county of San Francisco.

Killian, however, had become fascinated with computers in graduate school, and Millard needed a good programmer who also knew hardware. After dropping out of a graduate school physics program, Killian was looking for a job in the Bay Area when a friend introduced him to Bill Millard. The *est* training formed a bond between the two, but Killian was not the model IMSAI executive Millard was seeking. Young and enthusiastic, Killian nevertheless had a shell of deliberation about him. He was open to new ideas and attacked new technical problems with a hobbyist's zeal. But always there was that moment of hesitation before he expressed an opinion on a new idea, the moment it took him to fit it into his existing knowledge and beliefs. Later Millard discoveries would be more willing to take risks.

It took a New Mexico auto dealer to turn Millard and Killian toward building microcomputers. Early in 1975, one of their customers provided both a problem and a maddening challenge for Millard. The automobile dealer had commissioned Millard to find a computer to do his accounting, and Millard thought he saw an inexpensive way to satisfy him. MITS had just announced the Altair, and Millard planned to buy the rudimentary machine and tack on whatever extras the dealer needed.

Unfortunately for his plan, Millard did not fully grasp the MITS situation. Roberts's little company, overwhelmed by orders, was not yet ready to deliver complete Altairs, and Roberts had given no thought to quantity discounts. The idea of selling Altairs at a discount to Millard, who would dress them up as business systems with the appropriate software and attachments, didn't appeal to him. When Millard realized that Roberts couldn't or wouldn't supply him with discount machines, he began to look elsewhere.

Had Millard been in tune with the hobbyist milieu, he might have come to some agreement with one of the new hobby firms just popping up. Instead, he drew on his contacts in the minicomputer and peripheral equipment areas. At a computer terminal company called Omron, which had coincidentally just bought the first two of Torode and Kildall's microcomputer systems, Millard talked with a soft-spoken man named Ed Faber. Faber was, in some ways, a kindred spirit. Like Millard, he was an ex-IBM salesman, in his mid-40s, and intrigued by risks. Millard took particular note of Ed Faber. But the immediate goal was to fill the auto dealer's order, and again, nothing acceptable to Millard emerged. Millard was growing frustrated.

Yet there was a great opportunity here, he realized. It wasn't just a matter of a single auto dealer in New Mexico. Once Millard's people had put together a complete system with programs and all the necessary hardware, they could sell it to auto dealers throughout the country. Millard *knew* they couldn't fail. He wasn't going to let the opportunity evanesce. Taking the auto dealer's money, he started a company called IMSAI Manufacturing for the express purpose of building a microcomputer.

Millard knew what he wanted. The Altair was the machine for the job, he was convinced, and if Roberts wouldn't sell Altairs to him at a reasonable price, he would build his own. Or Joe Killian would. A friend of Killian's had bought an Altair, and Killian studied it, but that wasn't enough. External examination was fine, he explained, but he basically needed to get inside the thing and dismantle it; his friend liked his Altair intact. Millard listened and then phoned Paul Terrell, whose nearby Byte Shop was one of the few Altair dealerships in the country. Millard ordered some Altairs for dissection. Over the next few months, Killian would tear the computers apart, figure out how they were made, and replicate them.

Millard's team was beginning to grow. Killian had worked many late nights on another project, and in February 1975, Millard gave him a vacation. In Killian's absence, Millard needed a programmer to take his place and advertised for one. The UC Berkeley computer science graduate school dropout who applied was young, brash, and willing to take risks; moreover, he knew how to sell himself. This Bruce Van Natta appealed to Millard. Here was, in many ways, the model of the IMSAI executive: tall, thin, bright-eyed, quick with an opinion, crisp and decisive in his speech, sharp in his attire, and willing to take outrageous risks. Van Natta fell naturally into the aggressive IMSAI mold.

When Killian returned, the three of them sat around a table at Jake's Blue Lion Restaurant in San Leandro talking late into the night about their plans — about microcomputers, about their new company, IMSAI, about making miracles. "Make a miracle" was an often used phrase and one of Millard's favorites. If Killian or Van Natta objected that he was asking the impossible, Millard would say, "Make a miracle."

While Killian worked on the IMSAI computer, Bruce Van Natta was promoting the Hypercube, a product idea he had come up with and hashed out during the Blue Lion talks. The Hypercube was a proposed device to link several microprocessors together to produce results similar to those of a large computer. Van Natta received warm acclaim for this concept. He was soon giving lectures around the San Francisco Bay Area, at one point even speaking before several hundred electrical and electronics engineers. But he was proudest of his invitation to lecture to the UC Berkeley Computer Science Department he had so recently left.

The Hypercube also caught the attention of the computer media, stealing the front page of *Computerworld* and the Product Spotlight in *Datamation*, two mainframe computer publications. This was a great deal of attention for a product that never existed except in Van Natta's head, but to those editors, who were trying to keep abreast of all the rapid innovations, some such linking scheme may have seemed the only way by which the tiny microcomputers could be useful.

In December 1975, with IMSAI's computer in the first stages of production, Millard talked again to Omron's Ed Faber. This time he asked him to come to work for IMSAI. Faber was skeptical. Killian's computer was, like the Altair, a kit. Kits were ridiculous, Faber thought. He had never heard of building your own computer, let alone selling it through mail order via ads in *Popular Electronics*. But the number of calls coming in when he visited IMSAI changed his mind. He soon got swept up in the excitement and started as director of sales in January 1976.

Faber was not exactly of the IMSAI mold. He was knowledgeable, experienced, and used to giving orders rather than taking them. Most of the other key people were more malleable. Millard, the gambler, had wanted his eager band of executives to follow him in his high-risk excursions. Would Faber follow?

Faber was willing to take risks. He was a veteran IBM employee who had specialized in two fields: sales and start-up operations. Having started a number of new ventures for IBM, Faber had found that he enjoyed the exhilaration. Millard needed someone to organize a sales force, and Faber was willing. It was a critical post; the sales team was the heart of the company.

Bill Lohse, one of the first salesmen Faber hired, was a vitamin seller with a degree in philosophy. But he was of the IMSAI mold: a recent and enthusiastic *est* graduate, tall, thin, brash, and fond of the kind of suits that Van Natta and Millard favored. He knew nothing about computers but was convinced he could sell them to anyone.

Many more employees were hired, including a crew to produce the machines, and some of these, like ex-rock music roadie Todd Fisher, were of a different mold. By fall of 1976, the production crew was turning out Killian's computer, the IMSAI 8080, in quantity, and MITS, which until then had seen competition only for its circuit boards, suddenly had a serious rival.

&

Building One was primarily the adminis-
trative building. Building Two was the pro-
duction building. There was always this
thing of Building Two versus Building One.

Todd Fisher

Building One and Building Two

Todd Fisher liked to fix things. When high school ended and many of his classmates went to college or engineering school, Fisher drove to the Air Force recruitment center and enlisted. The Air Force taught him to repair electronic equipment. He wanted the training, but he didn't want to make a career of the Air Force. When his hitch was up, Fisher went to work briefly for IBM repairing typewriters and keypunch machines. He quit in 1967. It wasn't that Fisher didn't like the work. He did. But the idea of working for a corporation as huge and powerful as IBM got to him.

After leaving IBM, Fisher discovered that he could make money from music—not by playing it, but by fixing equipment. He drifted into the San Francisco rock music business in the late 1960s. This was Fisher's milieu and he loved it. From 1968 to 1971 Fisher worked with dozens of local rock groups. He became a roadie for drummer Buddy Miles and then for the rock band Uriah Heep. Fisher traveled around the world repairing electronic equipment. He was in heaven.

Eventually he had to return to earth. Back in the Bay Area and short of funds, Fisher opened an electronics repair shop but closed the shop when he couldn't find enough customers. He was working in a stereo store doing repairs when a friend invited him to come to work in the service division of a one-year-old computer company, a place called IMSAI Manufacturing. Repair computers? Well, why not? he thought. After touring with Buddy Miles it was a letdown, but Fisher liked to fix things.

IMSAI had grown fast and showed no signs of decelerating. The company already occupied two buildings on Wicks Boulevard in San Leandro: Administration, Sales, Marketing, and Engineering were located in one building, and Production and Support in the other. Millard had put together a driven organization, a fact nowhere more apparent than in the sales department in Building One. Telephone salespeople like Bill Lohse came in promptly at 8:00 A.M. and, after a brief sales meeting, got on the phones and stayed there, logging every call until lunch. Lohse would take an hour off, during which he compared notes with other sales representatives on how many thousands of dollars of equipment each had sold that morning, and then jump back on the phones again until the end-of-day sales meeting. The meetings were results-oriented. Lohse learned not to talk about problems, but about challenges and opportunities. Exhortations to "make a miracle" were common.

Under Millard's encouragement—some say insistence—the IMSAI executives and sales staff did the training, made the miracles, and met the goals. IMSAI employees learned to focus on what they wanted to do and then to do it; they learned that lesson well, and it intensified their performance in meeting goals and in working with co-workers and customers. Focus on what you want to do and do it: this was a powerful message to put in the head of a recent graduate in his or her first serious job in a rapidly expanding company that could apparently go bankrupt next week or grow as big as IBM. And the message was delivered under the leadership of a compelling entrepreneur, a high-roller who told the new employee that he or she could perform miracles—*would* perform miracles.

Millard's exhortations created an atmosphere calculated to drive his staff to superhuman efforts, and those who breathed that atmosphere were certainly driven. It created a style among IMSAI management of almost manic optimism. They regularly worked into the night, living and breathing IMSAI, almost losing sight of the sublunary world. Focus on what you want to do and do it was Millard's standard. Yet from where Bill Lohse stood, eyebrow-deep in the work, it was often difficult to see anything to do but what he was already doing. There was nothing on the horizon but this week's sales goal.

The goal was the sales department's Holy Grail. One experience drove that point home for Bruce Van Natta.

Van Natta had held a number of jobs at IMSAI, working in purchasing, programming, engineering, and product planning. One day, to the sales director's surprise, he walked in and announced that he wanted to be a sales representative. It seemed an odd thing for a co-founder of the company to do, but before long, he was the company's top agent.

Around this time, Bill Millard set a sales goal of one million dollars for the month. Two days before the end of the month, Van Natta checked the sales figures: $680,000—well short of one million dollars, and there was nobody left to call. He wouldn't say it was impossible to make the goal; one didn't talk that way at IMSAI. But he thought it as he went home that night.

Van Natta's wife Mary was IMSAI's sales coordinator and she knew the figures too. Her birthday was approaching, and she wasn't sure she could enjoy it in the wake of their failure to reach the goal. When Van Natta asked her what she wanted for her birthday, she could think only of one thing.

"I want the goal," she told him.

They talked it over. Van Natta reminded her that there were just two days left, that they had called everybody they could possibly call, and that they would be lucky to ring up another dime that month. Besides, $680,000 was a long way from a million dollars.

She said that she wanted the goal.

OK, Van Natta said. He did some mental calculations. If he could convince the firm's biggest customer to place a 90-day order instead of a 30-day order, and if.... He was one of a dozen or so on the sales team, and he accounted, he estimated, for about 30 or 40 percent of sales. But it just seemed impossible.

At ten minutes before 5:00 P.M. on the last day of the month, Van Natta walked slowly over to Mary's desk. He added his latest sales into the current total. It came to $990,000. Could they stop now? Was that OK?

No, she told him. It's the goal or nothing. We've got to have the goal. No falling short by $10,000. Bruce went back to the phone and called a dealer. Would the dealer take $10,000 worth of equipment that he didn't really want as a personal favor? The dealer reluctantly agreed. They made the goal.

Selling a million dollars worth of computers and building a million dollars worth of computers were two different things, and the production people had trouble keeping up. But one spring month the company actually shipped a million dollars' worth of machines, and the production crew had a party in Building Two. Operations Manager Joe Parsialli brought in some beer, and there was pizza for everybody. Nancy Freitas was a production technician, and Todd Fisher had become the supervisor of production testing. Both got drunk.

Freitas noticed that they weren't the only ones responding to the alcohol. After working long hours for weeks on end, succumbing to a few beers was easy. They were tired. The production team arrived at work at 6:00 A.M. and labored till 8:00 at night. Lots of overtime was expected of everyone. But it wasn't just the hours. It was the push, the emotional strain. They were frazzled. Fisher recalled that after working 12 or 14 hours straight they would sometimes go sit in a bar and drink to stop their hands from shaking. Small wonder a beer or two at the party loosened them up.

This group could have fun together, Fisher found. Others shared his interest in music, and sometimes, when the pressure slackened, a bunch of them —and not the same bunch every time — would go out back and throw a Frisbee around. They'd go out for lunch and 20 or 30 of them would sit around together. He appreciated the camaraderie. And he realized something about IMSAI's two buildings. There was a definite cliquishness, he thought, to Building One. But in Building Two, in the production department, the people were laid back. There were some musicians, some dope smokers, and not many *est* graduates. IMSAI definitely had two factions, and it seemed that neither could relate to the other. In production they worked together to do the job, but the people in Building One were very competitive.

Millard believed competitiveness was no handicap for a salesperson. Indeed, he did all he could to encourage it. And probably no one else at IMSAI, in Building One or Building Two, was more aggressively competitive than the company's director of marketing, Seymour Rubinstein.

&

> *What [IMSAI] needed was a way to sell*
> *floppy-disk drives; CP/M is what did it. I*
> *personally consummated the CP/M contract.*
> *[Kildall] got a good deal, considering that*
> *the Navy was supporting him and he didn't*
> *have any other expenses.*
>
> **Seymour Rubinstein**

Miracles and Mistakes

Seymour Rubinstein was a programmer for Sanders Associates, a military defense electronics firm in New York, when he first met Bill Millard. Rubinstein's ambition and self-confidence must have been obvious to Millard; and so was something else Millard admired: a willingness, born perhaps of that same supreme self-confidence, to take on tasks others rejected as impossible.

Rubinstein considered himself a self-made man. Born and raised in New York City, he had put himself through Brooklyn College in night classes where he took the school's only computer course. With the lever of his own boldness, Rubinstein turned that one course into a job as a technical writer, then a programming job, and finally the position at Sanders. By the time he left, as he would tell people later with a chuckle, he had a staff of programmers working for him.

In 1971 Millard had formed his own company, System Dynamics, to sell an IBM-compatible telecommunications terminal, and he recruited Rubinstein to come to work for him in California on this short-lived venture. When System Dynamics folded the next spring, driven out of business by IBM, Rubinstein and Millard went separate ways.

But Rubinstein was enthusiastic about the technology. If Ed Faber was initially skeptical about selling kit computers, Seymour Rubinstein was not. He had settled in San Rafael, north of San Francisco, and when System Dynamics took down its tent he became a consultant. Returning from a consulting trip to Europe at the end of 1976, Rubinstein was unaware of the infant microcomputer industry. He was surprised to see a new business on a main street of sleepy, suburban San Rafael. It was called a Byte Shop, and it sold computer kits. Rubinstein bought one, put it together in a few weeks, and began programming. It was a real computer! He was amazed. Later, he learned that his computer was manufactured by the same man who had brought him to California, Bill Millard.

By February 1977 Rubinstein had joined IMSAI Manufacturing as a software product marketing manager. Within a few months, he moved up to the position that he would hold throughout his tenure at IMSAI: director of marketing. Millard got Rubinstein to do the training and felt even better about him.

As software marketing manager Rubinstein came to know programmer Rob Barnaby—at least as far as one *could* know Barnaby, a slim, taciturn young man who liked to work alone into the early hours. Barnaby and Rubinstein both realized that the IMSAI machine needed software since the software originally supplied was scanty. Barnaby had proposed to write a version of BASIC for the IMSAI, but Millard vetoed the project when he found out how long it would take. Since then, Barnaby had been doing miscellaneous programming, helping hire other programmers, like Diane Hajicek and Glen Ewing, and negotiating software deals from outside sources. Millard wanted fast results, and buying software was quicker than writing it. When Rubinstein arrived, Barnaby was negotiating two software contracts with people from the Naval Postgraduate School in Monterey, where Glen Ewing had studied. Rubinstein took over these negotiations from Barnaby.

IMSAI needed a disk operating system. From the start Millard saw the IMSAI machine as a disk-drive machine, that is, one that would use magnetic disks for permanent information storage. The Altair had initially used slower and less reliable cassette tapes. Disks were essential for the business applications Millard intended for the machine. But a disk drive was useless without a program, a kind of software reference librarian to handle the storage of information on the disks.

IMSAI bought an operating system called CP/M from a professor at the Naval Postgraduate School, Gary Kildall, the same man who had sold computers with John Torode to Omron. CP/M was brand new. Kildall had given Barnaby the third copy in existence. Rubinstein negotiated with Kildall and his partner and lawyer, Jerry Davis, and closed the deal for a flat $25,000. It was theft, he exulted; if Kildall had had any sense, he would have sold on a royalty basis, not charged a flat fee. After closing, Rubinstein told Kildall that his marketing approach was naive. "If you continue this practice, you are not going to make nearly as much money as you are entitled to," he said. Kildall shrugged it off. He thought he had made a good deal.

One of Kildall's students had written a version of BASIC, and IMSAI picked that up too. Gordon Eubanks settled for even less than Kildall. In fact, he gave IMSAI his BASIC for the price of a computer and some technical support. IMSAI supplied him with a computer, disk drives, and a printer, and encouraged him to develop the language further, with the understanding that IMSAI would have unlimited distribution rights. Eubanks developed CBASIC, which would work with the newly purchased CP/M. It was just what IMSAI wanted. The cost to IMSAI of CBASIC was so low that IMSAI didn't even consider, then, buying the BASIC—MBASIC—that Gates and Allen were selling under the company name Microsoft.

Later, when IMSAI did begin buying software from Microsoft, Seymour Rubinstein handled the negotiations from start to finish. Rubinstein was a clever, remorseless negotiator and he brought all his skill to bear on Microsoft's young president, Bill Gates. Gates left their meeting thinking that he had done well for Microsoft, but a few days later he began to have doubts. Rubinstein, on the other hand, knew at once what kind of deal he had made. "Everything but the kitchen sink," he chuckled, "including the stopper and the faucets."

Seymour Rubinstein was making his own miracles in his own way.

But for the production and service people in Building Two, Building One's glorification of the impossible dream was creating problems. It was easy, Todd Fisher found, to think of the departments as individuals in conflict since the Building One and Building Two departments had such different personalities. The way Sales dictated what Production had to do, with no concern about what could be done, was, in Fisher's view, just too disruptive. Sales would set a production quota of, say, 27 for some item, Fisher recalled. Production would set aside the parts for 27 and build 27. Then someone would come running across the parking lot from Building One saying, "I've just sold 30 more of those things! We've got to have 30 more by Friday." Sales didn't care that Production didn't have the parts or the people free to do it; at least, that's how it looked from Fisher's viewpoint in Building Two. Sales had to have them out by Friday, so Production would shift gears and get them out by Friday. Make a miracle.

Fisher didn't like the way schedules got jerked around. Jarring changes in the work threw people off psychologically. Production could never tell when it would have to work longer hours or salvage something to obtain the needed parts. The uncertainty affected Production people's pride in their work, because often machines had to leave the shop without proper testing. Fisher once got a call from a customer wondering why the machine had a screwdriver in it. Someone had sealed the computer up and shipped it before the technician had had a chance to remove one of his tools from it.

But Production was better off than Support. Nancy Freitas's brother, Ed, who worked in Inventory, could see that the Customer Support department was getting short shrift. Often when Support needed a part to repair a customer's machine, the need received the lowest priority. Production got the parts first, a practice that failed to charm customers waiting for their machines to return from repair. Thus, informal Building Two procedures went into effect. Fisher or Freitas would spot a problem, Freitas would mention it to her brother, who would work his inventory magic. The part Support needed would then materialize. Freitas and Fisher found themselves resorting to this procedure often. Together they had started an underground.

Freitas had worked in both Inventory and Production and had once drawn a flowchart of operations, contacting all departments and detailing the course of parts through the manufacturing and repair phases. So she knew what could be done. All the talk of making miracles irritated her. She'd explain that a goal was actually, physically, and materially impossible. Management wouldn't want to hear "impossible." Make a miracle.

This reluctance to acknowledge limitations also caused friction within Building One, where Engineering resided. After the release of the IMSAI 8080,

Engineering's big new project was a computer called the VDP-80. The VDP-80 had a novel design, with the screen built into the box, and Killian wanted to see the machine tested thoroughly. But it soon appeared that such testing would not take place. The order came down that the machine had to be shipped, and it didn't matter that the whole department, including Joe Killian, said it wasn't ready. The prototype seemed to work, the orders were coming in, and the company needed cash.

Engineering threw up its hands. If you want the machine, Killian's group told Millard, it's your baby. Engineering didn't want responsibility for a machine that would soon be clattering with problems. Millard didn't want to hear about problems. Sales was getting more orders for the VDP-80 every day. The company needed the money to start shipping. That was that.

Sometimes it seemed to the people in Engineering, Production, and Support that Sales was blindly selling the ground right out from under them. IMSAI cared about success, all right. But Management measured success by sales figures first, rather than by the quality of production or service, it seemed to many. IMSAI was a selling machine and, viewed that way, was doing very well.

For Bill Lohse in Sales, this time seemed endlessly exciting and challenging. Lohse thought the company was constantly changing, taking risks, and scoring some big successes. Millard thrived on change and new risks. The sales team expanded and improved. Salespeople with experience and plenty of IMSAI drive and initiative, like Fred "Chip" Poode, were coming in. Then there was the franchise idea.

The computer store was emerging as a serious channel of distribution for microcomputers. Ed Roberts had trapped MITS by demanding that MITS's stores sell only Altairs, and Bill Millard was not going to make the same mistake. Still, how could he ensure loyalty? Millard liked the notion of an independent but friendly franchise, and the idea also interested Ed Faber. Perhaps Faber was chafing in Millard's organization, seeking more autonomy, or perhaps the initial start-up excitement had worn off. At any rate, in the summer of 1976, Faber told Millard that he wanted to start a franchise operation. Lohse watched this development with special interest, and when Faber left to start the franchise, Lohse replaced Faber as director of sales.

Lohse immediately confronted two challenges. Chip Poode saw Lohse as a kid fresh out of college and resented being passed over for the job. And Seymour Rubinstein, in Lohse's view, thought that Marketing and Sales should both report to one person: often Seymour Rubinstein. Lohse and Rubinstein locked horns frequently.

Still, Lohse thought, IMSAI was a great place to be. Lohse enjoyed working for Bill Millard, and liked being around him. And he enjoyed working in Sales. IMSAI's people sold when nobody thought they could and made sales goals that were obviously impossible. They performed miracles. It was unreal.

&

72

It was a bunch of heavy est *people.*

Jim Warren

est and Entrepreneur's Disease

Millard was busy throughout 1978 creating new companies. IMS Associates, the parent company for IMSAI, spawned ComputerLand, Faber's franchise operation. Millard also went to Luxembourg for several months to set up IMSAI Europe, a separate corporation that would buy computers from the California operation for resale in Europe. As a result of his absences, he failed to see the dramatic tailspin that IMSAI had begun.

IMSAI's high-handed stance regarding support was finally starting to hurt it. The company had misconceived its market. The notion was that IMSAI was selling computers to serious business users, but the quality of the IMSAI machine, like that of every other early microcomputer, was erratic, and the individual who bought the machine for purely business purposes was likely to be disappointed. The IMSAI 8080 had a distressingly high failure rate, and the instructions that came with the machine were written by engineers and were virtually opaque to anyone else. Bruce Van Natta, with tongue in cheek, summed up IMSAI's attitude toward documentation: "You got the schematic? Then what's the problem?" There existed no software for even the simplest business applications when the IMSAI 8080 was first released. The computer, viewed as a desktop adornment, was large, unwieldy, and suggestive of nothing so much as a pile of electronic test equipment. It took a large dose of imagination to believe that businesses would rush to install this assemblage in their offices or would entrust their business records to this unproven, unreliable artifact. Thus, most "business" users were actually hobbyists who hoped to use the machine in business and tolerated its deficiencies because they were learning and having fun. But IMSAI's poor customer support proved too much even for these tolerant hobbyists. Word spread fast through the hobbyist community, whose opinion IMSAI disdained. Sales soon started falling behind projections, and the game of funding current expenses with orders for future products began to falter.

While Millard was away, Wes Dean was in charge. Though IMSAI's president, Dean was beginning to despair of the company's future. Looking beyond the day-to-day crises, Dean concluded IMSAI was failing to deal with critical long-term problems of support, image, and cash flow. Dean finally gave up and left and was succeeded by John Carter Scott, who presided over layoffs in early October 1978.

IMSAI's financial problems had reached a crisis in the fall, and it became clear to Scott that drastic steps were necessary. The company had enough orders for machines and repairs to keep everyone busy, but meeting payroll appeared impossible. In October Scott initiated the first of a series of layoffs. Building Two suffered particularly. When he learned that Nancy Freitas would be cut in the layoff, Todd Fisher, who had moved to a key position in the Service department, resigned leaving an unanticipated gap in that already struggling department.

For IMSAI, Fisher's chivalry could not have been more badly timed. The company had started shipping the untested new VDP-80, and the machines were coming back almost as fast as Production could push them out the door. The reduced Service department struggled with the variety of defects in the machines, while the Sales team sold more and more of them. Since the repairs were done under warranty and were often extensive, the company was making very little, if any, profit on the VDP-80. The options were two: send the design back to the drawing board and stop selling the machines until the design problems were solved, or continue selling them and repairing them when they came back. IMSAI chose the latter.

Releasing the VDP-80 so soon was a bad decision, but not utterly inexplicable. Except for Killian and Engineering, Building One did not believe that the VDP-80 really had serious problems. Such a belief would have been tantamount to an admission of failure. Millard had taken pains to surround himself with people who would not admit the possibility of failure: enthusiastic amateurs, miracle makers, and *est* graduates. Whatever *est* might have meant to others, at IMSAI it became tied to an inability to admit the possibility of failing and to a narrowing of vision. Focusing on The Goal came to mean losing track of the customer and of the very nature of the market.

The blinders of positive thinking had contributed to the decision to release the VDP-80, but Millard and the IMSAI executives had another reason for pushing the defective computers out the door: cash. Even if the machines cost them money in the long run, they brought in cash with every sale. Since IMSAI financed present production with future orders, the company desperately needed the cash.

Even with its reduced payroll, IMSAI had severe cash-flow problems. In April 1979, the company took in $20,000 more than it paid out. In May, it took in $12,000 *less* than it paid out. By June, Millard was looking for investors, but by then it was too late. No one was willing to sink money into his company.

Earlier, when IMSAI had looked healthy, Millard had turned down several investment offers. He was not alone in his reluctance to take on investment capital. Many early microcomputer executives feared that selling even a part of the company would cause them to lose control of their organizations. They abhorred the prospect. "Entrepreneur's disease," many call it today — the determination of the founder not to release any corporate control to anyone for any price. As he neared the end, Millard began regretting his malady and wished he had accepted a little investment. The two million dollars offered by one hopeful would have come in handy in 1978.

Among others, Charles Tandy had made an investment foray at IMSAI looking for a microcomputer to sell in his nationwide chain of Radio Shack electronic equipment stores. Tandy didn't want his company, essentially an electronics distribution firm, to build a microcomputer, but he was interested in carrying a computer in the stores. He could do so by either buying computers from a company or buying a computer company. IMSAI was the biggest seller and it seemed the logical choice. Bill Lohse watched Tandy walk into Millard's office one day and knew the discussion inside would be crucial to IMSAI's financial state. It depressed him when he learned that Tandy had wasted his time in talking to Millard and that the companies would do no business together.

Now Millard thought IMSAI's cash-flow problem serious enough to require his presence. Soon, Bill Lohse was packing for Luxembourg to oversee IMSAI Europe.

&

*ROD SMITH SAYS THAT HE DOES
WANT ONE OF MY VDP80S AND
SENT A 4.6K CHECK AND THATS
NICE. BUT IT FEELS A LITTLE LIKE
EVERYTHING WE DO IS CORRECT
AND RIGHT BUT NOTHING PRO-
DUCES THE RESULT.*

Bill Lohse
(Telex from IMSAI
Europe to IMSAI San Leandro)

Death and Rebirth

Millard found IMSAI to be in a terrible cash-flow bind with a machine on the market that was blackening the company's reputation. To turn things around, he first authorized redesign of the VDP-80. He still felt, and Engineering agreed, that the computer was basically sound and would sell well if it worked, and if its reputation had not already been irredeemably hurt.

Another hopeful project was Diane Hajicek's IMNET, a software package that could link several IMSAI machines together. The machines would share resources, such as disk drives and printers. Together, IMNET and the revised VDP-80 would, Millard hoped, give IMSAI a viable office product. Every step was a gamble now, and time was the opponent. If IMSAI could get the VDP-80 and IMNET earning dollars soon enough, the company could make the miracle it needed. If not—well, Millard didn't like negative thinking.

When Millard thought he could safely return to Europe, he left Kathy Matthews in charge. Matthews was Millard's sister and had been an executive in the corporation for some time. The money situation didn't improve. Finally, in the spring of 1979, the company filed Chapter XI—the provision of Federal bankruptcy law that keeps a company's creditors at bay while it cuts back drastically, attempting to dig itself out of its financial hole. Kathy Matthews still believed IMSAI could recover.

Now, if ever, IMSAI needed a miracle. Matthews was doing all she could to generate orders. When Diane Hajicek said IMNET was ready, Matthews went on the road for three straight days to show off the product. The demonstrations were sometimes embarrassing: IMNET wasn't really quite ready. A presentation at one of Faber's ComputerLand stores went well though. Matthews sent IMNET back to Hajicek for more work, but expressed to the Luxembourg group her wish that they could see "how wonderful and exciting it is."

Layoffs continued, and IMSAI retreated to a single building. Its executives had been living like the big business officers they dreamed of being, but they now faced grittier prospects. The interior walls of Building One were rearranged, and the resulting narrow hallways made people claustrophobic. Functions of offices became more flexible, as did those of company officers. One day company vice-president Steve Bishop came across president John Carter Scott lying on his back on the floor of the former marketing office assembling machines as Joe Killian soldered wires.

The European operation wasn't flourishing either. Lohse pronounced the situation "grim." The money just wasn't coming in fast enough. In San Leandro, "We need a great August," Matthews said, as July of 1979 ended. Steve Bishop—the veep—examined the records and noted that they had lost less than he had feared. IMSAI could meet payroll for another month.

The July issue of *Interface Age* carried a column by industry watchdog Adam Osborne, who called IMSAI a "financial victim." Matthews felt she was reading her own obituary. They weren't dead yet! She wanted "so very much to produce a miracle and create a butterfly from a caterpillar."

Bill Millard decided San Leandro needed his firsthand attention again. He arranged a flight and sent telexes on July 31 to Ed Faber, Steve Bishop, and his daughter, Barbara Millard, all saying "I would like to meet with you Wed. 8/2" and naming time and place. Within a week of Millard's return, IMSAI Manufacturing suspended all sales and manufacturing operations. Steve Bishop told Lohse to advise European dealers of the situation. Meanwhile, Millard was desperately looking for someone with the money to keep IMSAI afloat.

On August 7, Steve Bishop telexed Lohse.

"YOU NEED TO CONSIDER YOUR PAY. YOU WERE BEING PAID OUT OF SNLO [IMSAI San Leandro] AND ONLY ONE PERSON IS LEFT ON THE PAYROLL HERE. THE WAY WHM [Bill Millard] IS SAYING IT IS THAT WE CAN STICK AROUND AND MAY GET PAID BUT NO ASSURANCE. ALSO YOU NEED TO CONSIDER YOUR RETURN EXPENSE TO THE U.S. NOT BEING NEGATIVE JUST WANTED YOU TO BE THINKING."

Things hadn't worked out for Lohse. He had seized the European job in part to escape the problems looming at IMSAI, but there was no avoiding the ultimate collapse. Lohse had two choices: abandon ship or ride out the storm. Somehow, after all he had experienced, quitting didn't make sense now. But if he stayed, Lohse had to wait for developments in San Leandro. The future was up to Bill Millard. If Millard could find an investor, the sparkle would return to all their lives. But Lohse wasn't very good at waiting, and most of the items on his to-do list said, "Wait for further info."

A week later, on August 14, the telexes between Kathy Matthews and Lohse were terse.

Lohse: ANY NEWS?

Matthews: NOT A THING.

Lohse: RATS.

Lohse assessed IMSAI Europe's financial position. It was bad. No matter how he figured, the European office could not guarantee payment of its September bills. Lohse would have to sell essential equipment just to keep a legal minimum balance in the bank.

Lohse had told his staff that there was no longer money to pay them. He had worked closely with these people for six months and it was a hard thing to say.

"WE ARE WAITING," he telexed to Matthews.

She said, "WELL, WE HAVE ANOTHER DAY."

Lohse paused, then answered, perhaps thinking of the time difference, perhaps of something else, "WELL, OURS IS ABOUT OVER."

On August 21, Lohse requested to come home. Bill Millard telexed back his permission, asking Lohse to bring along the Norelco shaver Millard had left behind.

Back in San Leandro on September 4, 1979, Millard called a meeting. The building, once the base for more than 50 people and several divisions of the company, was now vacant except for the small group of people sitting around the table. There wasn't much to say. The VDP-80 redesign was complete and it was solid. But the machine on which the company pinned its hopes was too late. IMSAI had been dying for a long time, and the final miracle hadn't come through. When the meeting ended, everyone got up and walked out, and a little later a policeman came and put a padlock on the front door.

But IMSAI was not dead yet. Before lockout, Todd Fisher came in and picked up some equipment. Along with Nancy Freitas, Todd had formed an independent repair company after leaving IMSAI, and they were doing most of the IMSAI repairs when the company filed Chapter XI. Recovery from Chapter XI almost requires a miracle, and IMSAI hadn't made one. Nevertheless the company did recover—or was reborn—in a most ironic fashion. While IMSAI was foundering, Fisher-Freitas was showing a profit. John Carter Scott didn't want customers' equipment tied up in judicial wrangling, so he asked Fisher to take it all along with whatever tools Fisher needed to keep his operation going. Plenty of IMSAI computers remained in the field, and they would all need service someday. Scott couldn't think of a better person to repair them than Todd Fisher.

After a month, Fisher bought most of the remaining IMSAI inventory at a low-key auction. Still later, finding the company name also apparently available, he took that too. He and Nancy Freitas, now husband and wife, brought in an old music-industry buddy of Fisher's and incorporated as IMSAI Manufacturing. Operating out of a few hundred square feet in the warehouse district of Oakland, California, they began to build IMSAI computers once more.

The IMSAI of Fisher and Freitas was a small company with little resemblance to the frantic original. It focused on support rather than sales and made efforts to get to know the actual customers.

But the old IMSAI had been remarkably successful with the IMSAI 8080, selling thousands over its three-year existence. IMSAI's brief triumph—as well, no doubt, as its ultimate failure—stemmed in large part from the managerial philosophy of Bill Millard, a philosophy marked by big goals and intolerance of failure, an exceptionally aggressive sales effort, a refusal to attend to problems, an unwillingness on Millard's part to relinquish any control, and a perhaps fatal scorn for the entire hobbyist community. Many have found a lowercase acronym for that philosophy: *est.* One outspoken computer company president pronounced that *"est* killed IMSAI," and as *est* was understood and practiced at IMSAI, at least, many industry insiders would agree.

IMSAI represents an apparent detour in the growth of the personal computer industry. But, in fact, IMSAI's rise and fall was a significant development. If the IMSAI decision-makers failed to understand the hobbyist nature of their market, they nevertheless fanned the fires of the revolution by giving hobbyists a better Altair. At the same time, IMSAI's attempt to make the industry into something it was not helps to illuminate what that newborn industry actually was: a grass-roots movement of hobbyists fully conscious that they were bringing on a social, not just a technological, revolution.

&

Thomas J. Watson, Sr., founder of IBM
(Photo courtesy of United Press
International)

John Mauchly, co-creator of ENIAC,
speaking at the 1976 Atlantic City
Computer Festival
(Photo courtesy of David Ahl, *Creative
Computing*)

David Ahl, who left Digital Equipment
Corporation and started *Creative Computing*
magazine to popularize personal computers
(Photo courtesy of David Ahl, *Creative
Computing*)

Les Solomon's basement with a collection
of computers designed by microcomputer
pioneers
(Photo courtesy of Les Solomon)

Ed Roberts, founder of MITS and creator
of the Altair computer
(Photograph by Charlotte Wilkes, courtesy
of *The Courier Herald*)

Opposite page, top,
Les Solomon at his desk at *Computers
and Electronics* with the MITS programmable
calculator, which predated the Altair
computer
(Photo by Paul Freiberger)

Opposite page, bottom,
Art Salsberg and Les Solomon, Editorial
Director and Technical Editor of *Popular
Electronics* (now *Computers and Electronics*), with
historic Altair cover
(Photo by Paul Freiberger)

Ed Roberts with his invention, the Altair;
at lower left is an Altair disk drive
(Photograph by Charlotte Wilkes, courtesy
of *The Courier Herald*)

Steve Dompier, an early Homebrew
Computer Club member, who made the
Altair play music
(Photo courtesy of Steve Dompier)

Cromemco's Cyclops camera, which
was designed to work with the Altair
(Photo courtesy of Roger Melen)

Bill Gates during the early days of his
company, Microsoft
(Photo courtesy of Bill Gates)

Bill Lohse of IMSAI
(Photo courtesy of David Ahl, *Creative
Computing*)

Lee Felsenstein with an intercom device
at a Philadelphia science fair in 1961
(Photo courtesy of Lee Felsenstein)

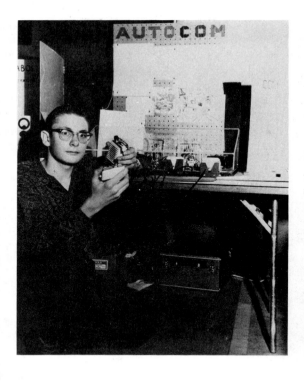

Following page, top,
Lee Felsenstein in the lab of an optometry
professor while a student at UC Berkeley
(Photo courtesy of Lee Felsenstein)

Following page, bottom,
Lee Felsenstein in 1977
(Photo courtesy of Lee Felsenstein)

Lee Felsenstein in 1962 discussing his
intercom device on a local television
program
(Photo courtesy of Lee Felsenstein)

Ted Nelson, computer pundit and author of *Computer Lib*
(Photo courtesy of David Ahl, *Creative Computing*)

Seymour Rubinstein, an early IMSAI employee, who later founded MicroPro International and published WordStar
(Photo courtesy of MicroPro International)

Promotional ad for People's Computer
Company
(Courtesy of Jim Warren)

Front and back covers of the first issue
of People's Computer Company newsletter
(Courtesy of Jim Warren)

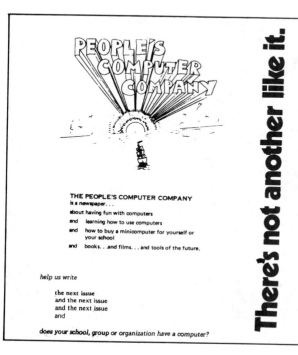

Bob Marsh of Processor Technology
entertaining children at a computer show
(Photo courtesy of Bob Marsh)

Opposite page, top,
Cartoon from a subscription ad for
People's Computer Company
(Courtesy of Jim Warren)

Opposite page, bottom,
Gordon French, one of the founding
members, addressing a meeting of the
Homebrew Computer Club in 1979
(Photo courtesy of Lee Felsenstein)

Steve Dompier (*far left*), Bob Marsh, and
Lee Felsenstein at a meeting of Processor
Technology dealers in 1979
(Photo courtesy of Lee Felsenstein)

Harry Garland (*left*), co-founder of
Cromemco, discussing computer standards
with colleagues on route to New Jersey
for PC-76, an early computer show
(Photo courtesy of Roger Melen)

Roger Melen at the Great Wall of China
(Photo courtesy of Roger Melen)

Harry Garland (*left*) and Roger Melen
of Cromemco
(Photo courtesy of Roger Melen)

George Morrow in a pose for an early
advertisement
(Photo courtesy of George Morrow)

Chuck Grant (*left*) and Mark Greenberg,
founders of Kentucky Fried Computers
and North Star Computers, with a
North Star Horizon
(Photo courtesy of North Star)

Homebrew

Chapter 4

It had its genetic coding in the '60s, in the anti-establishment, anti-war, pro-freedom, anti-discipline attitudes.

Jim Warren

Computers for the People

The Altair and IMSAI computers created excitement when they were introduced, but not because they were technological marvels — in fact they weren't. Understanding the popularity of these machines requires understanding the personalities of those hobbyists who bought them, and who soon founded computer companies of their own. Understanding the popularity of the Altair and IMSAI computers also requires understanding the social and political milieu into which the first microcomputers emerged.

The late 1960s were a turbulent time on American college campuses, a time when many were questioning received values and structures and building their own. The era had a strong anti-technological flavor, but to call the 1960s anti-technological is to ignore a countercurrent in the counterculture, a force that shaped the early development of the microcomputer industry. The iconoclastic styles of the early microcomputer companies in the San Francisco Bay Area, the way those companies communicated with one another, and even the kinds of machines they built owed something to the 1960s and to counterculture engineers like Lee Felsenstein.

Lee Felsenstein had dropped out of engineering school at the end of the 1960s and had gone to work for a company called Ampex as a junior engineer designing non-computer circuitry. Ampex didn't require him to work with computers, and that was fine with Felsenstein, who had been cool toward computers since an overly ambitious attempt in high school to build a computer of his own. Felsenstein was willing to work hard, but, as a true student of the 1960s, he didn't like ploughing his efforts into corporate America. He left Ampex in 1969 to write for the *Berkeley Barb*, a counterculture publication that achieved nationwide attention. For a time, he was listed on the masthead as "Friday" (as in Man Friday).

When internal politics split the *Barb* staff, he went to another underground publication, *The Tribe*. Felsenstein was brought in for his "technical knowledge," a condition which left his job definition flexible. For a while, he functioned as business manager, but also did some layout work. Although enthusiastic at the beginning, Felsenstein came to see *The Tribe* as "an exercise in applied adolescence." He cut back to part-time work with *The Tribe* and returned to Ampex around 1970, where he became involved with computers, designing an interface for a Data General Nova computer. There he decided that computers weren't so bad after all. Felsenstein saved his money, and in 1971 re-enrolled at UC Berkeley where he completed his engineering degree. In 1972, he moved into an urban commune in a factory building in San Francisco.

The building was a magnet for counterculture engineers like Felsenstein. He occupied it with a group from the San Francisco Switchboard, a volunteer referral agency, along with assorted other "computer junkies" who had left UC Berkeley protesting the American invasion of Cambodia. All were involved in a project called Resource One, an attempt to unify — via computer — the switchboards in the San Francisco Bay Area.

The Switchboard had a computer, a large, $120,000 XDS 940, a remnant of Xerox Corporation's abortive attempt to enter the mainframe computer industry, inherited by Resource One from the Stanford Research Institute, where it had seen service running one of the first computer-controlled robots, "Shakey." Felsenstein moved in as part of the second generation at Resource One, and he signed on as chief engineer to run the computer. The job paid "$350 a month and all the recrimination you can eat," as he put it. It was a frustrating job, but he believed in the project, and would later recall being annoyed when two Berkeley graduate students, Chuck Grant and Mark Greenberg, refused to get off the system so he could do maintenance.

Resource One put Felsenstein in touch with Cal students and faculty and other researchers. He visited Xerox's Palo Alto Research Center (PARC) and saw innovations that verged on microcomputers, but which were more sophisticated than microcomputers would be for many years — and much more expensive. However, Felsenstein's sympathies lay with a growing, grass-roots computer-power-to-the-people movement.

The movement was developing in the San Francisco Bay Area out of the general spirit of the times and out of an understanding by those, like Felsenstein, who knew something of the power of computers. They resented that such immense power resided in the hands of a few and was jealously guarded. These technological revolutionaries were actively working to overthrow the computer hegemony of IBM and the other computer companies, and to breach the "computer priesthood" of programmers, engineers, and computer operators who controlled access to the machines.

Many of these revolutionaries had been a part of the priesthood. Bob Albrecht had left Control Data Corporation in the 1960s because of its reluctance to consider personal computers, and had, with friends, started a non-profit alternative education organization called the Portola Institute. From Portola sprang, under the orchestration of Stewart Brand, *The Whole Earth Catalog*, which inspired actress Celeste Holm's son Ted Nelson to write a book similar in spirit, but about computers. Nelson's *Computer Lib* proclaimed, before the Altair was announced, "You can and must understand computers now!" Nelson's book was the *Common Sense* of the revolution. The other significant publication bringing information about computers to the general public in the Bay Area at the time was a tabloid called *People's Computer Company* (PCC), which, as its publisher Bob Albrecht said, was a company "in the same sense that (rock group) Big Brother and the Holding Company was a company."

Albrecht's Portola Institute had a rapidly growing influence throughout the Bay Area on the developing movement to bring computer power to the people. Albrecht wanted to teach kids, in particular, about the machines, and he split off from Portola to form Dymax, an organization dedicated to informing the general public about computers. Dymax gave rise to a walk-in computer center in Menlo Park and the thoroughly irreverent *PCC*, non-profit both by design and in practice. Computers had been mainly used against people, *PCC* said. Now they were going to be used for people. Albrecht was never paid, and others worked for little. The 1960s value structures that pervaded the company exalted enjoyment of the work and accomplishment of something worthwhile beyond the attainment of money, power, or prestige. If *Computer Lib* had the most revolutionary philosophy and the most brilliantly original ideas, *PCC* had solid practical advice for the person who wanted to learn more about computers.

Albrecht and company were not writing about personal computers yet since personal computers didn't exist. They wrote about personal access to computers. In the early 1970s, users generally gained access to a computer via time-sharing; that is, by using a terminal connected to a mainframe computer that was usually kept in a locked room. In the East, DEC sold a PDP-8/F minicomputer programmable in BASIC and featuring an I/O teletype machine for under $6000, a remarkably low price for a minicomputer and a hint to the visionary of what was to come; but virtually no individual owned a computer. Computers like the DEC minicomputer could, though, be purchased by schools. David Ahl, editor of DEC's newsletter on educational uses of computers, *EDU*, spent a lot of time writing about small computers like the $6000 system. He argued that children learning about computers should be able to get their hands on the real machines, not just terminals connected to a remote, impersonal time-sharing system.

On the West Coast, Lee Felsenstein was trying to humanize those time-sharing systems. He helped organize Community Memory, an offshoot of Resource One that installed public terminals in storefronts. The terminals gave anyone who walked in the front door immediate free access to a public computer network. It was rather like an electronic bulletin board, where messages, names, and addresses could be left and changed instantly. There were problems though. The Community Memory project taught Felsenstein a lot about bringing the power of the computer to people. Access wasn't enough; releasing the power of a computer depended on making it understandable and required freeing the users from depending heavily on a trained repairer. People didn't know how to use the Community Memory terminals, and the terminals needed frequent repair.

Felsenstein approached this challenge in a way characteristic of his general approach to technological problems. Instead of merely fixing the terminals, he began looking for the underlying philosophical problem in their design. His father had recommended the book *Tools for Conviviality*, by Ivan Illich, author of *Deschooling Society*. Pointing to radio as an example, Illich argued that technologies become really useful only when people can teach themselves about the technologies. Felsenstein had built his own radio in Philadelphia as a child and appreciated the point. Truly useful technologies must be, Illich said, convivial. They have to stand up under the abuse people put them through in learning how to use and repair them.

Felsenstein wanted computers to spread like crystal radio technology had done, and he took Illich's message to heart and began soliciting ideas for a convivial terminal, looking, in the spirit of Community Memory, for a communal design. He put a notice in *PCC* and placed on Community Memory a call for a meeting to discuss the Tom Swift Terminal. One of those responding was Bob Marsh. Marsh and Felsenstein discovered they had already met, but this meeting via computer was the important one.

Bob Marsh had been an engineering student at UC Berkeley, where he and Felsenstein lived in Oxford Hall, the University Students' Cooperative Association building. To Felsenstein, Bob Marsh still looked much the same with his boyish grin and his dark hair falling across his forehead, but Felsenstein noticed that Marsh had grown up. While Felsenstein had not always been as serious about school as about political events, Marsh hadn't seemed to be serious about anything. He had been a desultory student. Pool and beer got more of his attention than did classes, and he had dropped out in 1965.

Two weeks of pounding the pavement in Berkeley led to a job clerking in a grocery store. Marsh labored there just long enough to save up the minimum cash for a trip to Europe. When he returned, it was with an altered outlook. "I was more motivated," he said. He went to a community college to build up a grade point average to return to Berkeley; he planned to be a biology teacher. But one visit to a teachers' meeting ended that dream. Marsh didn't like the way principals and administration treated teachers and returned to an engineering major.

Marsh worked on a series of engineering projects with his friend Gary Ingram. They had known each other since they had worked together on their first project, one based on a *Popular Electronics* article by Harry Garland and Roger Melen. Marsh had also read the Don Lancaster TV Typewriter article in *Radio Electronics* and tried to devise an improved version of it with some success.

Ingram was now working at Dictran International, an importer of dictation equipment, and there he gave his friend Marsh a job. When Ingram quit a month later, Marsh found himself chief engineer. He liked it. Eventually that job disappeared, but he later said of his stint as a chief engineer, "It changed my life." Being a Berkeley student in the 1960s, being on his own in Europe, seeing in teaching what it was like to work under others, and getting a shot at being an engineer at Dictran had all contributed to creating in Marsh an entrepreneur.

In 1974, he was also broke and out of work. Felsenstein said Marsh had worked himself up to the level of unemployed electronic engineer. With house payments to make, a family to support, and one child and another child on the way, Marsh was looking for a project around which he could build a company. His meeting with Felsenstein about the Tom Swift Terminal led to a discussion about electronic products and about launching a corporation; Felsenstein, though, was involved in social revolution. He wasn't interested in starting a company.

Marsh decided he needed work space and talked Felsenstein into renting at least a garage with him. In January of 1975, they rented 1100 square feet at 2465 Fourth Street in Berkeley, which cost them $170 a month. Felsenstein set up his workbench and commenced the free-lance engineering projects he was picking up. He was still involved in Community Memory, and the Tom Swift Terminal was on hold. Marsh also set up shop, making plans with a friend who could get cheap walnut planks and with an electronics distributor named Bill Godbout, for a proposed digital clock.

Then the January issue of *Popular Electronics* came out, announcing the Altair and changing the lives of the counterculture engineer and the unemployed entrepreneur. It did so in part because it brought into existence the Homebrew Computer Club, an extraordinary gathering of engineering expertise and revolutionary spirit from which would spring dozens of computer companies.

&

There was a strong feeling [at the Home-brew Club] that we were subversives. We were subverting the way the giant corpora-tions had run things. We were upsetting the establishment, forcing our mores into the industry. I was amazed that we could con-tinue to meet without people arriving with bayonets to arrest the lot of us.

Keith Britton

The Homebrew Computer Club

Felsenstein and Marsh weren't there during Homebrew's gestation. Early in 1975, a number of San Francisco Bay Area counterculture information exchanges existed for people interested in computers. Community Memory was one. There was also *PCC*, and the *PCC* spin-off, the Community Computer Center. In addition, peace activist Fred Moore was running a non-computerized information network out of the Whole Earth Truck Store in Menlo Park, matching people with common interests about anything, not just computers. Moore became interested in computers when he realized he needed a machine and a base of operations, and he talked to Bob Albrecht at *PCC* about both. Soon, Moore was teaching children about computers and learning about them himself.

At the same time, Albrecht had been looking for someone to write certain assembly language programs and found Gordon French, a mechanical engineer and computer hobbyist, who then supported himself building slot car motors.

When the Altair story appeared in *Popular Electronics*, the need for a more direct information exchange became clear. The *PCC* people took the Altair seriously from the beginning. Keith Britton, a demolition consultant and *PCC's* treasurer, thought its arrival foretold the eventual demise of the computer priesthood. "All of us were champing at the bit to get an Altair," French recalls. So Fred Moore pulled out his list of the computer curious, the revolutionaries, the techies, and the educational innovators, and sent out the call. "Are you building your own computer? Terminal? TV Typewriter? I/O device? Or some other digital black box? Or are you buying time on a time-sharing service?" Moore's flyer asked. "If so, you might like to come to a gathering of people with like-minded interests. Exchange information, swap ideas, talk shop, help work on a project, whatever." The announcement tentatively called the group the Amateur Computer Users Group or Homebrew Computer Club, and it met on March 5, 1975, in Gordon French's garage.

Felsenstein read about the upcoming meeting and intended not to miss it. He collared Bob Marsh and they drove in Felsenstein's pickup truck through the rain across the Bay Bridge to the peninsula that stretches from San Francisco in the north to Silicon Valley in the south. Gordon French lived in suburban Menlo Park, a town jogging distance from Stanford and right on the edge of Silicon Valley.

At the first meeting, Steve Dompier reported on his visit to Albuquerque. MITS had shipped 1500 Altairs and expected to ship 1100 more that month. The company was staggering under the weight of the orders and couldn't begin to fill them, Dompier said. Bob Albrecht displayed the Altair that *PCC* had received that week — *PCC* was just behind Harry Garland and Roger Melen, over at Stanford, on MITS's list — and passed out the latest issue of *PCC*.

Dompier, like Marsh and Felsenstein, had driven down from Berkeley, but most of the 32 or so attendees were from the San Francisco Peninsula. Albrecht and Gordon French, who chaired the meeting, and Fred Moore, who took notes for a newsletter, and Bob Reiling, who soon took over that newsletter, all lived in Menlo Park. Many other people had come from farther south — from deeper into Silicon Valley: Mountain View, Sunnyvale, Cupertino, San Jose — people like Allen Baum, Steve Wozniak, and Tom Pittman, who described himself as a microcomputer consultant, perhaps the first in the world.

As the meeting concluded, one Homebrewer held up an Intel 8008 chip, asked who could use it, and gave it away. Many people present that night sensed the opportunity in this Homebrew spirit and in Dompier's words. One of them was Bob Marsh. Marsh went immediately to see Gary Ingram about forming a business enterprise. I've got a garage, he said. It seemed enough. They decided to call themselves Processor Technology, or Proc Tech. Marsh designed three plug-in circuit boards for the Altair: two I/O boards and a memory board. They looked good, he thought. He devised a flyer announcing Proc Tech's products, made hundreds of copies of it on a campus photocopying machine, and took 300 of them to distribute at the third meeting.

By this time the club was flourishing. Fred Moore was exchanging newsletters with Hal Singer, who put out the *Micro-8 Newsletter* in Southern California and had formed a Micro-8 club shortly after Homebrew started. Other publications were passed around. *PCC* and Hal Chamberlain's *The Computer Hobbyist* attracted special interest. A Denver organization identifying itself as a provider of support for Micro-8 and TV Typewriter hobbyists and calling itself The Digital Group, offered subscriptions to its newsletter. The movement was getting hard to keep up with. Intel, with its 4004, 8008, and 8080 chips, and at least 15 other semiconductor manufacturers had introduced microprocessors into the market, and the newly-formed club tried to keep its members informed about them all.

The third Homebrew meeting drew several hundred people, too many for Gordon French's garage. It was moved to the Coleman mansion, a Victorian building serving as a schoolhouse. There Marsh gave a brief talk, explaining that he was selling memory and I/O boards for the Altair. He hoped to present

Proc Tech as a serious company, not just the fancy of an unemployed electronics engineer with access to a copying machine. He offered a 20% discount for cash prepayment. To his disappointment, no one came to talk to him at or after the meeting.

The next week the first order arrived. Garland and Melen were seeking Processor Technology's cheapest advertised product. Their request was written on the stationery of their new company, Cromemco. They sent no check, just a purchase order requesting 30 days net credit, hardly what Marsh had expected. He had made Proc Tech look like a real company, all right.

After the Cromemco order, many others followed, most enclosing cash. Ingram fronted $360 for an advertisement in *Byte*. With the cash streaming in, Marsh and Ingram could afford to advertise in *Popular Electronics*, and they did, spending $1000 for a one-sixth-page ad. They incorporated, and Ingram was made president. As corporate headquarters and factory, they had half of an 1100-square-foot garage, no products, no schematics for proposed products, no supplies, no employees, and thousands of dollars in cash orders. It was beginning to appear that they had some work ahead of them.

Meanwhile, Lee Felsenstein was getting more involved with Homebrew. He took over from Gordon French as the master of ceremonies—he refused to think of himself as a chairman. The meetings were now held in the auditorium at the Stanford Linear Accelerator Center. Over the years, Felsenstein became intimately associated with the club and fostered its anarchic structure. The group had no official membership, no dues, and was open to everyone. Its newsletter, offered free after a nudge from Felsenstein, became a pointer to information sources and a link between hobbyists. As group toastmaster, Felsenstein performed with a curious kind of populist showmanship. As one attendee, Chris Espinosa, said, "People call him the Johnny Carson of Homebrew, but he's more than that. He kept order, he kept things moving, he made it *fun* to go to the meetings. There were 750 people in that room at one time, and he worked it like a rock concert. It's hard to describe, but to see him work a crowd like a Baptist preacher.... He was great."

The meetings didn't follow Robert's *Rules of Order* with Felsenstein running them: he gave them their own special structure. First came a mapping session, during which Felsenstein recognized people who briefly proffered their interests, questions, rumors, or plans. Felsenstein sometimes had quick answers to their questions or witty comments on their plans. A formal presentation followed, generally of someone's latest invention. Finally, there was the Random Access session, in which everyone scrambled around the auditorium to meet those they felt had interests in common with them. It worked brilliantly, and numerous companies were formed. A remarkable amount of information was exchanged at those meetings, and much information had to be exchanged; they were all in unfamiliar territory.

About this time, a San Francisco branch of Homebrew started. It held its first meeting at the Lawrence Hall of Science in Berkeley. Although it was called the San Francisco branch, Berkeley was a logical place for it to meet. Universities were becoming hotbeds of self-taught microcomputer expertise. Professors with grant money now found it cost-effective to buy minicomputers rather than buy time on the university mainframe computer, which was invariably out of date and overworked. DEC was selling PDP-8 and PDP-11 minicomputers to professors as fast as it could build them. They were particularly popular in psychology labs, where they were used for experimenting on human subjects, automating rat and pigeon labs, and analyzing data. The invasion of the psych lab by minicomputers created a new kind of expert: one who might know something about psychological research, but who was more clearly a hacker and a computer nut—someone to figure out how to run the computer and make it do what professors, who were generally ignorant about the machine, wanted.

Howard Fulmer was such a person. Fulmer worked in the Psychology Department at UC Berkeley running PDP-11s, selecting minicomputers for professors to buy, building interfaces, and programming experiments. In early 1975, one of Fulmer's professors bought an Altair, and Fulmer learned to use it. Soon after, Fulmer left his job to devote more time to microcomputers.

He was not alone: the Altair raided the University of California at Berkeley. George Morrow, a graduate student in math, worked at the university's Center for Research in Management Science with two other students, Chuck Grant and Mark Greenberg. They were trying to develop a language to use with a microprocessor in computer-controlled research.

Morrow, Grant, and Greenberg found that they worked well together. All three were perfectionists, although in different ways. Morrow, thin, prematurely balding, and with a twinkle in his eye and an irrepressible wit, seemed always to be enjoying himself, perhaps especially when he was hard at work. Grant and Greenberg appeared cut from a darker cloth. They were more businesslike. Although Grant and Greenberg often attended Homebrew meetings and profited from the free, open exchange of information, they never considered themselves part of the hobbyist community. Technically, the three formed a good team. Morrow knew hardware, Grant preferred software, and Greenberg was at home with either.

The trio considered making boards for the Altair or even a kit computer of their own. They knew that they were a good design team, but they also knew they lacked sophistication in marketing. So Morrow sought the advice of Bill Godbout. Middle-aged, blunt, opinionated, with a paunch that he joked about and an airplane that he flew stunts in, Godbout was the electronics distributor whom Bob Marsh had tried to interest in his walnut digital clock when he and Felsenstein had first worked in the garage. Morrow told Godbout about their plans.

Godbout was then selling chips and minicomputer memory boards by mail, and Morrow asked if he intended to sell Altair memory boards. Godbout scoffed. He wouldn't so dignify the product, he said. Morrow wondered if he might be interested in distributing a good computer, the creation of a top-notch design team. "You guys?" Godbout asked. He looked Morrow over. Godbout believed he was good at sizing people up, and Morrow looked all right. They agreed to split profits down the middle and shook on it. No written contract, Godbout said. Written contracts were a sign of mistrust and an invention of lawyers, and if there was anybody Godbout didn't trust, it was a lawyer.

By this time a motley group of engineers and revolutionaries had assembled in Silicon Valley in the infancy of a billion-dollar industry: irascible Bill Godbout, who suspected lawyers; ex-*Berkeley Barb* technical editor and current Homebrew toastmaster Lee Felsenstein; Bob Albrecht, who left a high-paying career to teach children about computers, who smoked cigars, and called himself "The Dragon"; Bob Marsh, testing his own abilities, turning his love for electronics into a garage corporation; and Keith Britton, who saw himself and the other Homebrewers as pivotal in "an equivalent of the industrial revolution but profoundly more important to the human race." A surprising number of them held political views that would have shocked the local Rotary Club, and almost all had no love for IBM and the computer establishment. But they and others like them were pulling off the most startling entrepreneurial achievement in recent times. And much of the action took place at Homebrew.

The Homebrew Computer Club was not merely the spawning ground of many Silicon Valley microcomputer companies. It was also the intellectual nutrient in which they first swam. Presidents of competing companies and chief engineers would gather there to argue design philosophy and announce new products. Statements made at Homebrew changed the directions of corporations. Homebrew was a respected critic of microcomputer products. The Homebrewers were sharp, and could spot shoddy merchandise and items that were difficult to maintain. They blew the whistle on faulty equipment and meted out praise for solid engineering and convivial technologies. Homebrewers soon developed the power to make or break new companies. In part due to Lee Felsenstein, Homebrew encouraged the conviction that computers should be used for and not against people. Homebrew thrived in a kind of joyous anarchy, but the club was also an important step in the development of a multi-billion dollar industry. Processor Technology was one of the children of Homebrew.

Processor Technology was a nexus for hobbyists making a transition, trying to be serious about it all and not always succeeding.

Lee Felsenstein

Wildfire in Silicon Valley

The Fourth Street garage in Berkeley was a busy place in the spring of 1975. Lee Felsenstein was making a meagre living from odd jobs like repairing friends' Altairs, and Bob Marsh was tearing open checks, writing ad copy, and doing his best to convince hobbydom that Processor Technology was a million-dollar company, when in fact it still existed mostly in his head.

Felsenstein had gotten himself in trouble that spring. Writing about the Altair for *PCC*, trying to get the word out, he described the machine's workings and capabilities based on information he received from Homebrew and from a telephone interview with Ed Roberts. Irate letters soon poured into *PCC* contending that Roberts, and thus Felsenstein, were too sanguine about the product. It had serious problems, the letters claimed. Dompier showed Felsenstein the difficulties he had had with the front panel of his Altair and got Felsenstein to fix it.

In a *PCC* article he titled "Criticism and Self-Criticism," Felsenstein then apologized: "I lied folks; this thing has problems." He detailed the computer's flaws and how to correct them. He also began fixing Altairs for friends and *PCC* readers, working on them in his half of the garage. Loyal to other hobbyists and feeling guilty about misinforming people, Felsenstein did the work cheaply. In the process, he learned a great deal about those early Altairs.

Meanwhile, Marsh and Ingram were using their half of the garage to create the Altair boards they were getting checks for. But they needed a sharp engineer to draw up the schematics for the boards that Marsh had conceived. The engineer had to be willing to work in a cramped and messy garage and had to work cheap. Marsh thought he knew someone like that.

Felsenstein had made it clear that he did not want to join Processor Technology or any other company. He had better things to do. Although working long hours for little pay, he was doing what he wanted and felt beholden to no one. Marsh, though, now put forward a new proposal. Would Felsenstein just do the schematic for the first board, as a consultant, rather than an employee? Consulting was indeed different. Felsenstein agreed and offered to do the schematic for $50.

This price, Marsh thought, was pathetic. It was a $3000 job, and Felsenstein, the poor goof, was offering to do it for $50. Marsh refused to go below $500. Felsenstein thought it over and accepted the compromise.

It was fast work, and by June they were shipping boards. One of them was at first meant to be a 2K memory board, an ambitious project when MITS was shipping only an eighth as much memory. But at the last minute Marsh changed the design, doubling the capacity to 4K. MITS's first real competition came from those 4K memory boards, and Ed Roberts wasn't pleased.

But MITS's poor memory boards and delivery backlog had already kicked the door open. When Bruce Seals, a Tennessee hobbyist, flew to Albuquerque in July to discuss an East Coast dealership, he returned to Tennessee with the entire state as his territory and a promise of three-day delivery. But MITS couldn't move the products out fast enough, especially memory boards, and Seals saw the same need—and opportunity—that Bob Marsh had. He too designed and began to sell a 4K memory board.

Processor Technology continued to market memory boards while moving on to new designs. The VDM, Felsenstein's next contract for Proc Tech, was a video display module, an interface board that allowed the Altair to display output on a television screen. Chuck Grant and Mark Greenberg, who had left UC Berkeley with George Morrow and were now doing business as G & G Systems, did the software for the module, and Steve Dompier wrote Target, a video game that showed off the VDM. Dompier later asserted that it was the VDM that first made such video-based games possible.

That fall, a local computer show took place at Berkeley's Lawrence Hall of Science. MITS was represented by two area Altair dealers, Paul Terrell and Boyd Wilson, who proudly showed Felsenstein and Marsh the hoops their machine could jump through. Marsh was more interested in the fact that the Altair was full of Processor Technology memory boards. Harry Garland and Roger Melen were also there, showing how their Cyclops camera could be used with the Altair.

Before Homebrew had grown big enough to need the auditorium at the Stanford Linear Accelerator Center, Les Solomon visited it in the nearby SLAC Orange Room. He was the star of the evening, a temporary king in the anarchy, telling somewhat far-fetched stories of his own experiences. Sometimes he sounded like a counterspy, other times like a vaudeville magician. "It was unclear what country he was working for," Lee Felsenstein joked, but he was among Solomon's large cadre of admirers. At one point, Solomon led the Homebrewers outside, did some hocus pocus, and instructed them to lift the huge stone table in the yard. They were surprised to find that they could hoist it right up, although Felsenstein noted dryly that no one had tried lifting it without the hocus pocus.

Some nights at Homebrew, a tall, dapper, and charismatic man could be found selling books out of a cardboard box. A chemical engineer born in Bangkok of British parents, he was the same Adam Osborne who had been doing technical writing for Intel. He had written a book called *An Introduction to Microcomputers* and was publishing it himself. It was, in fact, an introduction to *microprocessors*, such as the Intel 8080. The microprocessors were commonly referred to, especially by the public relations departments of the semiconductor companies, as microcomputers.

Although the IMSAI people almost never attended club meetings, Bruce Van Natta was at Homebrew one night and bought a copy of the book. His decision to include a copy of Osborne's book with every IMSAI allowed Osborne to start a publishing company that would eventually be purchased by McGraw-Hill. Ironically, it would be Osborne who would first announce IMSAI's demise in a column in a computer magazine.

After Homebrew meetings, the most fanatical of the members went to a local beer-and-burger place known as the Oasis—everyone just called it "the O." They sat in wooden booths at wooden tables, surrounded by the deeply carved initials of generations, and drank beer and argued computer design. They ignored the fact that they were competitors. There were a lot of things to learn in developing this new kind of product, and they weren't about to let economic issues get in the way of learning all they could. Marsh and Melen regularly traded insights on design, and Grant and Greenberg sometimes joined them at "the O."

By the end of 1975, new microcomputer companies were poking up everywhere, though the most furious activity was still in the San Francisco Bay Area. IMSAI was located in San Leandro. Cromemco was designing boards for the Altair. MOS Technology had released its KIM-1 hobby computer, based on its bargain-basement 6502 microprocessor, with a hexadecimal keyboard instead of binary switches. Microcomputer Associates in Los Altos had its Jolt, a 6502 kit.

Southern California was also a growing center of hobbyist activity. In Gardena, Dennis Brown was selling his Wave Mate Jupiter II, a computer based on the Motorola 6800 microprocessor, "for serious hobbyists" for less than $1000. Although the Altair had sold for less than half of that, a realistic price for an assembled Altair *system*, including some sort of I/O device, adequate memory, and a storage device, was well over $1000. Electronics Products in San Diego announced another 6800-based computer, the Micro 68. On December 31, 1975, Rich Peterson, Brian Wilcox, and John Stephensen quit their jobs to form a company. Peterson and Wilcox had built an Altair, Stephensen had built his own 8080 machine from scratch, and they found themselves designing boards to make the Altair run better. Deciding that their hobby could just as well be their vocation, they formed Polymorphic Systems and started working on a computer kit. They first called it the Micro-Altair, and later, under duress, changed it to Poly-88.

Elsewhere in the West, MITS in Albuquerque was offering a 4K static memory board for its 8080 system and was developing a computer based on what was emerging as the Southwest chip: Motorola's 6800. Systems Research in Salt Lake City sold a 6800 microcomputer board. Mike Wise's Sphere, operating out of a small factory near Salt Lake City, was offering its 6800 computer with a built-in terminal and plastic case. Southwest Technical Products, run by

Dan Meyer in San Antonio, Texas, also had a 6800 system. The Digital Group in Denver was selling a variety of boards.

In the Midwest, Martin Research was offering its Mike CPU boards with 8008 or 8080 chips. Ohio Scientific Instruments in Hudson, Ohio, had 6800 and 6502 kits. Heath Kit in Benton Harbor, Michigan, had a computer in the works.

In the East, the hobbyist movement grew up around the Amateur Computer Group of New Jersey. Scelbi, in Milford, Connecticut, put out a popular kit based on the 8008, and Technical Design Labs in New Jersey was developing a computer kit around a new chip, the Zilog Z80. Hal Chamberlain in North Carolina, Bruce Seals in Tennessee, Georgia Tech student, Ron Roberts were active hobbyists working on systems or components or software.

But the fire burned most strongly in Silicon Valley, and in its symbiotic atmosphere of information sharing, new companies to create circuit boards for the Altair were popping up almost daily. By the end of 1975, one of these, Processor Technology, was well on its way to parlaying its substitute for the defective Altair memory board into wealth and, within its curiously anti-corporate industry, a kind of corporate respectability.

&

Bob said he would pay me to design the
video section of the Tom Swift Terminal. He
knew how to manipulate me.

Lee Felsenstein

Nostalgia for the Future

In June 1975, Bob Marsh and *Popular Electronics* technical editor Les Solomon
were contemplating an "intelligent terminal" kit, a terminal with semiconductor circuitry inside it, to perform certain display and keyboard decoding functions that a computer would otherwise have handled. Marsh had some ideas
from his own experience and from discussions with Felsenstein about the Tom
Swift Terminal. "If you can get me a working model in 30 days, I'll give you a
cover story," Solomon said.

Marsh then asked Felsenstein, "Do you think it's impossible?" Felsenstein
appreciated the careful phrasing. To dodge the job would force him to pro-
nounce it impossible, an act distasteful to a self-respecting engineer. They discussed it. Marsh would pay Felsenstein to design the video portion of his
dream machine, the convivial terminal that would be one step in releasing the
power of computers to everyone. Felsenstein agreed. It soon turned out that
Marsh had really had a different project in mind. Marsh wanted an 8080-based
terminal that contained the chip that ran the Altair. They showed each other
proposed designs. Felsenstein thought his was better, but when he saw Marsh
was adamant, he gave in and started to work on Marsh's version. Neither
Felsenstein, Marsh, nor Les Solomon realized it, but the product they were
designing would become something more than just a terminal.

Felsenstein had to withdraw from another project when he agreed to design
the intelligent terminal. "The roof is falling in again," he told his ex-customer.
Up to now, he had paid his share of the rent by consulting for various people.
But Proc Tech was expanding to take up the whole garage, all 1100 square feet
of it. Felsenstein was being absorbed.

Marsh had already developed the terminal's architecture and continued to
change the design requirements as Felsenstein worked. Felsenstein had
enjoyed consulting, in part because he could get some distance from the person
he was working for and concentrate uninterruptedly on a problem. But this
advantage disappeared as he labored in the little garage with Marsh. Marsh
insisted on design changes and forced Felsenstein to junk much of his careful
work and start over. "The situation did," Felsenstein later said, "call heavily on
my sense of futility, absurdity, and ultimate irrelevance."

But despite his complaints, Felsenstein was enjoying himself. His comments
about being manipulated are more an ironic jab at himself than at Marsh, who

for all his entrepreneurial energy, was at least partly in it for the fun of it. At one point in the project, Felsenstein said, "Let's advertise it as having 'the wisdom of Solomon.'" He meant it as a sly reference to Les Solomon, and this whimsical sales tactic soon ripened into naming it "The Sol."

Marsh and Felsenstein could have used the wisdom of Solomon themselves. Not only did they argue over the design at Felsenstein's workbench and in the makeshift Proc Tech offices slapped up within the garage, but they argued about it over meals and while driving across the Bay to Homebrew meetings. On one trip to Homebrew, they redesigned an entire internal bus.

Once they started work, it dawned on Marsh and Felsenstein that they were designing a real computer. After all, it had an 8080 in it. But clearly it was also a terminal. Till then, computers had generally been rectangular boxes with accessor connections to terminals of some kind — Teletypes, cathode ray tubes, typewriters, or printers. But theirs was a keyboard and a computer in one case. Could they make it? The question was both technical and political. At this point the Altair dominated the tiny microcomputer industry, and IMSAI had not yet made its entry. And they were developing this terminal under the encouragement of the Altair's biggest booster outside Albuquerque — Leslie "Uncle Sol" Solomon. Would he rescind the cover story agreement if they told him they were doing a computer instead of a terminal? They decided not to tell him.

In spite of all their arguments, Marsh, Ingram, and Felsenstein were enjoying themselves. "This is a company that's going to have fun," Felsenstein said, "no matter how miserable I have to be." He described Marsh and Ingram as nostalgic for the future, like many computer hobbyists of the day, and often their discussions were quite visionary. But there were also the day-to-day decisions. Marsh's friend still had the cheap walnut, so Marsh, in designing the cabinet, gave it walnut sides.

Felsenstein had originally expected to hand the finished schematic to a layout artist. As it turned out, *he* was the chief layout artist. A light table for the layout work was installed in a loft above the Proc Tech offices. Felsenstein padded the forehead-level conduit, but wasn't sure how to prevent bumping his head on the rafters as he worked with the other layout artist 14 to 17 hours a day, 7 days a week. The other artist, pumping himself with cola while Felsenstein ran on orange juice, dropped out before the end and Felsenstein had to finish the job alone.

Marsh kept the pressure on and within 45 days of his first discussion with Les Solomon he had a circuit board, and within 60 days he and Felsenstein were nearly finished. Solomon had given them a 30-day deadline, but when they were nearing completion Marsh booked a flight to New York and informed a bleary-eyed Lee Felsenstein that he was coming along. They stuffed their Sol into two paper bags.

The demonstration for Solomon at *Popular Electronics* was a disaster. The thing just didn't work. They made excuses and flew on to an appointment at *Byte*.

The presentation there went no better. Felsenstein, dead on his feet from the breakneck schedule, fell asleep during the *Byte* demonstration.

Well-rested and back in California at his workbench, he found the problem quickly—a short. Marsh put him back on a plane to New York to demonstrate a working Sol with strict instructions not to reveal that it was actually a computer.

Felsenstein kept his mouth shut. But when he showed Les Solomon the Sol terminal, Solomon watched it work for a while, and then asked what was to stop him from plugging in a memory board with BASIC and running the Sol as a bona fide computer.

"Beats me," Felsenstein deadpanned.

Marsh and Ingram had realized that if the Sol was a computer, it needed software, particularly a BASIC. They contracted with Chuck Grant and Mark Greenberg to write it. George Morrow had previously had a difference of opinion with Grant and Greenberg—he didn't think they were taking their oral agreement with Godbout seriously enough—and Morrow decided to deal with Godbout alone, while Grant and Greenberg began business as G & G Systems.

As they worked on the BASIC, Grant and Greenberg found they were having the most trouble with the floating-point routines: arithmetic on real numbers, not integers. They couldn't process the operation as fast as they wanted. Finally, they decided to build the floating-point math into the hardware, and hired George Millard (no relation to Bill Millard) to help design a floating-point board.

About this time, contention arose over ownership of the BASIC. Marsh asserted that the BASIC was being developed for Proc Tech, while Grant and Greenberg, with growing ambitions, insisted that it was theirs and began soliciting other customers for it. Proc Tech took Grant and Greenberg to court, and the case lumbered through discovery and delay, doing, close observers felt, neither company any good.

Grant and Greenberg had other hot projects. They developed a cassette tape interface. Then Shugart, a Silicon Valley disk drive manufacturer, announced a drive that used 5 1/4-inch disks—smaller than the 8-inch disks in common use on bigger computers—and that cost less than any other disk drive. So Grant and Greenberg started designing a controller board to make the drive work with microcomputers. When they had their disk system together, they gave themselves a new name, North Star, perhaps an echo of Altair. Simultaneously, as Applied Computer Technology they contracted to sell IMSAIs together with their own BASIC and cassette interface to universities. The market, they discovered, did not want configured systems, but raw computers, so they began selling IMSAIs out of Mark Greenberg's garage. This operation, at Grant's suggestion, was called Kentucky Fried Computers.

Meanwhile, their ex-partner George Morrow had bought an Altair, studied it, and decided not to imitate it. He shared Godbout's estimate of the Altair. The computer that he and Godbout planned, and that he began to design, would be better. He would base a computer on National Semiconductor's PACE, a microprocessor they hoped to get for $50 from National. Godbout, however, had reservations about the project. He meditated over Altair's sales figures, and decided that memory boards for the Altair might do very well after all. Morrow, with some reluctance, put aside the PACE machine and commenced designing a 4K memory board with his own name on it, joining Proc Tech and Seals in the memory market. Godbout sold the board for $189, well under Proc Tech's price, and suddenly Morrow found himself making $1800 a month in royalties.

Godbout now became intensely interested in selling microcomputer boards. But when he vetoed one of Morrow's ideas, Morrow reevaluated their relationship. Couldn't he sell his boards just as well as Godbout, he asked himself. The only difference, he decided, lay in who placed the magazine ads, so he started Morrow's MicroStuff. The market was crazy, according to Morrow. "You could start a company, announce a product, and people would throw money at you."

Bob Marsh had already learned this lesson with Proc Tech's memory boards, but was willing to have the lesson rubbed in. Marsh and Felsenstein took the Sol to the PC Computer show in Atlantic City, New Jersey, in June 1976, to unveil it to the world. It went over big.

Back in California again, they continued to enhance and modify the Sol. While writing tutorial articles on computer design for *PCC*, Felsenstein added what they called, after Don Lancaster's term, a "personality module." This tiny circuit board had a ROM chip and could be plugged into the back of the machine, allowing the "personality" of the machine to be changed in a second. Felsenstein imagined employees popping in game modules for the business modules while the boss was out of the room.

Around this time, the winter of 1976-77, DEC was selling its LSI-11 bottom-of-the-line minicomputer for slightly over $1000. In Southern California, Dick Wilcox gave hard thought to a suggestion in *Dr. Dobb's* about interfacing the LSI-11 with an Altair or IMSAI. He came up with his Alpha Micro, an LSI-like multi-user CPU board, which he demonstrated to Homebrew in December.

New microprocessors continued to arrive. Toshiba had released the first Japanese chip, the T3444. National Semiconductor issued a new microprocessor and also supplied the development tools hobbyists needed to start building real computers or writing software.

Scores of microcomputer companies were appearing. Vector Graphic in Thousand Oaks, California, introduced an 8K memory board. Vector consisted of a Stanford engineering school graduate and two businesswomen. Men had founded almost all the microcomputer companies, though some had recruited wives or girlfriends as business managers. But Lore Harp quickly showed she was more than just a business manager as she guided the company with a shrewd sense of the market's needs and possibilities.

Vector, though, was doing no better than Proc Tech. During the winter of 1976-77, Proc Tech moved out of the garage to a much larger facility, 14,000 square feet next to a beef-rendering plant in nearby Emeryville. The atmosphere was uninviting, but the new location proved, for a while, far roomier than the garage. A month after Proc Tech moved out, Felsenstein got new roommates. Grant and Greenberg moved into two-thirds of the space of the garage and placed their three company names on the door: North Star, Applied Computer Technology, and Kentucky Fried Computers. As Kentucky Fried Computers, they were now marketing IMSAIs, Polymorphic and Vector Graphic boards, and one Apple I that they were persuaded to take on consignment by a scraggly-bearded young man named Steve Jobs. That winter, though, sales of their disk system soared, and they closed Kentucky Fried Computers to concentrate fully on North Star. A letter from a certain fast-food poultry chain, demanding that they cease and desist from using the name Kentucky Fried Computers, made the decision easier.

By the end of 1976, Processor Technology, Cromemco, North Star, Vector Graphic, and Godbout were eminent among the Silicon Valley enterprises, building an entire industry where none had existed two years earlier. And that industry was growing with amazing speed.

&

*The first part of the meeting we were
involved in open combat with Intel. Intel was
out to torpedo any standardization effort on
the S-100 bus.*

George Morrow

Home Rule

A continuing fear in the developing microcomputing industry was that "the big
boys" would come in and spoil all the fun. Sometimes "the big boys" meant
IBM and the other mainframe computer and minicomputer companies; sometimes it meant Texas Instruments, Commodore, and the other electronics
companies that had waged Pyrrhic price-cutting wars in the calculator industry; especially it meant Texas Instruments, known for its ruthless price-
cutting. Lee Felsenstein summarized the dread of the hobbyist entrepreneurs:
"Anyone but TI!" Intel and some of the other semiconductor companies,
although well situated to produce microcomputers from their own chips, had
expressed reluctance to do anything that could be construed as competing with
their own customers, and the hobby-born microcomputer companies had
developed enough clout by this time to be taken seriously as semiconductor
customers.

In December of 1976, Commodore International, an electronics firm with a
lot of market muscle, leaked information to *Electronic Engineering Times* about a
new product. Commodore, the story went, was ready to release a machine
very much like a low-cost Sol. Proc Tech was just shipping the first Sols and
Marsh was thinking about the company's next product, a new version of the
Sol with an integrated keyboard and 64K of memory, that would be cheap at
$1000. It was, unfortunately, essentially the Commodore machine.

Convinced that Commodore actually had the computer on the launch pad
and that Proc Tech could never compete with it, and even more worried by
news that National Semiconductor was also planning a microcomputer, Marsh
scrapped the project. The laws of battle in the semiconductor wars five years
earlier had been to cut prices to the baseline and push the technology madly,
even under threat of corporate extinction. Proc Tech couldn't compete with
National, especially in mortal combat. But in fact the Commodore machine
would not appear for some time, and the National computer never materialized
at all.

Many new hobbyist-born companies were starting to manufacture microcomputer products, but most of these were turning out boards for the Altair or
IMSAI, and practically all were small companies, start-ups like Proc Tech.

Howard Fulmer began such a firm in his Oakland basement. After reading an editorial by Ed Roberts in Dave Bunnell's *Computer Notes* that attacked the compatible board companies as "parasites," he considered calling his own company Symbiotic Engineering to emphasize his conception of the proper relationship between MITS's products and his own. But a group called the Symbionese Liberation Army was making a name for itself then, and he wanted to avoid confusion. He called his company Parasitic Engineering.

George Morrow and Howard Fulmer were both designing Altair-compatible products, and in the spring of 1977 decided to build a computer together. Morrow would supply Fulmer the boards he had designed at a cheap price, and Fulmer would devise the remainder of the computer. Fulmer called it the Equinox 100. It was a solid design, for they had listened to the ideas of Bob Mullen, one of the founders of Diablo Systems, a Silicon Valley disk-drive manufacturer, and of Bill Godbout about improving the S-100 bus.

The timing of the machine's release was unfortunate though. The Equinox was an 8080 machine, and Technical Design Labs in New Jersey, Garland and Melen's Cromemco, and The Digital Group in Denver were all known to be designing computers based on the new and apparently better Z80 chip. Cromemco had already produced a Z80 central processor board, and hobbyists were dropping it into the IMSAI chassis to create a mongrel Z80 machine.

Marsh wondered if Proc Tech shouldn't do a Z80 machine as well. But it seemed irrational to dump a successful design to achieve a marginal improvement in performance. Besides, the processor mattered much less than the software, he believed. The software made the computer work, and that would distinguish one machine from another.

Proc Tech called two programmers, Jerry Kirk and Paul Greenfield of MicroTech in Sunnyvale, who had produced high-level language compilers for minicomputers. They were hired to create a set of programmer's tools, programs that would make it easier to write, edit, and debug other programs on the Sol. Ingram developed their work into Software Package One.

Ownership of software was an inflammatory issue in the Valley and elsewhere. Processor Tech was aggressively pro-piracy, and its hobbyist founders swapped program tapes at Homebrew meetings along with everyone else. Gordon French, who after helping to start Homebrew had become Proc Tech's General Factotum (his official title), argued for an open system, that is, free dissemination of software code and internal workings to everyone. He wanted outside programmers and peripheral manufacturers to be able to create compatible products and expand the market. At that time, Ed Roberts and the entire mainframe and minicomputer industry held the opposite view. But the hobbyists were bringing their own values into their industry. An open architecture, the publicly-known physical design of the machine, was one emerging ideal. An open operating system was another. But at Proc Tech the idea of an open operating system was frowned upon. Marsh and Ingram wanted a proprietary operating system.

In fact, Proc Tech had its own disk operating system very early on. The company bought PT-DOS from its author, 19-year-old Bill Levy, who developed it at the Lawrence Hall of Science at Berkeley. Levy modeled PT-DOS after UNIX, a mainframe/minicomputer operating system in use at UC Berkeley. Marsh thought PT-DOS much better than CP/M, but PT-DOS was slow to reach the market because of "the drive fiasco."

Disk drives posed an alluring challenge in 1976, when the Sol was released. They existed and were used heavily on mainframe and minicomputers, but to mount a disk drive on a microcomputer was prohibitively expensive. Drives typically cost $3500. So Marsh was very intrigued when George Comstock, Bob Mullen's partner at Diablo Systems, declared at Homebrew one night that he wanted to develop a disk drive for microcomputers. Comstock thought that a drive, complete with a controller board and software, could be sold for about $1000.

But Diablo was not then involved in the growing microcomputer industry, and Comstock felt a disk-drive system would only flail around without close consultation with microcomputer companies. He later proposed a joint effort to Marsh. Diablo would develop the drives, the physical mechanisms that read and write information from and to disks, and Processor Technology would write the software and develop an S-100 board to control the drives. He also proposed that Proc Tech could market the board on its own.

Disk drives were so clearly destined to belong in any serious microcomputer system that engineers were already vying to develop a low-cost drive system with software and a controller board. Shugart's 5 1/4-inch drives seemed attractive, but they had one drawback. IBM had been using 8-inch drives and had established certain standards for the devices. There were no standards for small disk drives and no guarantees that disks written on one brand of machine would be readable on another. North Star had selected the Shugart drive and sold it for under $800. Using an idea of Eugene Fisher's of Lawrence Livermore Labs, both Morrow and San Francisco engineer Ben Cooper had begun developing relatively low-cost 8-inch disk drives. Cooper had perhaps the first commercial 8-inch disk controller for microcomputers. Morrow, shortly thereafter, had the first one available for the $1000 price Comstock was aiming for, and he negotiated with Digital Research and Microsoft for an operating system (CP/M) and BASIC to distribute free with the drive system. Both Morrow and Cooper continued to develop significant disk products, and Cooper created the first hard disk controller for microcomputers.

But at Processor Tech, the disk drive plans were crumbling. Diablo encountered trouble with the drives and dropped the project, leaving Proc Tech so far into development of the controller that it had to continue. Marsh and Ingram raised the price of the system to $1700 and substituted a more expensive drive offered by Perscii. The price was too high, and Proc Tech's drives didn't always work. Customers could find better deals from Cooper, Morrow, and North Star.

Despite such problems, Proc Tech seemed to be thriving. The executives were recycling their profits into the company. (Lee Felsenstein was investing his in the Community Memory project.) The Proc Tech staff in Emeryville now numbered 85, not counting non-employee/consultant Felsenstein, and headquarters was growing crowded. That year, 1977, Proc Tech moved south to the bedroom community of Pleasanton. The new offices boasted a spacious executive suite with large windows looking out over the valley.

But there was competition. As 1977 came to an end, Proc Tech found itself in a more serious industry. The trading of information, the shirt-sleeve management, the flashes of idealism, and the lack of detailed planning that had characterized the industry from the start still existed. The chief users and the designers and company presidents were still hobbyists at heart, and most of the world knew nothing of the revolution that was afoot. But new companies were emerging like mushrooms overnight. Among the computer and computer-related companies at the end of 1977 were Apple (which some insiders thought had great promise), Exidy, IMSAI, Digital Microsystems, Alpha Micro Systems, Commodore, Midwest Scientific, GNAT, Southwest Technical Products, MITS, Technical Design Labs, Vector Graphic, Ithaca Audio, Heathkit, Cromemco, MOS Technology, RCA, TEI, Ohio Scientific, The Digital Group, Micromation, Polymorphic Systems, Parasitic Engineering, Godbout Engineering, Radio Shack, Dynabyte, North Star, Morrow's Microstuff, and, of course, Processor Technology.

Many companies were located in the Bay Area and were associated with the Homebrew Club. The club had become large, and by 1977 tended to assemble in fairly predictable groups. In front, performing, was Lee Felsenstein. Bob Marsh and the Proc Tech group were usually assembled along one wall. Steve Wozniak and the boys from Apple and the other 6502 processor fans sat in the back. Jim Warren of *Dr. Dobb's* sat on the aisle three seats from the back, stage left, ready to stand during the Mapping session and do his Core Dump, an extemporaneous outpouring of all the news and rumors he had heard. The front row always had Gordon French, who maintained the software library, and Bob Reiling, who wrote the newsletter.

In December 1977, Reiling wrote, "The development of special-interest groups has probably been the biggest change during the past year. At the beginning of the year the 6800 group was holding regular meetings. At the end of 1977, the groups include not only the 6800 group, but also the F8 Users, North Star Users Group, Sol Users Society, and PET Users." At that time, the Homebrew attendees (the club did not have members) included key people from Apple, Cromemco, Commodore, Computer Faire, *Dr. Dobb's*, Itty Bitty Computers, M&R Enterprises, Mountain Hardware, IBEX, Mullen Computer Boards, North Star, *PCC*, Proc Tech, and the Bay Area computer stores. The most significant of these then was Proc Tech. Marsh had, to some extent, realized his dream. The company seemed to be doing very well.

And in December, Reiling could report optimistically, "The IEEE now has a standards group to sort out the various hardware and software standards." That blithe statement subsumed a wrangling struggle and a remarkable achievement which brought new legitimacy to the industry. The sorting out had been no simple matter.

Bob Stewart was a consultant in optics and electronics and a member of the Institute for Electrical and Electronics Engineers (IEEE). He had bought an Altair and had become frustrated with it. At a meeting at Diablo Valley College to discuss the S-100 bus he met some company presidents: Harry Garland of Cromemco, Howard Fulmer of Parasitic Engineering, Ben Cooper of Micromation, and George Morrow of what he was then calling Thinkertoys. *Byte*'s Carl Helmers was also there. The idea was to cure the obvious problems of the bus and to establish common standards, so that one company's board would work with another's. Garland explained the virtues of his and Melen's shielded bus, but Morrow thought he had a better approach. No immediate agreement was forthcoming. Stewart suggested creating an official IEEE standard for the bus. With the group's encouragment, he petitioned the IEEE to form a microcomputer standards subcommittee of the computer standards committee. The petition succeeded, and the group became official.

Roberts was invited to participate in the microcomputer standards subcommittee, but declined to send a representative or even to respond directly. He did say in print that he felt MITS had the sole right to define the bus. The subcommittee ignored him. At first, the meetings involved contention with Intel, which fought standardization. Morrow got the impression that Intel wanted no standards unless Intel was setting them. But when the subcommittee decided to formulate standards whether Intel liked them or not, Intel acquiesced. This was outrageous cheek. A bunch of hobbyists turned entrepreneurs had simply ignored the biggest microcomputer company of that time and had faced the leading chip manufacturer and not been struck by lightning.

In spite of its solidarity, the subcommittee had no guarantee that it could really create standards. The subcommittee had 15 assertive, opinionated people disputing an issue about which they held legitimate and conceivably irresolvable differences. Each of the members had a product that would be incompatible with anything likely to be proposed. As the meetings went on, Roger Melen came in for Cromemco. Alpha Micro was represented. Elwood Douglas appeared for Proc Tech and judged the standard against the memory board he was designing. George Millard spoke for North Star. Someone arrived from IMSAI to read its formal position, which resembled Ed Roberts'. The subcommittee ignored that position too. Most of its members had written IMSAI off as a place where training in *est* mattered more than training in engineering.

At times the subcommittee members weren't too fond of each other. They argued for hours, with no one yielding an inch. They would then return to their companies and discuss how to compromise their own designs to achieve a standard. At the next meeting, they would find themselves closer to agreement. Little by little, these creative, independent people subordinated their egos and short-term economic gains for the good of the entire microcomputer field.

The committee was attempting guerrilla design. In mainframes and minicomputers, the bus was always whatever the bus designer said it was. Although the IEEE suggested subtle variations in tolerances during the process of formalizing the company bus into a standard, independent committees did not assemble to redesign the whole bus. Timing parameters and other features were dictated by the companies. IBM and DEC worked this way. In a way their method was certainly easier than communal design. But the S-100 committee members dug into the Roberts bus, figured out how it worked, and were scrapping it in favor of a new, independent bus open to all. This was a populist revolt against the tyranny of the big company, with MITS hoisted as a poor but adequate symbol of the big company. The revolution was succeeding.

That's where the source of this industry
has been. It hasn't come out of TI, IBM,
Fairchild. It's come from people who are on
the edge, who have an alternative vision.

Fred Moore

Homebrew Legacy

In 1979, Proc Tech was in trouble. Marsh and Ingram, caught off balance by the Commodore and National threats and worried about the promising Apple, had become hesitant about their product line. Their worries showed. Felsenstein kept coming into their offices to talk about new products, but they seemed unable to decide on any. Finally, he asked them, "Look, what the hell do you guys want?" They said they wanted to see what he could come up with, and Felsenstein then understood that they really had no product planning.

Proc Tech also lacked the flexibility that more money would have given, but Marsh and Ingram, green executives, suffered, like Bill Millard, from "entrepreneur's disease." Adam Osborne had once talked with them about accepting investments. But soon the investors were the ones who were reluctant to talk. Proc Tech was not developing new products, and "the Sol" was an 8080 machine in a brand-new world of computers built around the Zilog Z80. Was the Sol out of date? Not really. But since technology was developing rapidly, and since Proc Tech had nothing new in the works, it was hard to see "the Sol" as the computer of the future. When potential investors asked Felsenstein how much work "the Sol" needed to keep it technologically advanced, he told the truth: quite a bit. That didn't help.

On May 14, 1979, the wolf came to the Pleasanton factory door and found nobody home. Proc Tech had cashed in its chips and gone away.

Theories abounded to explain the problems of Processor Technology: too many revisions of the basic product, too much reliance on one product, failure to develop new products, and failure to keep abreast of the technology. Steve Dompier held that the company looked inward too much, tried to deal with all its problems as though they were simply organizational ones. Proc Tech did shuffle people around. According to one (presumably apocryphal) story, the company had hired a full-time employee merely to relocate phones in the Pleasanton plant. Felsenstein has always contended that Proc Tech's boat sank because it was full of small holes and the management had a policy of making more of them.

Maybe it was Gary Ingram's desk. When Proc Tech held its bankruptcy auction, Parasitic Engineering founder Howard Fulmer drove to Pleasanton to look at the former enterprise. He walked through the building, past small, slapped together cubicles, the signs of a company on the skids. At the top of the building, Fulmer found what he could only call the penthouse suite. He had never been there before. He was impressed. There, in the middle of a huge room with large windows, was Gary Ingram's French Provincial desk. Fulmer glanced over his shoulder, then went to the desk and sat down. He settled back in the chair, put his feet up on the desk, looked out across the valley, and sighed contentedly. "I feel rich," he murmured. "Everything must be fine."

Certain fundamental problems at Processor Technology seem clear in retrospect. The Sol did not spring from a single mind, and as a result was not designed as cleanly and coherently as it might have been. Despite the talk of the Sol growing out of Felsenstein's Tom Swift Terminal ideas, Felsenstein didn't design the machine to satisfy himself, but to fill a contract.

A second problem was entrepreneur's disease. Ingram refused to surrender any control of Proc Tech, and as a result the company suffered both from his and Marsh's managerial amateurishness and from undercapitalization. An experienced manager, some investment capital, and greater freedom for the designer might have given Proc Tech's story a happier ending. Indeed, the story might as yet have no ending.

Nevertheless, Proc Tech and companies like it — that operated in ways that baffled seasoned executives — were constructing the microcomputer industry. Soon that industry was shifting its orientation from the hobbyist to the consumer. Market niches were being established. By 1979, Cromemco was known for its square steel boxes full of solidly engineered boards that sold primarily to engineers and scientists. Vector Graphic was selling business machines that started with the turn of a key and immediately ran a business application program. Apple's computer in its plastic case was the premier game machine. And encroaching on the territory of the minicomputers was Alpha Microsystems, offering microcomputer systems that could support several users.

The Homebrew legacy remained discernible in product designs and marketing principles. Homebrew had been catalytic to and actively formative at the microcomputer's creation. But since computers were becoming affordable to large numbers of people, another kind of creative effort was needed to make the hardware useful to as many people. Computer power to the people, the dream of computer revolutionaries like Felsenstein, required software. Useful, affordable programs and the means for producing them were essential to turn the microcomputer into the personal computer. The newborn microcomputer industry brought with it a sibling, the software industry, the outgrowth of the hacker spirit that motivated Gates and Allen to write Altair BASIC.

&

The Software Factor

Chapter 5

I think that most people's real motivation
for getting a computer was to learn — they
wanted to see what they could do with it.

Dan Fylstra

The Altair's First Recital

On the evening of April 16, 1975, at an early Homebrew meeting held in a Menlo Park, California, elementary school, Steve Dompier put on a show. He had an Altair, and few had ever seen one. Certainly, none had ever seen anything like this one.

MITS wasn't delivering yet, but Dompier had earned his Altair. He had flown to Albuquerque to pick it up personally. It might have seemed odd, even fanatical, for Dompier to travel a thousand miles to get a $397 toy. But somehow Dompier made it seem reasonable. This *was* a computer, he was saying to the Homebrewers. It was real and it was here now. And all of them could buy it. Own their own computers? Only a rare few had been able to afford them, but the technofreaks in the audience that night caught Dompier's excitement and began to imagine what they could do if they had computers of their own. What they *would* do *when* they had their own. No, Dompier didn't seem at all fanatical to the crowd in the old school building. He seemed entirely reasonable. They envied him.

But Dompier had quickly learned that the Altair was not quite the final dream machine. When he brought it home and put it together, it failed to run. After six hours of work he identified the problem as a scratch on the main circuit board. He was lucky. It was a relatively minor flaw for that time.

Then Steve Dompier faced the big problem. He had to figure out a use for the machine when all he could do was flip the front switches and watch the lights flash. But quite by accident he discovered something. Playing around with his discovery, he soon had an amusing effect, which he refined and decided to demonstrate to the Homebrewers.

The Homebrewers were interested in the machine, but hardly expected it to do much since it had no display, no keyboard, and only a teaspoonful of memory. But some of them knew Dompier. He was a likeable, rational fellow around whom the universe crackled. If some people are accident-prone, Dompier was wonder-prone, Lee Felsenstein thought. Felsenstein was curious to see what Dompier could do with the Altair.

As the audience watched in puzzlement, Dompier set up his computer and placed a portable FM radio next to it. Then he began flipping switches, the laborious means by which one entered a program in the first Altairs. It took several minutes of this painstaking switch-flipping for Dompier to enter his program. One mistake, he knew, and it would have to be done over. Just as he finished, someone bumped the power cord and erased all his work. Dompier plugged the machine back in and started over, patiently reentering his program.

Suddenly tones came out of the nearby radio. It had been quiet, and now it was playing music: first the Beatles' "Fool on the Hill," and then as an encore, "A Bicycle Built for Two." The radio was apparently controlled by Dompier's Altair. But how? There were no wires connecting the two. What was going on?

In fact, Dompier had simply exploited a characteristic of small computers that was to annoy the neighbors of their owners for the next five years. The machines emitted radio frequency interference, the stuff that makes snow in television pictures and static on the radio. When Dompier realized that the Altair made his own radio buzz, he decided to play with the static. He discovered what he had to do with his program to control the frequency and duration of the noise, and his tiny program, which would have looked nonsensical to any programmer who didn't know about its accidental side effect, turned the static into recognizable music. The Homebrewers gave Dompier a standing ovation.

Dompier described his accomplishment a year later in an article entitled "Music of a Sort" in *Dr. Dobb's Journal of Computer Calisthenics & Orthodontia*, calling the event "the Altair's first recital."

Clever as it was, Dompier's program was short and simple. The machine did not have the memory to do anything complicated. At the time, hobbyists were more interested in hardware than software. After all, many of them had dreamed of owning a computer for some time now, and they couldn't start programming a machine that did not exist. But with the advent of the Altair, software became not only feasible, but essential.

So they all wrote their own. No one thought anyone would actually buy software from someone else. Hobbyists wrote small programs that weren't applications of the machine so much as demonstrations of its capability, one step removed from soldering it together.

Before the microcomputer could begin to change the times, software had to transform the toy into a useful tool. A few pioneers worked within the tightly constrained memory of the first machines and created some ingenious programs. But as more memory became available, more complicated and useful programs became possible. The first of these were often frivolous, but serious applications and business and accounting software soon followed, and programming, a hobby at first, quickly became an earnest commercial enterprise.

The two kinds of programs the new machines needed immediately were operating systems and high-level languages.

The collection of programs that controls I/O devices like disk drives, shunts information into and out of memory, and performs all the other operations that the computer user wants done automatically is called an operating system. In practice, it is usually via the operating system that users work with a computer. Large mainframe computers had operating systems, and it was clear to many people that a microcomputer needed one too.

Every computer has a language known as "machine language," which is simply a set of commands the machine is built to recognize. But such commands merely trigger the fundamental operations of which the machine is capable, like moving data between its internal storage registers, storing data in memory, or performing simple arithmetic on it. The details of machine language make it cumbersome and complex. The computer only becomes widely useful when a command can set off groups of these fundamental operations. Collections of these more powerful and meaningful commands are called high-level languages. High-level languages thus elevate the user one step above the plodding minutiae of machine language and make using the computer faster and more interesting.

Beyond these programmers' tools lay applications programs, the software that would make the computer actually do something. Word processing programs would turn the computer into the replacement for the typewriter, business accounting programs would keep track of payroll records and print checks, educational programs would introduce computer users to new ways of learning.

For the moment, though, operating systems and high-level languages were not available, and applications software was even farther off. Hobbyists looked at their new machines and asked themselves what they could do with them. Play games, they answered.

&

Man is a game-playing animal and a computer is another way to play games.

Scott Adams

Pleasure Before Business

Long before high-level languages and operating systems simplified programming, computerists created games. Nearly everyone is familiar with *Pac Man* and *Ms. Pac Man,* along with the hundreds of other arcade computer games. The early games were much simpler but just as entertaining.

Moreover, games gave the early hobbyists justification for having a computer. When their friends questioned the utility of the machine, they could show them a clever game, perhaps Steve Dompier's *Target* or Peter Jennings' *Micro Chess,* and listen to the oohs and aahs.

Dompier was among the most creative when it came to programming games on the Altair. With no I/O but the front switches, making the Altair do anything was a challenge. Several people, Dompier included, wrote programs in which the player chased the 16 blinking lights up and down the front panel, attempting to hit a switch that would make the lights flash on and off "real pretty."

Creating games was also a way to learn to program, especially after a BASIC was introduced. Several books were available that listed game programs. An Altair, KIM-1, IMSAI, or Sol owner could type in the program and be playing the game in no time. The first such book was David Ahl's *101 BASIC Games,* compiled while Ahl was still at DEC and originally intended for use on minicomputers. Often displaying nothing more graphically sophisticated than patterns of asterisks printed out on a Teletype machine, the early games were primitive compared to today's multimedia arcade spectacles.

Many of the first games jumped to micros from large mainframes. Perhaps it is true that the earliest ancestor of modern computer games with their flashy graphics was a tennis-like game played on an oscilloscope, but games were not new to the early hobbyists. Many had played them on larger computer systems at their jobs, sometimes loading games into memory on large time-sharing systems. Of course, if they were caught playing, they faced trouble, but somehow they couldn't resist the temptation. Today, many business computers hold hidden games in their memories.

One of the more popular of the large machine games was *Star Trek,* which allowed the player to pretend to be Captain Kirk of the *Enterprise* and command the ship through a series of missions, usually involving search-and-destroy missions against Klingon warships. *Star Trek* was an underground phenomenon, hidden in the company or university computer's recesses, played surreptitiously when the boss wasn't looking. No one paid for copies of the game; no royalties were ever paid to the writers or creators of the television show from which it took its name and theme. Scott Adams, an RCA employee working on satellite recognition programs at Ascension Island, recalls playing *Star Trek* on the radar screens, an act which did not endear him to the government officials in charge.

It was only natural that *Star Trek* became one of the first microcomputer games. It was everywhere on larger machines. Many different versions of it already existed, and many more were soon written for microcomputers, including Dompier's *Trek* for the Sol. When the technology made graphics possible on the micro, *Star Trek* programs added visual simulations of "the final frontier."

By late 1976, graphics capability was rapidly growing important. Cromemco, with its Dazzler board, and Processor Technology, with its VDM, gave the Altair its first graphics. The VDM video display module, released in 1976, also worked on the IMSAI, Sol, and Polymorphic computers and on any other machine with an S-100 bus structure.

Graphics software was frequently designed to test or show off the capabilities of a machine. The kaleidoscopic images and changing patterns of the game of *Life* were popular for this reason. Steve Wozniak's *Breakout* for the Apple and Steve Dompier's *Target* for the Sol were two real games that showcased the computers well. A clever programmer such as Dompier could easily make games to highlight a computer, and *Target*, described by its author as a "shoot-down-the-airplane type game," became a phenomenon. People at Processor Technology played it during lunch, and others gave it broader exposure.

One evening Dompier was at home playing *Target* while glancing occasionally at a color television across the room. Suddenly the television screen lit up with video graphics, and there was his game, blazing away in full color on the set. He jerked his hands off the keyboard in amazement. There was no physical connection between the TV and the computer. Had the computer somehow started broadcasting? But the television screen showed a different stage of the game from that on his terminal, although both were certainly *Target*. Then the game on the screen dissolved into Tom Snyder's face, and Dompier realized that the talk show host had been playing *Target* on the air, showing the Sol's capabilities from coast to coast.

Another kind of game was getting a lot of publicity at about this same time, and it also depended on microelectronics, although it was not played on a computer. A brilliant engineer and entrepreneur named Nolan Bushnell had created the successor to pinball machines in the form of an electronic game machine. He sold it through his start-up company, Atari. *Pong* made Bushnell rich and famous and eventually spawned millions of arcade and home video game machines. Bushnell sold Atari to Warner Communications in 1976 when Atari was doing 39 million dollars in sales. While the game machines Atari specialized in were not general-purpose computers, those who wrote games for personal computers took much inspiration from these devices. (Atari would later make its own personal computers.)

But while occasionally a program like Dompier's received mass attention, and while the game machines were enjoying great popularity, microcomputer programmers in 1976 generally didn't believe they were on the brink of creating an industry to compare with hardware manufacturing. In 1976 very few programmers sold software to anyone other than a computer company, and, in this narrow market, they sold cheaply.

Peter Jennings foresaw earlier than most that microcomputer owners would gladly buy software from independent companies. Jennings, a Toronto chess enthusiast, had often toyed with the idea of designing a chess playing machine. In fact, while still in high school he built a computer that could make the opening moves in a chess match. When he learned of the microprocessor, he figured he could program it to play the ancient game. Jennings bought a KIM-1 microcomputer with less than 2K of memory at the PC'76 computer show in Atlantic City, brought it home, and boldly declared to his wife: "That's a computer and I'm going to teach it to play chess." Writing a chess program compact enough for a few hundred bytes of memory is the sort of challenge most people would happily avoid. Chess is an intricate game, and this task could use up much of a mainframe's memory. Jennings was undeterred: he enjoyed the challenge. Within a month he had written most of the code, after a few more months he had perfected it, and before long he was selling it through the mail. For $10 Jennings sent a stapled 15-page manual that included the source code for *Micro Chess*. His advertisement for it in the *KIM-1 User Notes* newsletter was one of the first ads for applications software on microcomputers. And when Chuck Peddle, president of MOS Technology, maker of the KIM-1, offered Jennings a thousand dollars for all rights to the program, Jennings declined, saying, "I'm going to make a lot more money selling it by myself."

One day, while Jennings waited for the money to come in, his phone rang and the caller identified himself as Bobby Fischer. The reclusive chess Grand Master wanted to play a match against *Micro Chess*. Jennings knew how it would come out, but agreed gladly. Later, after Fischer had trounced the program, he graciously told Jennings that it had been fun.

It was fun for Jennings too, and it was also lucrative. The orders poured in. Jennings found that people who couldn't play chess, who didn't even want to learn, would buy the program. *Micro Chess* legitimized the machines. With it they could show their friends that this thing they had, this computer, was powerful, was *real*. It could play chess.

One of the first buyers of *Micro Chess* was Dan Fylstra, who ordered the program while an associate editor at *BYTE* magazine. Later, when Fylstra started a company called Personal Software, he called on Jennings and the two agreed to work together. Soon they were investing money from sales of *Micro Chess* in the marketing of a business program called VisiCalc, written by Dan Bricklin and Bob Frankston. The pairing of Fylstra and Jennings created one of the most important software companies in the industry. And Bricklin and Frankston's VisiCalc was Personal Software's biggest hit. The transition from games to business software has occurred frequently in the microcomputer industry. Games led to profits, and profits led to business applications. Several early game companies went on to add business software departments.

Another game that gained surreptitious stardom was *Adventure*. Written originally on a mainframe computer at the Massachusetts Institute of Technology by Will Crowther and Don Woods, *Adventure* involved a simple form of role-playing: exploring mazes, fighting dragons, and finding treasure. There were no graphics. The player typed in terse verb-object commands like "GET GOLD" and "OPEN DOOR," and the program responded by describing the objects and beings in the player's immediate vicinity in the maze. By storing large vocabularies of verbs and nouns and tying them to certain responses, the programmer was able to create the sense that the program could understand these simple two-word sentences. No one but the programmer knew the program's vocabulary, and learning to communicate with the program was the best part of the game. The game achieved cult status, and a San Francisco Bay Area programmer named Greg Yob wrote a limited *Adventure*-type game called *Hunt the Wumpus*, played in a maze of tetrahedral rooms.

By 1978 Scott Adams decided that he didn't have to restrict his game promotions to coffee breaks but could launch a company and sell them full-time. Well-meaning friends told him that programming *Adventure* on a microcomputer was impossible. Storing the structure of the maze and the vocabulary of its commands would require too much memory. Adams did it in two weeks and started a company, Adventure International, that became a small computer game empire, attracting huge crowds at computer shows.

Adams became convinced that games like his *Adventure Land* and *Pirate Adventure* served to introduce computers to people. Other companies began selling adventure games also. Even Gates and Allen at Microsoft, who until then had shown no professional interest in game software, released a version of *Adventure*. In addition to *Star Trek* and *Adventure*, other games such as *Lunar Lander* made the transition from big to small computers.

When customers walked into computer stores in 1979, they saw racks of software, wall displays of software, and glass display cases of software. Most of it was games. Many of these were outer space games—*Space, Space II, Star Trek*. Many games appeared for the Apple, including Programma's simulation of a video game called *Apple Invaders*. Companies such as Muse, Sirius, Broderbund, and On-Line Systems reaped great profits from games.

Programma amassed a huge and diverse supply of software—not a wise policy as it later turned out. Programma sold plenty of programs, mostly games, but not all of them were good, and its reputation suffered. When serious competition arrived, Programma's reputation for second-rate wares killed it. Nevertheless, many personal computer programmers got their start writing programs for Programma. Few of the early software companies were anchored in the business savvy of Personal Software or achieved the wide acceptance that Digital Research won for its operating system.

&

> *CP/M has been the cornerstone of the development of software for micros because it provided a standard that changed the way people thought.*

Thomas Lafleur

> *CP/M was 5K and it gave you no more and no less than what an operating system should do.*

Alan Cooper

The First Operating System

The operating system that eventually qualified as a standard in the developing microcomputer industry had actually appeared before the Altair itself. CP/M was not the result of a carefully designed project involving years of research by dozens of software specialists. Like most of the early significant programs, it originated with one person's initiative.

In mid-1972, Gary Kildall, computer science professor at the U.S. Naval Postgraduate School in Monterey, California, came across an advertisement on a bulletin board that said "MICROCOMPUTER $25." It was actually a microprocessor — but still a bargain in 1972. Kildall decided to buy it and thus obtained one of the first Intel 4004 microprocessor chips.

If many founders of microcomputer companies didn't fit the image of industry leaders, Gary Kildall acted as if he didn't even want to be one. After finishing his PhD at the University of Washington, he moved to Pacific Grove, California. Kildall loved the scenic coastal town, and its relaxed, fog-draped ambience seemed to suit him. He had a soft voice and a disarming wit, and was most at ease in sport shirt and jeans. When he had a point to make he would often cast about for chalk or a pencil; he was an incurable diagram drawer. In the early 1970s Kildall was happy in his job at the Naval Postgraduate School. He enjoyed teaching and his job left him time to program. Kildall had no particular business skills and no real desire to leave academia. He was comfortable where he was.

Gary Kildall liked to play with computers; after all, he *was* a computer science professor. After purchasing the Intel 4004, he began to wonder what he might do with the "bargain basement" chip. Recalling that his father, who owned a small navigation school in Seattle, had always wanted a machine that would compute navigational triangles, Kildall wrote some arithmetic programs to run on the 4004, thinking idly that he might come up with something his father could use. He was just fooling around with it, trying to see how far he could go, and with what speed and accuracy. The processor was pretty limited, he decided.

Although frustrated with the 4004, Kildall found that he loved working with a small machine. Early in 1973 he visited the microcomputer division at Intel. He was surprised to see that the pioneering firm had set aside only a few rooms for the entire division. Kildall and the Intel people got along well, and the professor began working as a consultant there on his one free day a week. In this new role, he tinkered with the 4004 for a few more months until he "nearly went crazy with it." He realized that he would never go back to work on large computers.

Soon Kildall was dabbling with Intel's first 8-bit microprocessor, the 8008. He was working in the same two-level mode that Gates and Allen used, developing the software for the microprocessor on a minicomputer. Like Paul Allen, he wrote programs to simulate the microprocessor on a larger machine and then used this simulated microprocessor, with its simulated instruction set, to write programs to run on the microcomputer. But unlike Gates and Allen, Kildall had the benefit of a development system, essentially a full microcomputer design spun out around the microprocessor, so that he could check his work as he went along, trying it out on the development system. In a few months he had created a language called PL/M, a version of a mainframe language called PL/I and significantly more elaborate than BASIC.

As partial payment for his work, Kildall received a small computer from Intel. He put the machine in the back of his classroom, creating the Naval Postgraduate School's first microcomputer lab. Curious students would wander back there after class and tinker with it for hours. When Intel upgraded the Intellec-8 from an 8008 processor to an 8080 and gave Kildall a display monitor and high-speed paper tape reader, he and his students were working with a system comparable to the early Altair before the Altair was even conceived.

Kildall realized, however, that he was still missing an essential ingredient of a successful computer system—an efficient storage device. Two common storage devices on large computers were paper tape and magnetic disks. Considering how slow the microprocessor was, paper tape storage was simply too cumbersome and expensive. Kildall set out to get a disk drive and did a little programming in exchange for one from Shugart. But in order for the disk drive to work, a special controller was needed—a circuit board to handle the complicated task of making a computer communicate with a disk drive.

Kildall tried to design such a controller several times. He also sought to create an interface that would allow his system to connect to a cassette recorder. But he found he needed more than programming talent to solve the complex engineering problem of interfacing the two machines. The project failed, and Kildall decided he was totally inept at building hardware. Yet he had shown a lot of vision. It would be years before disk drives came into common use on microcomputers. Finally, at the end of 1973, Kildall approached John Torode, a friend of his from the University of Washington, who would later found his own microcomputer company. "John," he said, "we've got a really good thing going here if we can just get this drive working." Torode got the drive to work.

Meanwhile, Kildall polished the software. At one point late in 1973, during his months of frustration with the disk drive, Kildall had written a simple operating system in his PL/M language. It took a few weeks to complete, and he called it CP/M, for Control Program/Monitor. CP/M underwent further development, although it already provided the software needed for storing information on disks.

Some of CP/M's enhancements arose under curious conditions. While he continued teaching, Kildall became involved in a project with Ben Cooper, the hardware designer in San Francisco who had worked with George Morrow on disk systems and had later started his own computer company, Micromation. Cooper thought he could build a commercially successful machine to cast horoscopes, and he enlisted Kildall's help. They had no interest or belief in astrology, which they both saw as patent nonsense, but Cooper had ideas about the hardware and Kildall wanted to do the math that calculated star positions. Then, too, they could see that it might be a commercial success. So Cooper built and Kildall programmed, and they came up with their astrology machine, which would stand in grocery stores eating quarters like an arcade game and printing out horoscopes. Kildall thought the machine was just beautiful.

Commercially, however, the astrology machine was a failure. Its makers placed machines in various locations around San Francisco, but the fancy knobs and dials that excited the two hobbyists irritated customers—and with good reason. They would drop their quarters in and the paper would jam up. Kildall and Cooper didn't know what to do. "It was a total bust," Kildall later said.

Still, the astrology machine gave Kildall his first commercial test of portions of his program, CP/M. In the process of programming the astrology machine, he rewrote the debugger and the assembler, two tools for creating software, and began work on the editor. These were the essential parts of the operating system. In addition, he created a BASIC interpreter that allowed him to write the programs for the astrology machine. Some of the tricks he learned in developing the BASIC he would pass on to his pupil, Gordon Eubanks.

As they worked on interfacing the disk drive, Kildall and Torode exchanged views about the potential applications of microprocessors. They didn't say much about microcomputers. They still felt, along with the designers at Intel, that the microprocessor would wind up in this nation's blenders and carburetors, and they thought they could perhaps provide a combined hardware and software development system to encourage these uses. Kildall's belief in the future of such "embedded applications" of microprocessors was undoubtedly fostered by his colleagues at Intel. At one point he and a few other programmers had written a simple game program using the 4004 microprocessor. When they approached Intel chief Robert Noyce with the suggestion that he market the game, he vetoed it. Noyce was convinced that the future of the microprocessor lay elsewhere. "It's in watches," he told them.

So Torode and Kildall, without forming a company, sold their hardware and software together—not as a microcomputer, but as a development system. And when Kildall, encouraged by his wife Dorothy, finally incorporated and began to offer CP/M for sale, he had no idea how valuable a program he had written. How could he? There were few software developers around that could use it.

At first the Kildalls called their company Intergalactic Digital Research. The name was quickly shortened to Digital Research, and Dorothy, who was by this time running the company, began using her maiden name, McEwen, because she didn't want customers thinking of her as just "Gary's wife." Digital Research's earliest customers received some startling bargains. For instance, Thomas Lafleur, who helped found an early microcomputer company called GNAT Computers, made one of the first corporate purchases of CP/M. For $90 he gained the right to use CP/M as the operating system for any product his company developed. Within a year, a license for CP/M cost tens of thousands of dollars.

Dorothy saw the contract with IMSAI in 1977 as the turning point. Until then IMSAI had been purchasing CP/M on a single-copy basis. Its ambitious plans to sell thousands of floppy disk microcomputer systems caused marketing director Seymour Rubinstein to negotiate seriously with Gary and Dorothy. He finally purchased CP/M for $25,000. It was a lot more than the $90 that GNAT had paid, but Rubinstein gloated. He thought Gary Kildall an outstanding programmer but a babe-like businessman and was convinced he had virtually stolen the operating system from its author. The Kildalls' perspective was different; the IMSAI deal made Digital Research a full-time business. After IMSAI bought CP/M, many other firms followed suit. CP/M was such a useful program that not until IBM introduced a microcomputer with a different operating system did Digital Research face any serious competition.

And the programmers who would provide that competition were still working at MITS in Albuquerque.

&

If anyone had run over Bill Gates, the microcomputer industry would have been set back a couple of years.

Dick Heiser

Getting Down to BASIC

The emergence of BASIC as a popular high-level language foretold the development of the personal computer. Once the development of the microprocessor and the exploitation of that technological advance by hobbyist/entrepreneurs gave computing power to the people, BASIC gave them a tool for harnessing that power.

Two professors at Dartmouth College, seeking a better way of introducing their students to computers, had used a grant from the National Science Foundation to give birth to BASIC in 1964. The language John Kemeney and Thomas Kurtz created was an instant success. Compared with the slow, laborious and complex process of programming in FORTRAN, the comparable computer language in common use at the time, BASIC was a winged delight.

During the following two years the National Council of Teachers of Mathematics debated whether to support FORTRAN or BASIC as the standard educational language. FORTRAN, widely used in scientific computing, was considered better for large computational tasks. Yet, BASIC was far easier to learn. Bob Albrecht was an important supporter of BASIC. As a pioneer of computer education for children, he had been frustrated with FORTRAN. The Council's ultimate selection of BASIC was a watershed. The personal computer and the BASIC language would be the two most important products in the effort to convince educators that computers could help students learn.

Bob Albrecht wanted to create software for reasons other than personal ambition. Always interested in turning kids on to computers, he asked himself when Altair came out, "Wouldn't it be nice to have something called Tiny BASIC that resided in 2K and was suitable for kids?" Such a program would fit within the Altair's limited 4K memory and could be used immediately.

Albrecht pestered his friend Dennis Allison to develop Tiny BASIC. Reports of progress on the program appeared in the *PCC* newsletter and its outgrowth, *Dr. Dobb's*. "The Tiny BASIC project at *PCC* represents our attempt to give the hobbyist a more human-oriented language or notation with which to encode his programs," wrote Allison. In an early issue of *PCC*, Allison "& Others" explained their goal:

"Pretend you are seven years old and don't care much about floating-point arithmetic (what's that?), logarithms, sines, matrix inversion, nuclear-reactor calculations and stuff like that.

"And...your home computer is kind of small, not too much memory. Maybe it's a Mark-8 or an Altair 8800 with less than 4K bytes and a TV typewriter for input and output.

"You would like to use it for homework, math recreations and games like NUMBER, STARS, TRAP, HURKLE, SNARK, BAGELS,...

"Consider then, Tiny BASIC."

Many of *Dr. Dobb's* and *PCC's* readers did more than consider it. They took Allison's program and modified it, often creating a more capable language. Some of those early Tiny BASICs allowed large numbers of programmers to start using the machines. Two of the most successful versions came from Li-Chen Wang and Tom Pittman. They were "successful" in terms of the stated goal for Tiny BASIC—to give users a simpler language. The Tiny BASIC authors were not trying to use it as a path to wealth.

Another, more ambitious BASIC was also in the works. In the fall of 1974, Bill Gates had left Washington for Harvard University. Gates's parents had always wanted him to go to law school, and now they felt he was finally on the right track.

But as precocious as he might have been, Gates found himself rooming with a math student who was even sharper than he, and Gates was shocked when his roommate told him he had no intention of majoring in math but planned to study law. Gates thought, "If this guy's not going to major in math, I'm sure not." Examining his options, he immersed himself in psychology courses, graduate courses in physics and math, and long, extracurricular nightly poker games.

Then the *Popular Electronics* article came out. Gates's friend Paul Allen ran through Harvard Square with the article to wave it in front of Gates's face and say, "Look, it's going to happen! I told you this was going to happen! And we're going to miss it!" Gates had to admit that his friend was right; it sure looked as though the "something" they had been looking for had found them. He immediately phoned MITS, claiming that he and his partner had a BASIC language usable on the Altair. When Ed Roberts, who had heard a lot of such promises, asked Gates when he could come to Albuquerque to demonstrate it, Gates looked at his childhood friend, took a deep breath, and said, "Oh, in two or three weeks." Gates put down the receiver, turned to Allen and said: "I guess we should go buy a manual." They went straight to an electronics shop and purchased Adam Osborne's manual on the 8080.

For the next few weeks, Gates and Allen worked day and night on the BASIC. As they wrote the program, they tried to determine the minimal features of an acceptable BASIC—the same challenge Albrecht and Allison faced except that Tiny BASIC was to be a minimal language, usable on a variety of machines. There was no established industry standard for BASIC or for any other software. There was no industry. By deciding themselves what the BASIC required, Gates and Allen set a pattern for future software development that lasted for about six years. Instead of researching the market, the programmers simply decided, at the outset, what to put in.

Both men threw themselves completely into the project, staying up late every night programming. Gates even made the ultimate sacrifice and abandoned some of his nightly poker games. They were programming half-asleep sometimes. Once when Gates nodded off, head on the keys, he woke up suddenly, glanced at the screen, and immediately began typing. Paul Allen decided Bill must have been programming in his sleep and kept right on when he awoke.

They slept at their terminals; they talked BASIC between bites of food. One day while eating in the dining hall of Gates's Harvard dorm, they were discussing some mathematics routines—subprograms to handle non-integer numbers—that they felt their BASIC needed. The floating-point routines were not especially difficult, but they weren't very interesting either. Gates said he didn't want to write them; neither did Allen. From the other end of the table a hesitant voice called out, "I've written some floating-point routines." Both their heads turned in the direction of this voice, and over lunch in the college cafeteria Marty Davidoff joined their programming team.

At no time during the project did Gates, Allen, or Davidoff ever see an Altair computer. They wrote their BASIC on a large computer, testing it with a program Allen had written that caused the large machine to simulate the Altair. At one point when Gates phoned Ed Roberts to ask how the Altair processed characters typed on a keyboard, Roberts must have been surprised that they were actually pursuing the project. He turned the call over to his circuit board man, Bill Yates, who told Gates that he was the first to ask this obviously essential question. "Maybe you guys really have something," he told Gates.

In six weeks, Gates and Allen thought the effort was nearing an end, and when they called Ed Roberts, he invited them out to demonstrate what they had. Paul Allen booked a plane reservation as he and Gates scrambled to finish up the BASIC. On the night before Allen was to catch a 6 A.M. flight for Albuquerque, they were still working. At about 1 A.M. Gates told his friend to get a few hours of sleep, that when he awoke, the paper tape with the BASIC would be ready. Allen took him up on the offer, and when he awoke, Gates handed him the tape and said, "Who knows if it works. Good luck." Allen crossed his fingers and left for the airport.

Allen was sure of his and Gates's abilities, but as the plane approached Albuquerque he began wondering if they had forgotten something. Halfway into the landing he realized what it was: they had not written a loader program to read the BASIC off the paper tape. Without that, he couldn't get their BASIC into the Altair. It had never been a problem on their simulated Altair—the simulation had not been that exact. He took out some scrap paper, and as the plane descended, began writing in 8080 machine language. Somehow by the time the plane touched down, he had scribbled a loader program. Now when he wasn't worrying about the BASIC, he could fret about this impromptu loader program.

Not that he had much chance to worry about anything. Roberts was right there to meet him. Allen was surprised at Ed Roberts's informality and at the pickup truck he drove. He had expected a man in a business suit and a fancy car. Equally surprising to him was the dilapidation of MITS's headquarters. Roberts ushered him into the building and said, "Here it is. Here's the Altair." On a bench before them sat the microcomputer with the largest memory in the world. It had 7K of memory, on seven 1K boards, and it was running a program that tested memory by writing random information into it and reading it back. The memory needed testing, but this program was also the only one they had. As it ran, all the Altair's lights would blink. They had just gotten it working with 7K that day.

Roberts suggested that they postpone testing the BASIC till the next day and took Allen to "the most expensive hotel in Albuquerque." The next day Roberts had to pay the bill because the embarrassed Allen hadn't brought along enough to cover it.

That morning Allen held his breath as the machine chugged away, loading the tape in about five minutes. He threw the switches on the Altair and entered in the starting address to invoke the program. As he flipped the computer's RUN switch he thought "If we made any mistake anywhere, in the assembler or the interpreter, or if there was something we didn't understand in the 8080, this thing won't work." And he waited.

"It printed 'MEMORY SIZE?'" said Ed Roberts. "What does that mean?"

For Allen it meant that the program worked. In order to print this message about 75 percent of the code had to be accurate. He entered the memory size — 7K — and typed "PRINT 2+2." The machine printed "4."

Roberts was convinced and explained to Allen some additional features he thought a BASIC needed. A few weeks later, he offered, and Allen accepted, the position of MITS software director.

Gates soon decided that Harvard was less interesting than Albuquerque and moved to join his friend. Although never a direct employee of MITS, Gates spent most of his time at its quarters, where he and Allen were beginning to realize that a large market for software existed beyond the Altair. They signed a royalty agreement with Ed Roberts for their BASIC but began looking for other customers for it as well. And they began calling themselves Microsoft.

&

Studying computer science was the Navy's idea.

Gordon Eubanks

The Other BASIC

While only one operating system would dominate the early years of the personal computer industry, the ease of creating different BASIC capabilities led to competition for preeminence between two higher-level languages. One was Gates and Allen's. The other was developed by a student of Gary Kildall.

In 1976 a young nuclear engineer named Gordon Eubanks had almost finished his U.S. Navy service. As a civilian he had had nine months experience with IBM as a systems engineer. The Navy offered him a scholarship to take a masters degree in computer science at the Naval Postgraduate School in Pacific Grove, California. Why not? he thought. It sounded good to him.

Attending class was tamer than most things that sounded good to Eubanks. His glasses and soft-spoken manner belied a love of adventure. He thoroughly enjoyed working on a nuclear-powered, fast-attack submarine in the Navy. A friend, software designer Alan Cooper, summed it up: "Gordon thrives on tension."

Gordon also liked to work hard. When he arrived at the Naval Postgraduate School, he soon heard about a professor named Gary Kildall. Kildall was teaching compiler theory, and everybody said he was the toughest instructor. Maybe he'd learn something, Eubanks thought. He signed up for Kildall's class.

For Eubanks, hard work paid off. He became interested in microcomputers and spent a lot of time in the lab in the back of the room, working with the computer Kildall had received for his work at Intel. When he approached his professor for a thesis idea, Kildall suggested that he expand and refine a BASIC interpreter Kildall had begun. That sounded good to Eubanks.

The BASIC that emerged from Eubanks' work, called BASIC-E, differed from Microsoft's in an important way. While Microsoft's was an interpreted language, in which statements were translated directly into machine code, Eubanks' was a pseudo-compiled one. This meant simply that programs written in BASIC-E were translated into an intermediate code, which was then translated by another program into machine code. This same general idea was being used in a BASIC compiler under development at Ohio State University. There were various merits to each approach, but BASIC-E had one critical advantage. Its programs could be sold in the intermediate code version, and the purchaser, while able to use the program, would not be able to modify it or steal the programming ideas it incorporated since the intermediate code was not human-readable. Thus software developers could write programs in

BASIC-E and sell them without fear that their ideas would be stolen. With a pseudo-compiled BASIC, it made sense to start selling software.

For Eubanks this was just an academic project, and he placed his BASIC-E in the public domain and returned to the Navy for a new assignment. But before he did, he had two important meetings. The first was a visit from two young programmers, Alan Cooper and Keith Parsons, who were interested in starting an applications software company and, as they put it, "making $50,000 a year." They wanted his BASIC-E. Eubanks gave them a copy of his source code and never expected to see them again.

In addition, goaded on by Glen Ewing, another ex-student of the Naval Postgraduate School, Eubanks visited IMSAI to see if the young microcomputer company might be interested in his BASIC. At first IMSAI was not, and Eubanks was not particularly disappointed. Later, however, he received a telegram from IMSAI software director Rob Barnaby asking for a meeting. And soon after that, early in 1977, Eubanks was negotiating a contract with IMSAI's director of marketing, Seymour Rubinstein, to develop a BASIC for the company's 8080 microcomputer. Rubinstein gave the young programmer no quarter. Ultimately, Eubanks agreed to develop the BASIC and give IMSAI unlimited distribution rights to it in exchange for an IMSAI computer and some other equipment. However the Navy engineer retained ownership rights to his program.

That trade sounded good to Eubanks. This was his first software deal, and he was very innocent. Explained Alan Cooper: "Gordon was saying 'Oh! They're giving me a printer too!'"

Eubanks did aspire to something bigger than a printer; he dreamed of making $10,000 on his BASIC so that he could buy a house in Hawaii.

In April 1977, the first West Coast Computer Faire was taking place in San Francisco, and Eubanks demonstrated his BASIC-E in a booth he shared with his former professor, who had started Digital Research. Alan Cooper and Keith Parsons showed up there and reintroduced themselves to Eubanks. They explained that they had made some modifications in his BASIC and had begun developing some business applications software. Eubanks asked the young programmers if they had suggestions for his IMSAI project. Soon the three of them decided to work together. As Eubanks refined the BASIC and Rob Barnaby, a demanding and meticulous taskmaster, tested it, Cooper and Parsons began writing Structured System Group's General Ledger software, perhaps the first serious business software for a microcomputer.

The development of Eubanks' BASIC was a late-night crash project like Microsoft's. Cooper had a place in Vallejo, California, and Cooper and Parsons would drive there and sit until three in the morning drinking cokes, poring over listings, and trying to decide what statements to put in the language. Like Gates and Allen, Eubanks determined the contents of the BASIC by his own ongoing judgment. Sometimes selection was less than scientific. Sitting there in the Vallejo house staring at the code, Alan Cooper would suddenly say,

"Why don't you put a WHILE loop in?" Eubanks would answer, "Sounds good to me," and in it would go.

All the long nights paid off. The result for Eubanks was CBASIC, which later made possible his own company, Compiler Systems. Cooper and Parson's Structured Systems Group became his first distributor. But Eubanks didn't know how much to ask for his BASIC. Cooper and Parsons suggested $150; Kildall suggested $90, the price CP/M first sold at. Eubanks roughly split the difference and charged $100.

They needed to develop packaging and documentation for the product. Cooper and Eubanks wrote the manual and ordered 500 copies of it from a printer. They immediately got an order for 400 copies and had to order another batch. They knew they were on their way.

As for Gordon Eubanks, he got his house in Hawaii. In fact, he underestimated the amount of money he would make on CBASIC, almost to the same degree that he underestimated the cost of houses in Hawaii.

A software industry was still in its nascent days, but some of the important bricks had been set in place. Another was developed independently of either BASIC or CP/M.

&

*Electric Pencil was like Kleenex and Coke;
it was generic. [Shrayer] could have owned
the microcomputer word processing business
if he'd wanted to. But he didn't.*

William Radding

*When I started doing business, I started
with an unlisted phone number.*

Michael Shrayer

The Electric Pencil

At one of the early meetings of the Southern California Computer Society in
the fall of 1975, visitor Bob Marsh offered attendees a present, a copy of Proc
Tech's public domain software package called Software Package One. It was a
collection of programmers' programs — tools to make writing and modifying
programs easier. Marsh said, "Here you are guys, enjoy it."

In the opinion of Michael Shrayer, Software Package One was the most
important package then in existence because it effectively enabled people to
write software. Shrayer, an admittedly "laid-back sort," had moved from New
York to California several years earlier. He had tired of a hectic life in the
commercial film world, where, among other jobs, he worked as a camera operator for Allen Funt's *Candid Camera*. One day, while shooting a soft drink commercial, Shrayer suddenly realized that the rat race was no longer for him.
After moving to California, he became involved with the Southern California
Computer Society and in this way saw Software Package One.

But Shrayer was not fully satisfied with the editor portion of the package
and felt he could do better. So he created Extended Software Package 1 (ESP-1)
and the beginnings of a pioneering software firm. Almost overnight, the laid-
back New Yorker found himself in a brand new rat race. Other computer hobbyists, in numbers that amazed Shrayer, began wanting to buy the program. In
most cases he had to reconfigure the program for each customer's
particular machine.

Soon Shrayer found that he was making enough money to live on. It was a
nice hobby, and remunerative, and he found that he liked to program. He'd sit
around with other members of the club, endlessly talking about computers.
And he'd send out copies of ESP-1. He was just having fun.

Shrayer's next idea proved more significant. Tired of having to type out the
documentation for his assembler on a manual typewriter, Shrayer decided to
add a novelty to his Executor (an upgrade of ESP-1). He had a computer, he
thought. Why couldn't he use *it* to type a manual? There was nothing like a

word processor available—and Shrayer didn't even know what a word processor was. He had to invent one.

By Christmas of 1976, after nearly a year of work, Electric Pencil was ready. Although written first on the Altair, Electric Pencil won its first fame on Proc Tech's Sol. "The Pencil," as it became known, was soon selling quickly. The former camera jockey called his company Michael Shrayer Software, a decision he later regretted because it publicized his name so widely as to sabotage his privacy. Nevertheless, at the outset he visited computer clubs to talk about his program and enjoyed the admiration lavished upon him.

The popularity of Electric Pencil created a demand for it on all microcomputers then available. Shrayer spent much of his time rewriting the program for different systems. Not only did each computer require a different version, so did each kind of printer or terminal. Moreover, Shrayer was constantly increasing The Pencil's capabilities. In all, he wrote about 78 different versions.

Had Shrayer been a more experienced programmer, he would have made the program easy to rework. Had he been an experienced businessperson, he might have begun selling it in an organized fashion. But Shrayer was neither, so the rewriting devoured his time, and sales often took place through single mail orders. Shrayer grew tired of Electric Pencil and irritated that it was becoming a serious business. He began to hire programmers to write some of the versions for him.

All of his versions ran on systems with direct video displays. Instead of writing information on the screen a line at a time, as serial terminals did, such systems allowed direct access to individual characters on the screen. But not all microcomputers had such direct video displays. It remained for others to develop word processors for a serial terminal.

Shrayer's experience shows that in 1977 the hardware manufacturers had still not recognized the importance of software. Perhaps they felt the marketplace would remain dominated by hobbyists. In any case, none were willing to pay Shrayer to adapt The Pencil to their machines, although they certainly wanted him to do so.

As Kildall, Eubanks, Gates, and Allen had done before him, Michael Shrayer proceeded according to his own fancy and wrote programs for whatever machines he wanted to. And when he lost his enthusiasm for the whole enterprise, he went back into retirement and reclusion.

Years later, Electric Pencil still seemed touched with an immortal quality. Thousands of personal computer owners continued to use it on such machines as North Stars and Radio Shack TRS-80s. Shrayer was successful because his program allowed non-technical people to use personal computers to perform practical tasks.

&

*In working with the Altair dealers around
the country, we saw there was a good opportunity for software distribution.*

Ron Roberts

My unemployment had run out.

Alan Cooper

The Rise of General Software Companies

After helping Eubanks write CBASIC, Alan Cooper and Keith Parsons set out
to achieve their own dream of making $50,000 a year. The two had known
each other since high school. Parsons had taught Cooper to tie a necktie, a skill
he shelved at college, where he became a self-described "long-haired hippie."
Cooper intensely wanted to "get into computers," and he asked the older Parsons for advice. "You're overtrained," Parsons told him. "Drop out of school.
Get a job." And he did. After work, he and Parsons would get together and talk
about starting their own company. Nirvana, they thought, was $50,000 a year.

When the Altair came out, Cooper and Parsons laid their plans. They decided
to market business software for microcomputers, hired a programmer, and put
him in a tiny room and told him to write. They wrote too. For a while, they
tried to sell turn-key systems—computers with sophisticated software that
came into action when the machine was turned on. They got nowhere. They
really needed an operating system—of which there were none, as far as they
knew—and maybe a high-level language. Talking with Peter Hollinbeck at the
Byte Shop led them to Gary Kildall, CP/M, and Gordon Eubanks. Now after
months of development on Eubanks' BASIC and on their business software,
they were ready to start making $50,000 a year. They placed their first ad for
CBASIC in a computer magazine. After much agonizing they also decided to
mention their business software in little letters at the bottom of the ad: "General Ledger $995." Then they waited for the hobbyists to attack them for sell-
ing a program for almost triple the cost of the Altair itself.

A response did not take long. A businessman in the Midwest sent in an
order for the General Ledger. Cooper made a copy of the program and inserted
it in a zip-lock plastic bag along with a manual, a method of packaging software
that became common. Before they knew it, back came a check for $995.
Cooper, Parsons, and the whole Structured Systems Group staff went out for
pizza.

Meanwhile, they kept working on software. The atmosphere was giddy and
the style far from corporate. Parsons paced the office shirtless, while Cooper,
hair down to mid-back, guzzled a coffee that "would dissolve steel." The two of

them, wired on caffeine and the excitement of the $995 check, wrangled about potential markets and dealer terms. Parsons' girlfriend made phone sales while sunbathing nude in the backyard behind their "office."

Three weeks later another order came in and the staff had another pizza. The pizza ritual continued for two months. People were sending in checks for thousands of dollars. It seemed to them that they were eating pizza for breakfast, lunch, and dinner.

Another early software company started up soon after the Altair announcement, and this one was far from Silicon Valley. In the suburbs of Atlanta in December 1975, several computer enthusiasts including one Ron Roberts (no relation to Ed Roberts) who met as graduate students at Georgia Tech opened an Altair dealership called the Computersystem Center.

These enthusiasts quickly realized that, as much as their customers wanted the Altairs, they also wanted software to use with the machines. Business was slow at the outset and they had lots of time to program.

They soon contacted other Altair computer stores throughout the country and discovered that the need for software was nationwide. In 1976 the group approached Ed Roberts with the idea of using the Altair name for software distribution. Roberts saw that software could help sell his machine and he agreed. Ron Roberts became president of the Altair Software Distribution Company (ASDC). The idea was to distribute other people's Altair software and to write a little of their own.

The Georgians called a meeting of Altair dealers in October 1976, and nearly 20 stores (nearly all that existed) sent representatives. MITS attended the meeting as well because the dealers wanted to inform the company how delays in deliveries and mechanical failures were affecting their business. Ron Roberts found that Altair dealers had a lot in common. They all suffered from a lack of software, hardware delivery delays, hardware malfunctions, and a meager awareness of microcomputers on the part of the general public. But "software was the biggest item on the agenda," according to Roberts.

At the meeting, several dealers agreed right away to purchase ASDC software. Its initial programs were simple business packages: accounting, inventory, and later a text editor. The accounting and inventory programs sold for $2000 retail, a price Roberts and his colleagues considered reasonable because they had worked previously in the minicomputer and mainframe industry where such charges were thought modest. Given the software vacuum of the time, they were able to find buyers at that price. "We were making quite a bit," Roberts recalled.

The sale of MITS to Pertec in 1977 and the subsequent fade-out of the Altair caused Ron Roberts to unhitch his wagon from that star. CP/M was gaining popularity and he decided to convert the programs to run with Kildall's operating system. This move allowed for sales to more than one brand of computer, since CP/M was not machine-specific.

As the word "Altair" no longer belonged in their business name, they changed the name to Peachtree Software after a downtown Atlanta street. "In the Atlanta area it's a quality name," Roberts said. Peachtree employees were more businesslike in their approach than the SSG crew; not only did they wear shirts, but they even wore ties. They called their software Peachtree Accounting and Peachtree Inventory. In the fall of 1978 Roberts and one of his partners took the software part of the business and merged with Retail Sciences, a small computer consulting firm in Atlanta run by Ben Dyer, who had previously worked for a hardware store chain (of the nuts and bolts variety). Following the merger, Peachtree released a general ledger business package. Sales increased rapidly, as did the number of dealers carrying the Peachtree label, and soon it became one of the best known and respected in the software field. Eventually Dyer changed the name of the whole company to Peachtree Software.

With SSG on one coast and Peachtree on the other, the software industry was establishing itself as an independent entity.

&

*If they have a contest as to who is the best
negotiator in the industry, I'll withdraw to
Seymour's fine abilities. Seymour is a master. And I was just a poor child.*

Bill Gates

*They had no concept of product distribu-
tion, royalties, and so on. That's where I
saw an opportunity.*

Seymour Rubinstein

The Bottom Line

Seymour Rubinstein has said that he left IMSAI in order to establish a software firm. But as a man of sharp business sense, Rubinstein must have seen
the dissolving financial foundation beneath the house of IMSAI. More important, however, he chose to bring his business skills to a software industry
characterized by haphazard marketing.

The lack of business expertise had held back the software industry, Rubin-
stein felt. He decided that his firm would not sell to manufacturers, as Kildall,
Eubanks, and Gates had been doing, nor would it sell by mail to end-users, as
Shrayer, Cooper, and Parson did. The number of computer stores was not
large, but it was growing. Rubinstein decided that his new firm, MicroPro
International, would sell only to retailers.

But first he needed the software, and for that Rubinstein knew where to
turn. The day he left IMSAI he visited another ex-IMSAI employee, Rob Barnaby, who had headed its software development division. Recalling Barnaby's
exhaustive programs to test Eubanks' CBASIC, and because of other examples
he had seen of Barnaby's clever, painstaking programming, Rubinstein knew
he wanted Rob Barnaby for his company, and he went out and got him. By
September, Barnaby had completed MicroPro's first two products, SuperSort
and WordMaster. The first was a data sorting program, and the second was a
text editor that Barnaby had begun working on while still at IMSAI.

Although sales for these two products grew rapidly ($11,000 in September
1978; $14,000 in October; $20,000 in November), Rubinstein felt the market
could handle much more; he realized that Shrayer had whetted the appetite of
the computer owner. MicroPro was inundated with requests for a word processor like Electric Pencil. Not one to scorn an opportunity, Rubinstein brought
out just such an item. Barnaby's new program, WordStar, was the elaboration
of WordMaster into an actual word processor, and it quickly sold more copies
than The Pencil or any other rival.

WordStar was also superior to Electric Pencil. Shrayer had offered word wrap, a feature that allowed users to continue typing even when the text arrived at the end of a line. But a fast typist could still type quickly enough to cause the software to miss one or two characters while the carriage was returning. WordStar overcame that problem and offered another improvement best described as "what you see is what you get." In other words, text appeared on the screen in virtually the same form as it did when it was printed.

Soon WordStar had rivals. By mid-1979, when MicroPro released WordStar, Bill Radding and Mike Griffin in Houston were almost ready to release their word processor, Magic Wand, a worthy competitor.

Rubinstein offered WordStar and his other programs to dealers on a per copy basis. Michael Shrayer had also done some work in this direction, but he had had few computer distribution centers and stores at the time. By late 1978, when MicroPro International commenced sales, the number of computer stores had grown exponentially. Along with two other companies — Personal Software, with its VisiCalc for the Apple, and Peachtree Software, with its General Ledger program — MicroPro established the standards for applications software developers to do business. By selling its product like any other consumer item, the software industry gained self-respect, credibility, and a financial bonanza.

If in many ways software was a product like, say, a clock, it was also different in one important respect. Software could be stolen without removing the original item. The thief simply copied someone else's program — a task easier and faster than taping a phonograph record. From the earliest days of the industry the unauthorized copying had outraged many programmers, who saw the fruits of their ingenuity copied and recopied without the slightest monetary return.

Bill Gates was the first programmer to call attention to the piracy problem. In January 1976, he wrote an "Open Letter to Hobbyists," which was published, among other places, in the "Homebrew Computer Club Newsletter," in which he lamented the widespread larceny of paper tape copies of his BASIC and called the hobbyists thieves. "The amount of royalties we have received from sales to hobbyists makes the time spent on Altair BASIC worth less than $2 an hour," Gates wrote. "Why is this? As the majority of hobbyists must be aware, most of you steal your software. Hardware must be paid for, but software is something to share. Who cares if the people who worked on it get paid?"

Gates' diatribe had no effect whatever on the hobbyists except to anger them further at the $500 charged for his BASIC. Hobbyists could see no justification for such a price — as much as the computer itself — and they knew that they needed BASIC to make effective use of their machines.

From time to time software developers tried to copyproof their programs by subtle software tricks that either prevented copying a disk or booby trapped the copied program. Generally copy protection has failed for one fundamental reason — if a copy-protected program can be written, it can also be cracked.

Most companies began to view piracy as a cost of doing business.

And business was good, very good. The microcomputer had tempted a few programmers into creating tools that allowed others to create applications software. Programmers quickly developed an impressive library of software applications that showed the general public microcomputers could be both fun and useful. Microcomputers had made a new software industry possible. Soon software became as good a reason as the computer itself to buy the hardware. At first the hobbyist/entrepreneur was only an amateur retailer, and that was bound to change if personal computers were to become a popular consumer product.

&

Retailing the Revolution

Chapter 6

The [computer] magazines basically defined
a nationwide small town.

Carl Helmers

The Magazines: Purveying the Word

Electronics magazines provided the first marketplace for microcomputers. A publication such as *Popular Electronics* would announce an innovation like the Altair or just carry a small ad for it, and the manufacturer would be swamped with mail orders. Normally mail order is a fairly unsophisticated means of selling sophisticated hardware, yet it proved almost too effective for MITS and other companies, and they were seldom able to keep up with the demand.

Mail order was a novel way to market computers. Mainframes and minicomputers were tailored to the needs of the buyer, usually an institution, after elaborate consultation. These machines were so expensive that customizing them made financial sense. But the micros were cheap, and providing specialized aid to every customer was out of the question. Fortunately for manufacturers, the earliest buyers scarcely demanded it. They were hobbyists, who would tolerate almost anything — including the mirage world of mail order — to get their own computers. That the machines were affordable was enough; it was more than enough.

But buying by mail was like buying blind. People were sending checks in to companies they had never heard of to get products they could not be sure existed. They were playing micro roulette. Knowing little more than that they wanted a computer, they mailed in money and waited. And waited. And waited. Products were commonly announced before they were even designed, let alone manufactured. Cover stories in *Popular Electronics* had passed off an empty box as the original Altair and a mock-up as Processor Technology's Sol. These excesses were probably harmless in themselves, but the same technique was used in ads. *Byte*'s Carl Helmers said, "I'm not saying it's legitimate, but it's certainly one that's used all over the place in technology. A product may be there to show in functional simulation form, and functional simulation is one step into making the thing actually happen."

But while useful in promoting the growth of the industry, such misrepresentations created anxiety in buyers. The prolonged delay—itself a frustration repeated day after day—was often followed by receipt of a product that looked quite different from the one expected. And the functional simulation was the least misleading kind of ad since it did give the buyer some idea of the machine to be built. Other ads were more fanciful. "A guy who is in love with writing copy about computers can dream up any kind of system," said Helmers. "And there were people who did that." Moreover, since there were at first no retail outlets where users could test products before buying them, mail-order items varied in quality. Even MITS did not hesitate to sell questionable memory boards or to hitch acquisition of its BASIC to the purchase. In this loose and eager market there were even some premeditated frauds, but there were many more cases of overzealous promotion, a compound of undercapitalization and an optimism that rode the wind.

The magazines played dual, somewhat schizoid roles in this frenzy. Editors encouraged it by reporting advances, printing ads, and sometimes refraining from alerting their readers to substandard items. Carl Helmers, for instance, based his refusal to assess product quality on the theory that "the products that don't fulfill over the long haul will sort themselves out and will die." At the same time, other magazines actively participated in the sorting out. Adam Osborne, who had been selling books out of a cardboard box at Homebrew meetings, started a muckraking column that appeared in *Interface Age* and later in *InfoWorld* alerting consumers to the shortcomings of the products. *Dr. Dobb's* took a strong consumerist stance, steering readers away from purchases they might later regret. The magazines made the mail-order madness possible, and they also sometimes tried to control it.

Byte is one of the great success stories among microcomputer magazines, but the success grew out of conflict and, perhaps, betrayal. *Byte* magazine began in mid-1975, the brainchild of Wayne Green, who had published the ham radio magazine *73* for 15 years. Part evangelist and part huckster, Green enjoys promoting what he believes in: ham radio, microcomputers, and himself. Some view him as a front-porch philosopher, fond of contemplative argument, fond of hearing his thoughts shape themselves into speech. But others see a more complex individual who can be difficult to work for. His busy, impatient mind can flit from the latest software to psychic phenomena, but it never strays far from the bottom line. He likes to make money and to be viewed as a success.

By 1975, *73* magazine had grown large enough for Green to computerize circulation, so he called the major computer companies. Each sent a representative, and every representative warned him of the dangers inherent in buying a rival's machine. Green found all their warnings convincing. The task of investment was starting to resemble a leap into darkness. He decided that before paying $100,000 for a computer, he should first learn something about the field. He discovered that none of the books or magazines was comprehensible to him at all. Only the newsletters put out by computer clubs were readily understandable. The more Green thought about that, the more he realized that he was not alone. The country was full of people who needed an introduction to computers.

Green saw his opportunity. He decided to create a magazine to ease beginners into microcomputing. And he ran it just as he had run the successful 73, focusing on whatever developments excited him. If he enjoyed playing with a gadget, he would try to get others to take it up too. He needed a name for the publication, one that was short and catchy and that would conjure up computers themselves. He called it *Byte*.

Green hired Carl Helmers, who had been issuing *ECS* (*Experimenters Computer Systems*) in Boston, as his editor. *ECS* was a solo operation. Since January 1975, just after the Altair announcement, Helmers had been writing about 20 to 25 pages per month about his own plans for building and programming microcomputers. He then shepherded them through photo offset and had them distributed to his 300 or so readers. Helmers accepted Green's offer and relocated in Peterborough, New Hampshire.

Green drew his contributors and his readers from the newsletters and from his own 73 readers, believing the latter to be a natural audience for *Byte*. The first edition appeared on August 1, 1975. The first 15,000 copies were sold out immediately. A new kind of publication had been born.

With his ex-wife, Virginia Green, as office manager, Helmers as editor, and much of the 73 staff as personnel, Green set about compiling a second issue. He estimated that 20 percent of *Byte*'s readership came from 73. In addition, Green took the first issue around to such manufacturers as MITS in Albuquerque, Sphere in Salt Lake City, and Southwest Tech in San Antonio. He said they were enthusiastic about it and supplied him with address lists of their customers. Green guessed that these lists provided *Byte* with another 20 to 25 percent of its subscriptions.

Wayne Green was exhilarated. But he had one problem. He didn't own the company. It belonged to Virginia, from whom he had been divorced for ten years. Green had been convicted of tax evasion and faced other legal troubles. "So the lawyers said we should set up the new magazine with a different corporation and have somebody keep the stock separate until the suits were resolved," said Green. He entrusted the magazine to Virginia.

The early days of the magazine did not go smoothly. Green and Helmers did not see eye to eye on the direction *Byte* should take. Helmers did not feel comfortable with the idea of a magazine for beginners. He wanted *Byte* to address the experimenters, to become rather like a computer-oriented *Scientific American*, with a vastly expanded "Amateur Scientists" section. Helmers believed that Green was not merely simplifying complicated concepts, but also altering them, doing violence to them. This disturbed him.

The rift widened for several months. After the first issue had been published, Helmers, Virginia, and her new husband decided they didn't need Wayne Green and they moved out.

Green considered a legal challenge to his ouster but determined it would be too costly. His lawyers suggested he start a new magazine instead. He acquiesced. "I'm practical," he said.

By January of 1977, *Byte* had a readership of 50,000 and was the premier magazine in the field. Helmers remained as editor and owned part of the company, which he and Virginia sold to McGraw-Hill in April 1979. Helmers stayed on with the publication until September 1980.

Wayne Green did not sit still for long. In August 1976, he circulated among manufacturers, asking them if they would support a new magazine with himself at the helm. The response, he said, was unequivocally positive. He wanted to call it *KiloByte*, but *Byte* claimed it would infringe on its name. So Green christened his magazine *Kilobaud*.

Kilobaud was an expansion of a computer section called "I/O" that Green had been running within the pages of *73*. The new publication strove for the Wayne Green ideal: that anyone be able to pick it up and understand it within two or three issues. Green lamented that *Kilobaud* never overtook *Byte* in circulation or advertising, but it was nonetheless clearly a success.

Green watched his market. When he started *Kilobaud* almost all his readers were hobbyists, people who had no qualms about building accessories and modifying the equipment with a soldering iron. Around 1980, however, Green noticed that a new kind of hobbyist had emerged, one who still liked to use the equipment, but tended to shun the mechanical tinkering. To reflect this change, Green gave the magazine a broader name: *Microcomputing*. At about the same time, he started another journal, *80 Microcomputing* (later *80 Micro*), aimed at users of the Radio Shack TRS-80 computer line. Later, Green began other, even more consumer-oriented computer publications.

Carl Helmers saw the purposes of the early magazines as economic, educational, and social. The magazines defined a market, spread important news, and helped hobbyists meet. Moreover, the magazines created a nationwide community. He said, "Peterborough, where I live, is a small town, but it's geographically constrained." Just as one knew everybody and every occurrence in a geographically small town, one knew everyone and everything in the small town of microcomputer hobbyists. Curiously, no publication had more of the flavor of a small town than Wayne Green's early *Kilobaud*, with its chatty editorials, industry gossip, and events calendars.

To Helmers's purposes, Jim Warren would have added two more: making a contribution to society and encouraging enjoyment of the machines.

Though born in California, Jim Warren was raised in Texas and taught mathematics there for five years. He then moved to the San Francisco Bay Area, where he taught math for another five years as chair of the mathematics department of the College of Notre Dame, a Catholic women's college in Belmont, a small city north of Silicon Valley. At the same time, Warren was throwing huge nude parties at his home. "They were rather sedate by any common standards, except people didn't have to have clothes on," he recalled.

Bill Godbout, who started building S100 microcomputers early in the industry's development
(Photo courtesy of CompuPro)

The North Star staff in front of their Berkeley headquarters
(Photograph by Martin J. Cooney Studio, Oakland, California, courtesy of North Star)

Scott Adams, who created some of the
first games for personal computers
(Photo courtesy of Scott Adams)

Peter Jennings, programmer of
Micro Chess
(Photo courtesy of David Ahl, *Creative
Computing*)

Gary Kildall and Ben Cooper's astrology
machine
(Photo courtesy of Bob Reiling)

One of Gary Kildall's early offices with
stacked computers on the desks and
photos of airplanes taped to the wall
(Photo courtesy of Digital Research)

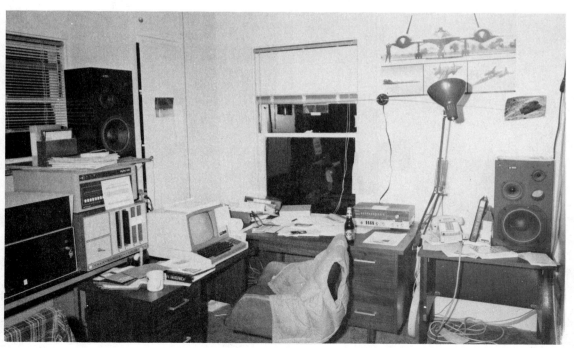

Gary Kildall at work in an early office
(Photo courtesy of Digital Research)

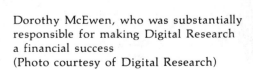

Dorothy McEwen, who was substantially
responsible for making Digital Research
a financial success
(Photo courtesy of Digital Research)

Gordon Eubanks, who began studying
computer programming and wrote
CBASIC while in the Navy
(Photo courtesy of Gordon Eubanks)

Gary Kildall clowning around
(Photo courtesy of Digital Research)

Gordon Eubanks, whose master's thesis became one of the industry's standard programming languages
(Photo courtesy of Digital Research)

Michael Shrayer, author of Electric Pencil
(Photo courtesy of Michael Shrayer)

Michael Shrayer with his pioneering word processor Electric Pencil
(Photo by Paul Freiberger)

An early board meeting of Structured Systems Group. *Left to right:* Richard Ellman, Alan Cooper, Peter Breeze, and Keith Parsons
(Photo courtesy of Alan Cooper)

Alan Cooper, co-founder of Structured
Systems Group
(Photo by Mr. Snoid)

Alan Cooper several years later with his
wife, Sue
(Photo by Ann Marie, courtesy of
Alan Cooper)

Bill Gates's attack on software piracy published in the Homebrew Computer Club newsletter
(Courtesy of Bob Reiling)

February 3, 1976

An Open Letter to Hobbyists

To me, the most critical thing in the hobby market right now is the lack of good software courses, books and software itself. Without good software and an owner who understands programming, a hobby computer is wasted. Will quality software be written for the hobby market?

Almost a year ago, Paul Allen and myself, expecting the hobby market to expand, hired Monte Davidoff and developed Altair BASIC. Though the initial work took only two months, the three of us have spent most of the last year documenting, improving and adding features to BASIC. Now we have 4K, 8K, EXTENDED, ROM and DISK BASIC. The value of the computer time we have used exceeds $40,000.

The feedback we have gotten from the hundreds of people who say they are using BASIC has all been positive. Two surprising things are apparent, however. 1) Most of these "users" never bought BASIC (less than 10% of all Altair owners have bought BASIC), and 2) The amount of royalties we have received from sales to hobbyists makes the time spent of Altair BASIC worth less than $2 an hour.

Why is this? As the majority of hobbyists must be aware, most of you steal your software. Hardware must be paid for, but software is something to share. Who cares if the people who worked on it get paid?

Is this fair? One thing you don't do by stealing software is get back at MITS for some problem you may have had. MITS doesn't make money selling software. The royalty paid to us, the manual, the tape and the overhead make it a break-even operation. One thing you do do is prevent good software from being written. Who can afford to do professional work for nothing? What hobbyist can put 3-man years into programming, finding all bugs, documenting his product and distribute for free? The fact is, no one besides us has invested a lot of money in hobby software. We have written 6800 BASIC, and are writing 8080 APL and 6800 APL, but there is very little incentive to make this software available to hobbyists. Most directly, the thing you do is theft.

What about the guys who re-sell Altair BASIC, aren't they making money on hobby software? Yes, but those who have been reported to us may lose in the end. They are the ones who give hobbyists a bad name, and should be kicked out of any club meeting they show up at.

I would appreciate letters from any one who wants to pay up, or has a suggestion or comment. Just write me at 1180 Alvarado SE, #114, Albuquerque, New Mexico, 87108. Nothing would please me more than being able to hire ten programmers and deluge the hobby market with good software.

Bill Gates
Bill Gates
General Partner, Micro-Soft

Wayne Green, founder of *Byte, Kilobaud,* and numerous other personal computer publications
(Photo by California Photo Service, courtesy of Wayne Green)

Carl Helmers, first editor of *Byte* magazine
(Photo courtesy of David Ahl, *Creative Computing*)

Carl Helmers, as the first editor of *Byte*, spreading the word about personal computers
(Photo courtesy of David Ahl, *Creative Computing*)

John Dilkes, who planned an early
computer show in New Jersey, PC-76
(Photo courtesy of David Ahl, *Creative
Computing*)

Jim Warren, a watchdog of the early
personal computer industry when he was
editing *Dr. Dobb's*, and a co-founder of
the most successful series of computer
shows, the West Coast Computer Faires
(Photo by C. Russell Wood)

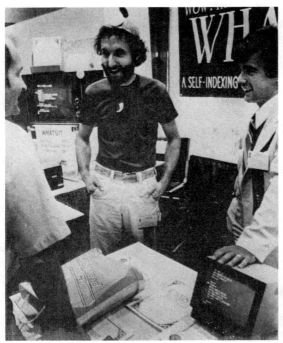

Bill Baker (*right*) of IUS with Lyall Morrill, who is wearing the trademark of his Computer Headware software company, at the Second West Coast Computer Faire (Photo courtesy of Paul Terrell)

Following page, top,
Paul Terrell in his Byte Shop
(Photo courtesy of Paul Terrell)

Following page, bottom,
Inside the original Byte Shop in Mountain View, California
(Photo courtesy of Paul Terrell)

Two pioneers in personal computer publishing: John Craig (*left*) publisher of *InfoWorld,* and Chris Morgan, editor-in-chief of *Byte* magazine, talking at a 1981 computer show
(Photo courtesy of John Barry)

174

Stan Veit, who founded an early
computer store in New York
(Photo by Paul Freiberger)

The first Byte Shop in Mountain View,
California
(Photo courtesy of Paul Terrell)

Ed Faber, who left IMSAI to found
ComputerLand
(Photo courtesy of ComputerLand)

Steve Jobs and Steve Wozniak examining
an early Apple circuit board
(Photo courtesy of Margaret Wozniak)

Steve Jobs and Mike Markkula
(Photo courtesy of Apple Computer)

Playboy magazine took some photographs there, the BBC filmed there, *Time* magazine did an article on these affairs, and the publicity forced the officials of the College of Notre Dame into action. They informed Warren that his conduct struck an unusual note at a Catholic school for women and asked him to leave. Warren shrugged. There *had* to be more interesting jobs in this enormous world, he thought.

So Warren began looking around. A friend asked why he didn't go into programming. "You'll pick it up," the friend said, so Warren went to work programming at the Stanford Medical Center and loved it. For pure fun, he found himself avidly following the state-of-the-art developments in the field. He had become an enthusiast.

The Stanford Medical Center was also the home of the Stanford Free University, which was providing an alternative, non-institutional approach to education much to Warren's liking, and of which he became executive secretary and newsletter editor. He met Bob Albrecht and Dennis Allison there.

For several years afterward, Warren did a variety of consulting jobs. Then the Altair was released followed by Gates and Allen's BASIC. Bob Albrecht, getting pudgy on beer and pizza at the Village Pub when he was not playing tennis or encouraging kids to use computers, and Dennis Allison, a member of the computer science faculty at Stanford, began seeking ways to bring their expertise to the people's computer cause. *Byte* had already appeared in September of 1975 and it was publishing information on hardware design, but there was no software magazine, and hobbyists turned to *PCC* to provide one. Dick Whipple and John Arnold of Tyler, Texas, sent in a long listing of a "Tiny BASIC," and Allison decided to publish a limited three-issue magazine to get this code into hobbyists' hands.

The response was overwhelming, and the magazine turned into an ongoing project entitled *Dr. Dobb's Journal of Tiny BASIC Calisthenics and Orthodontia.* "Dobb's" came from a collapsing of Allison's and Albrecht's first names — Dennis and Bob. The rest of the title was a computer in-joke about "running light without overbyte." They hired Jim Warren to run the publication. Warren thought its name too restrictive and changed it to *Dr. Dobb's Journal of Computer Calisthenics and Orthodontia.*

The magazine published classic Tiny BASIC implementations by Li-Chen Wang, Tom Pittman, and others, along with all the microcomputer news, rumors, and scuttlebutt Warren could unearth. *Dr. Dobb's* also adopted an irreverent, folksy tone that reflected the influence of the 1960s upon its editor. Warren believed in contributing to humanity; in fact, in the early 1970s he sometimes wondered whether he should continue working with computers at all. The machines were gadgets — toys as stimulating as a game of chess, but perhaps equally devoid of social utility, he felt. As he later put it, "Somewhere back there I'd been raised with a Puritan work ethic (if not all the Puritan values), a make-a-contribution-to-society ethic, which was certainly illustrated in ten years of teaching at destitute wages, over which I have no regrets at all."

Warren also had no regrets about earning $350 a month editing *Dr. Dobb's* when he could have been making more money consulting. Money wasn't paramount. He was making a contribution. He liked to quote Dennis Allison's slogan: "Let's stand on each other's shoulders and not on each other's toes."

Warren was also enjoying himself and believed others should too. Idle fun could ultimately ruffle his conscience, but delight was nonetheless one of the great rewards of existence. "Let's not worry about conformity and tradition. Let's just do whatever works. And let's have fun doing it," he said. He was attracted to *PCC* partly because it was the first newsletter to treat computers as objects of intellectual play. The merry spirit he injected into *Dr. Dobb's* became one of its keynotes.

There was a wide variety of other magazines. Some spun off from existing publications. *PCC* soon spun off another periodical, *Recreational Computing*, which addressed a broader and less technically-minded audience. Others came from corporations. MITS's *Computer Notes* emanated directly from the company and concentrated on the Altair line. Its editor, David Bunnell, later quit to run the slick *Personal Computing*, whose early issues carried articles for relative beginners. Still other magazines grew out of informal newsletters exchanged by hobbyists. Hal Singer and John Craig started the *Mark 8 Newsletter* to provide information for fellow users of the Mark 8, and Craig later became editor of *Kilobaud*. The Southern California Computer Society produced a newsletter called *Interface*. And many arose from various sources. After David Ahl left DEC, he started *Creative Computing*, which took on an intellectually playful air characteristic of its rumpled, bespectacled editor. *ROM* offered regular contributions from iconoclasts like Lee Felsenstein and Ted Nelson, as well as a technological centerfold with such chipcake as R2D2 from the movie *Star Wars*. It lasted less than a year.

The magazines spread the word and made staying abreast of events possible for hobbyists even in the remotest parts of the country. Magazines also served as vehicles for a volatile and often unpredictable system of mail-order marketing. Although some periodicals tried to warn buyers away from the less satisfactory products, the mail-order problem would not abate until the retail computer chains developed and customers could see and use the merchandise before buying it. Nevertheless, mail order survived and remained controversial. Although businesses might avoid it, hobbyists looking for the cheapest deal possible supported it fervidly. Some companies (like Apple in December 1981) forbade the sale of their products through mail order, asserting that dealers could provide better customer support.

However, in 1975 there were very few dealers. Careful consumers scanned the various publications for news of product quality. They also went to clubs and shows.

&

*The First [West Coast] Computer Faire was
definitely a torn T-shirt computer junkie
crowd. It was a gas. We didn't know what
the hell we were doing. The exhibitors didn't
know what they were doing. The attendees
didn't know what to expect. But we pulled it
off.*

Jim Warren

Word of Mouth: The Clubs and Shows

Clubs and shows were the forums of the early microcomputer world. They
offered hobbyists not only an interesting society, but otherwise unobtainable
news about products and innovations. The clubs provided ongoing support for
hobbyists and featured free and wide-ranging discussions about products,
which often led to publication of a regular newsletter. The fairs were technological spectacles. They gave hobbyists the chance to try out the latest innovations hands-on, and their carnival atmosphere fired attendees' enthusiasm for
the growing field.

The Homebrew was the prototype consumerist club. Its candid assessments of
market offerings had an impact far beyond the four walls of the meeting room
itself. This impact radiated to users' groups all over the country. When the
magazines emerged, they sent reporters to cover the meetings, broadcasting
Homebrew's voice even farther. Homebrew's opinion could be critical for a
company's success. Processor Technology, Apple, and Cromemco all profited
from Homebrew endorsements. Many other corporations received less flatter-
ing appraisals.

The first Homebrewers also realized they had the potential to affect the
image and future of the computer industry itself. Prior to 1975, computers
were associated with individuals in long white coats—the high priests of the
big computers—who would take a problem, retire to an air-conditioned environment, and return with a printout. The Homebrew Club helped replace this
vision with one of rugged, even ragged individualism, where solo mental
efforts could lead to multimillion dollar companies. Homebrew also understood
that it had an obligation to try to map out the future. The first edition of the
club newsletter in March of 1975 predicted that home computers would perform jobs ranging from editing texts and storing information to controlling
household utilities, doing menial labor (robotically), and instructing and divert-
ing the user.

The world's second major microcomputer club appeared only a week after
Homebrew began. In New Jersey, without knowing of Homebrew, Sol Libes
brought a small band of hobbyists together to form the Amateur Computer

Group of New Jersey (ACGNJ). The club resembled a mutual-help society, Libes thought. Like Homebrew, ACGNJ became something of an arbiter of new technology. The founders of Technical Design Labs of Trenton, New Jersey, for instance, started their company by attending ACGNJ meetings and selling used computer terminals there.

One club that took on a professional tone was the Boston Computer Society (BCS). Jonathan Rotenberg founded BCS in 1976, when he was only thirteen, and developed it into a 7000-member organization with 22 different sub-groups, a resource center, and a long list of industry and corporate sponsors. Rotenberg would later insist that BCS was a "users' group, not a club."

Yet BCS and the many other users' groups were really nothing more than clubs in a different stage of development. The clubs initiated the spirit of voluntarism and consumerism that continued to carry the users' groups. Indeed, the clubs protected buyers to an extent unprecedented in any new American industry. Vigilance committees against shoddiness and deception, as well as informal think tanks, social occasions, and arenas for information exchange, the clubs had a pervasive effect on the growth of the field.

But for the hobbyist seeking computer equipment there was no substitute for hands-on experience. For that, and for a sense of "the future is here" that sent the imagination into orbit, the computer hobbyist went to the computer shows.

The first big microcomputer fair was a one-company event. Early in 1976, David Bunnell of MITS began promoting the World Altair Computer Conference in his *Computer Notes*. The gathering took place in March and drew several hundred people. Among the speakers was *Computer Lib* author Ted Nelson, who delivered a scandalous and wildly entertaining speech on what he called "psycho-acoustic dildonics." Lee Felsenstein wondered if the audience would lynch Nelson at some point for his carefully analyzed explication of sex via telephone. After the address, Nelson talked to several people about setting up a computer store in the Chicago area. Nelson wanted to call it the Itty-Bitty Machine Company (after IBM). Among those interested was Ray Borrill, who was then building his own small network of computer stores in the Midwest.

Ed Roberts had planned the conference as a showcase for MITS and only MITS. He refused to give booth space to such competitors as Processor Technology. Lee Felsenstein and Bob Marsh were undaunted. Felsenstein suggested to Marsh that they rent a room in a hotel and sell products there. "Great idea," Marsh answered. "We'll get a *suite* at the hotel." They got the penthouse. They then posted signs on the conference floor inviting people to drop by. In the suite, they demonstrated Dompier's *Target*, using their VDM, a television set, and, since the Sol wasn't ready, an Altair. Ed Roberts came by, and he and Felsenstein met for the first time since Lee had criticized the Altair in *Dr. Dobb's*. David Bunnell tore down their signs.

Other shows soon followed. In May of 1976 Sol Libes of ACGNJ put together the Trenton (New Jersey) Computer Festival, something of a hardware swap meet and discussion session. Hal Chamberlain, one of the premier hobbyists, had come from North Carolina to give a talk. Other speakers included David Ahl and Dr. Bob Suding of Denver, whose Digital Group had received advance copies of the Z80 chip from Federico Faggin's new semiconductor company, Zilog. This fair pioneered the idea of the open conference, one not tied to a single manufacturer. It also showed California skeptics that the revolution was not confined to the West Coast.

In June of 1976 a loose confederation of hobbyists staged the first Midwest Area Computer Club conference. It drew 4000 people. Midwest dealer Ray Borrill shared a booth with Processor Technology, which displayed its new Sol-20 computer. The booth sold thousands of dollars worth of parts and supplies, and since the exhibitors hadn't thought to bring along a cash box, money lay in piles on the table. By the end of the show, people were buying whatever the booth had left because they wanted to buy *something*. Hobbyist fervor ran high at this fair, and Innovex, a well-known mainframe disk drive supplier, rewarded it with a discount. Its eight-inch floppy disk drive normally cost over a thousand dollars—a price well beyond the range most hobbyists could afford. But Innovex sold some 300 of them to fair-goers for under $500 each, the amount it charged bulk purchasers. This generous act gave a large push to the development of disk-based microcomputers.

The first national show took place in August 1976 in Atlantic City, New Jersey, where John Dilkes staged the Personal Computing Festival. This event helped popularize the term *personal computing*. Before the Festival, most people had spoken of "hobby computing" or "microcomputing." According to Wayne Green, the *Kilobaud* booth took over a thousand subscriptions to the incipient magazine there. And Peter Jennings bought the KIM-1 computer he would write *Micro Chess* on.

There were other shows in 1976, in Denver, Detroit, and elsewhere, leading to Jim Warren's First West Coast Computer Faire in April 1977.

Warren had watched these festive get-togethers with both appreciation and a gnawing sense that something was out of order. "My myopic contention was that all of this good stuff was happening on the wrong coast," he later said. About a week or two before the Atlantic City show, he commenced planning for one in the San Francisco Bay Area. He decided to call it a Computer Faire after the Renaissance Faire, a local summer spectacle in the manner of faires in Elizabethan England. The name was apt, he thought. The Renaissance Faire celebrated the past. The Computer Faire would celebrate the future.

Soon David Bunnell contacted him on behalf of MITS. Bunnell said MITS was also planning a West Coast show and suggested that they merge their efforts and stage a conference sponsored by *Personal Computing*. Warren could have 10 percent of the gate and profit further by his partners' greater experience and professionalism. Warren did not feel at all comfortable with this proposal. He replied that he did not think it would be appropriate for himself, as editor of *Dr. Dobb's*, to be involved in a show sponsored by *Personal Computing* or any other magazine. He was also uneasy about the emphasis on money. "I wasn't thinking about doing a bucks thing at all," he recalled. "I just wanted to have this event. I'd done be-ins in the '60s. I just wanted this stuff happening out here."

Warren attempted to reserve facilities at Stanford University but found he couldn't get the dates he wanted. So he looked into the San Francisco Civic Auditorium. It was great, he thought. It had excellent conference capabilities and a splendid exhibition room. Then he asked how much it would cost. Rental was $1200 per day. He was horrified.

Warren stopped off at a restaurant called Pete's Harbor with Bob Albrecht that day and they did some figuring on a napkin. If they could get at least 60 exhibitors, charge them each around $300, and perhaps draw about six or seven thousand people, they could break even. Hell, Warren thought, they could actually make money. That's when he founded his company, Computer Faire.

But Warren greatly underestimated the number of people who would attend. He had figured to draw between 7000 and 10,000 between Saturday and Sunday. Instead almost 13,000 showed up. For several hours on Saturday morning two lines stretched around one side of the Auditorium and three lines around the other. They met in the back. It was a clear, windy day, and Faire-goers stood there talking with each other. It took them an hour to get through the door, but they didn't care. For them, the Faire had begun outside in conversation with individuals who were as rabid about computers as they were.

Inside they found computer heaven: rows and rows of festive booths, many touting the latest advances in the field. Some were manned by the presidents of companies in their T-shirts and blue jeans. Hobbyists inquiring at a booth could easily find themselves talking to the person who had designed the product. The Apple II was unveiled in a large, attractive booth manned by Steve Jobs, Mike Scott, and other Apple executives. The Commodore PET was introduced. Sphere had failed to rent booth space, so it parked the Spheremobile, a 20-foot motor home modeled after MITS's Blue Goose, out front and sent an employee to walk the floor of the Faire with a placard saying, "Come see the Sphere." Gordon Eubanks demonstrated his BASIC-E in a booth shared with Gary Kildall. The excitement was tangible and exhilarating. "It was like a toy store. It was mobbed," attendee Lyall Morill said later. Among the many co-sponsors were the Homebrew Club, the Southern California Computer Society, *PCC*, and the Stanford Electrical Engineering Department. Science fiction writer Frederick Pohl spoke at the Faire, as did Ted Nelson, Lee Felsenstein, Carl Helmers, and David Ahl. Everyone agreed it was a gas.

Jim Warren spent most of the weekend in a whirl, racing around to smooth out little snafus. At subsequent Faires he took to getting around the convention hall on roller skates. Yet despite his administrative duties, he too was thrilled. "It was the excitement of turning all these people on," he recalled. He also felt justifiable pride in the accomplishment. The First West Coast Computer Faire was three to four times larger than any previous show. It also led to the first published proceedings of a personal computer conference. Warren had made his contribution, staged a watershed event. And he, like many others, had had fun.

Even before the first Faire opened, Warren had decided to hold a second one. It took place in March 1978 in San Jose, California. Exhibit space was sold out a month before it began. Lyall Morill was there again, but this time he represented his own software company, Computer Headware. "Either by the luck of the draw or the strange humor of Jim Warren, my booth was next to the IBM booth," he recalled. The contrast was striking. IBM had mounted a slick chrome booth staffed by men in suits and polished shoes and featuring its 5110, a relatively expensive desktop minicomputer that didn't impress the people at the show. Morill was showing his software package, a simple data base management program called WHATSIT, a loose acronym for "Wow! How'd All That Stuff get In There?", and had written all his signs in felt-tip pen the night before. Warren enjoyed the juxtaposition so much he had photos taken of Morill socializing with the IBM sales staff. The difference in the impact of the booths was as dramatic as the difference in their styles. IBM got few takers, while Morill was besieged. People lined up at his booth with credit cards to order Morill's program.

The second Faire was also a success, and Warren decided to do one every year. If, as Carl Helmers said, the magazines defined the microcomputer community, shows such as Warren's gave it a county fair.

&

*Dick was not what you'd think of as an
entrepreneurial type.*

Ed Roberts

*We didn't want to sell Altairs. We wanted
to solve problems.*

Dick Heiser

The First Retailer

On June 15, 1975, 125 hobbyists and novices collected in the recreation room
of the Laurel Tree Apartments in Miraleste, California. They had been
brought together by digital engineer Don Tarbell and a computer neophyte,
one Judge Pearce Young, to form the Southern California Computer Society.
The occasion was distinguished by lively debate about the structure and
purpose of the club. At one point, someone asked for a show of hands of
people who either owned or had ordered an Altair. A forest of hands appeared.

One of those present, Dick Heiser, was particularly struck by this response.
He realized that these people were going to have a lot of questions about Altair
assembly. Maybe he could help, he thought. Heiser, a systems analyst, had
recently spent $14,000 building a video word processor for a low-cost
minicomputer. When the Altair came out, he saw that he could construct a
similar processor on it for about $4000. He knew the insides of a computer,
and he was eager to work on the Altairs.

Why not, he thought, set up a small storefront to market the kits and
provide advice and support for buyers? Heiser had little business experience
and had never imagined himself working as a sales representative, but he knew
the opportunity to use his technical skills would be fun. Would it be profitable?
He devised a cash-flow plan. If he were to pay $200 rent per month and sell
about 10 to 20 computers at $439 each assembled, he could stay in the black. It
was worth a try.

In June 1975 he flew to Albuquerque to talk to MITS. The people at MITS
were not sure what to make of Dick Heiser. Ed Roberts thought he was a "nice
guy" but deficient in the aggressiveness that, he felt, marked the born entrepreneur. Roberts also worried about the profit margin. MITS was selling the
Altair kits for $395 ($439 assembled), which left only a thin profit margin.
Heiser would have to sell at a higher price, but MITS couldn't afford to discount to anyone. Roberts hadn't built discounts into the Altair's pricing. Nonetheless, Roberts took Heiser seriously. Others had approached MITS with the
retailing idea, but Heiser was the first to prepare a spreadsheet. "They thought

I was a little weird," Heiser recalled, "but they told me it sounded like a good idea, and we signed a contract."

By mid-July, Heiser had opened a small store in a low-rent area of West Los Angeles and was paying $225 per month for rent. In large letters across the front he put the outlet's official name: Arrow Head Computer Company. In smaller ones below he subtitled it "The Computer Store," because he thought it sounded "funky" and interesting. Soon everyone was calling it The Computer Store.

Curiosity-seekers—and the store drew them as well as the hobbyists—on walking into the store found themselves in a strange world of blinking boxes and shelves of books and magazines with obscure names like *Byte*. Some people walked in, looked around, and walked back out again with no clear notion of what they had seen. Heiser, in beard and cowboy hat, might be in a serious technical discussion with a hobbyist one minute and the next assuring a skeptic that the Altair, despite its low price, was truly a computer. In the back room, between attending to customers, he made repairs and worked on his own computer, which he was still soldering together.

Heiser quickly discovered that his spreadsheet had been seriously in error. He had anticipated a series of individual computer purchases at $439 each—the price of an assembled Altair. Instead, he found that a person who had bought a computer might easily spend another $4000 for accessories—extra memory, video terminals, and disk drives. Heiser, making the first small excursion into retailing, was amazed. These people were willing to spend real money on the machine. In his first month he took in between $5000 and $10,000, and in his first five months, over $100,000. By the end of 1975, he was ringing up over $30,000 in sales per month.

Heiser undertook little advertising other than posting flyers at large engineering firms such as System Development Corporation, Rand, and TRW. As a result, most of his early customers were engineers, often computer enthusiasts who had come to California to work on high technology. Later, celebrities such as Herbie Hancock, Bob Newhart, and Carl Sagan came to The Computer Store, but at the time his clientele consisted mainly of hobbyists.

Having hobbyists as customers was probably just as well since Altair assembly generated all the problems Heiser had anticipated. "It was really tough in those days," he recalled. "You had to know electronics as well as software. You had to bring up the raw machine, and you had to use the toggle switches to put in the bootstrap loader," he explained, describing the steps required before the Altair could be used. Buyers who stumbled at various points in the route came back to Heiser, who gave them careful instruction in assembly, repaired malfunctions, and lent a sympathetic ear, at the least, to the inevitable complaints about the MITS memory boards.

With the business prospering, Dick's wife Lois, also a systems analyst and a member of the board of directors of the Southern California Computer

Society, joined him in the enterprise. In addition, he was able to hire two employees. Dick Heiser did not have to run want ads. He had noticed a number of individuals simply hanging out at the store: hobbyists who soon developed the habit of explaining things to more transient customers. He asked them if they wanted work. They did. As it turned out, they already owned Altairs and had spent hundreds of hours experimenting with them. Their entire lifestyle revolved around the computer, and Heiser thought it was wonderful to be able to hire these experts for his store.

The Computer Store was not without local competition. Around Thanksgiving of 1975, John French opened Computer Mart in a small rented suite. French offered the IMSAI, which was simply a better piece of computer hardware, but Heiser, with Gates and Allen's BASIC, had the superior software. Software was the more important of the two, but since the BASIC could run on French's machines, French thrived. Eventually, French sold out, invested in his friend Dick Wilcox's company, Alpha Micro, and became involved in another business venture.

Heiser also faced competition from a group of Sikhs in Pasadena. Though American-born, they had embraced the Indian creed and adopted Indian names. The Sikhs did not disdain technology. "It wasn't, 'Let's sit by the river and meditate,'" Heiser said. Rather, in their turbans and white coats, the Sikhs sold computers from Processor Technology and later Apple. Heiser respected them immensely. Like himself, they cared more about working out their customers' problems than about moving the inventory.

In May of 1976 Heiser moved The Computer Store to Santa Monica and to a facility four times as large as the one in West Los Angeles. He now had five or six employees and was making $50,000 to $60,000 a month. He installed carpets and desks so it looked like the officers' side of a bank. Customers would sit across the desk from an employee, and they would discuss requirements and how best to meet them. Partly because of his experience with IBM and the customized method of selling computers, Heiser saw himself as a counselor more than an entrepreneur. But the problem-solving approach gave him personal satisfaction as well. "I'm a computer enthusiast and a compulsive explainer," he said.

There was one problem he couldn't solve. MITS was pressuring him into making bad deals with his customers. It tightly tied the purchase of Gates and Allen's BASIC to the purchase of the defective MITS memory boards. Heiser appreciated the value of the BASIC, but he realized that no one wanted to buy memory boards that didn't work, and he didn't even want to carry them. "We went through a lot of grief trying to make a viable computer system and a viable computer business when we didn't have any memories," he said. Then MITS decreed that Altair outlets sell its products and no one else's. MITS was worried that if its retailers also offered the wares of competitors, customers would buy MITS software and shun its hardware. The apprehension was probably unfounded, since most early stores quickly sold out of whatever hardware they could obtain. Heiser complained to Ed Roberts, but Roberts was adamant, and, according to Heiser, threatened to shut down dealers who disobeyed. This policy of exclusivity cost MITS many dealers, but Heiser remained and reluctantly abided by the edict until Roberts sold MITS to Pertec.

Heiser soon concluded that if MITS was out of touch, Pertec was roaming the ether. Pertec believed it would bring MITS needed capital and a proper business orientation so it called a meeting of MITS's 40 dealers. Heiser didn't think much of Pertec's marketing ideas. Pertec, he discovered, believed that if they could sell one computer to (for example) General Motors, General Motors would return to Pertec for its next 600 computers. Retailers would soon be making 600-item package deals all the time. The company would rocket up into the Fortune 500. Heiser was amazed. It was clear to him that Pertec was totally ignoring such problems as obtaining the proper software. At the end of the meeting, he stood up and said that the company would have to deal with immediate problems if it ever hoped to succeed financially. At that point, Heiser began making plans to go his own way and started stocking the Apple and the PET, among others.

Over the years, Dick Heiser saw the nature of retailing changing. Discounters entered the market, employing non-technical employees and selling machines "with the staples still in the box." "They might as well be selling canned peaches," Heiser said. It was becoming harder for him to maintain his standards of excellence, and in March 1982 he left the store.

Like many of the personal computer pioneers, Heiser had broken new ground in a spirit of enthusiasm for the technology. Even in retailing, the hobbyist ideal led the way. But retailing, unlike computer design, is an inherently commercial venture, and it quickly attracted individuals more entrepreneurial than Heiser.

&

They told me it would never snow in the Valley, and they told me you could never retail computers.

Paul Terrell

Snow in the Valley

In 1974, when Paul Terrell was running a sales representation company in Northern California, he got a call from friends who said they had seen a microcomputer in *Popular Electronics* for only $439. Terrell knew that no one could even get an 8080 chip on a PC board for that price, much less a power supply and a chassis and the rest. "My comment was that it was a paper tiger and forget about it," he said. "And a couple of months later, they called me back and told me to come on over and help them unwrap their paper tiger."

The Altair impressed Terrell. He contacted MITS in Albuquerque to see if it needed a sales representative in Northern California. MITS said it was primarily a mail-order company, but if he cared to meet MITS representatives at the National Computer Conference in Anaheim, California, that June, they'd be happy to talk. Terrell cared.

MITS showed up at the NCC with the MITSmobile. "You walked in and it had a refrigerator and a stove and a couple of computers set up," Terrell recalled. He talked with Ed Roberts and MITS's marketing manager. They got along well. Terrell felt Roberts did not really understand the sales representation business, but Roberts listened. In the end, they signed an exclusive sales representation contract whereby Terrell would promote the Altair and in turn receive a 5 percent commission on every MITS product shipped into Northern California, whether he had sold it or not.

After NCC, the MITSmobile toured the clubs in the Los Angeles area, meeting various people who had written in. Then it went north to the San Francisco Bay Area, where Terrell booked space in the Edwards Room at Rickey's Hyatt House in Palo Alto. The room held about 80 people. Between 200 and 300 showed up.

The following month, in July of 1975, Roberts called a sales representatives meeting in Albuquerque. Terrell and his partner, Boyd Wilson, along with the ten or so other Altair representatives in the country, flew to New Mexico, where Roberts showed them his shopping center factory, explained something of the history of MITS, and indicated the direction he wanted them to take.

Roberts also mentioned something else. "One of the principal things that came out of the meeting was that Ed had identified a crazy man in L.A. — Dick Heiser — who had approached him to try to retail computers across the countertop," Terrell said. Roberts wanted the sales representatives to find similar crazy men in their own territories. The retail idea was worth pursuing, he thought. Terrell asked what kind of deal retailers would get. Roberts said he would give them a 25 percent discount, no matter how much they sold. When they got back on the plane, Terrell and Wilson discussed this arrangement. "It was an easy task to figure that 25 percent plus 5 percent was 30 percent — a helluva lot more money than we were making as representatives," he said. They decided to open their own outlet.

Terrell and Wilson commenced the process in August. Soon after, *Byte* magazine appeared. "I told Boyd that this magazine is real significant," Terrell said. "There's a real following here. So let's be the Byte Shop, and we'll sell a helluva lot of *Byte* magazines in addition."

Friends told him retailing computers wouldn't work. And some people, Terrell later mused, said it never snowed in Silicon Valley. Terrell recalled his friends' warnings as he watched the snow falling on December 8, 1975 — the day he opened his Mountain View store in the heart of Silicon Valley.

Like most Altair dealers, Terrell quickly ran headlong into the MITS exclusivity policy. Terrell ignored it. He was selling all the Altairs he could get, about 10 to 50 per month, plus everything he could obtain from IMSAI and Proc Tech. The MITS edict, he concluded, was not only pointless, but, if he followed it, financially harmful as well. One day David Bunnell, then the MITS vice-president of marketing, called to cancel him as a dealer. Terrell argued that MITS should see the Byte Shop as rather like a stereo store, which carried many different brands and could turn a profit for them all. Bunnell waffled. It was Roberts's decision, he said. At the World Altair Computer Conference in March of 1976, Terrell approached Roberts directly. Roberts remained firm. Terrell was out.

At the time, Terrell was selling twice as many IMSAIs as Altairs, and he realized the MITS strategy of excommunication would ultimately hurt Roberts more than himself. He was still selling whatever he could get. He saw himself and John French, Heiser's Computer Mart competitor in Orange County, as conducting most of IMSAI's early business. They used to do battle for the product. Terrell would rent a van and drive it over to the back dock of IMSAI's manufacturing site in Hayward to collect his own and French's orders. Check in hand, he would ask, "You want cash on the barrelhead, boys?" It was hardware war.

Terrell had started his Byte Shop in December 1975. By January he was being approached by people who wanted to open their own stores. He signed dealership agreements with them, whereby he would take a percentage of their profits, and soon there were Byte Shops in Santa Clara, San Jose, Palo Alto, and Portland, Oregon. In March 1976, Terrell incorporated as Byte, Inc.

This was a hobbyist industry, and Terrell found the clubs critical to his business. They provided his customer base. Many of the hobbyists who attended meetings had not bought their machines yet, and those who had often wanted accessories. Club members proved particularly receptive to Terrell's message.

A single Homebrew meeting could have as many as six Byte Shop managers in attendance. "If I had a store manager that didn't go to the club, he wasn't going to be my store manager for long. It was important," Terrell said. At one Homebrew meeting, a long-haired youth approached him and asked if Terrell might be interested in a computer that a friend of his had designed in a garage. Steve Jobs was trying to convince him to carry the Apple I. Terrell said OK.

Like Dick Heiser, Terrell discovered that buyers needed help assembling the machines or obtaining the proper accessories. He offered them "kit insurance," where, for an extra $50, he would guarantee to solve any problems that arose in putting the computers together. Terrell understood that he was doing true specialty retailing and that he had to provide information and a certain amount of handholding. The computer stores were like the stereo stores of 15 or 20 years ago, he thought, when clerks routinely had to explain woofers, tweeters, and watts of power to puzzled customers.

The Byte Shops' success skyrocketed after the July 1976 issue of *Business Week*, which described the chain and suggested it offered significant opportunity to the investor. "We had something like 5000 inquiries come in," Terrell said. "You couldn't do anything in the store anymore." He found himself talking to people like the president of the Federal Reserve Bank. The chairman of Telex Corporation called to ask if Oklahoma was available for franchising. "The credentials were staggering," Terrell said.

The chain was adding eight stores a month, and Terrell had negotiated a price for an 8080 chip below that which IBM was paying. (IBM was not yet building a microcomputer.) By the time he sold the operation in November 1977, Terrell had 74 stores in 15 states and Japan. He valued the chain at $4 million.

By March of 1976, one could identify a Big Four among Altair retailers: Terrell, the Heisers, Peachtree in Atlanta, and Dick Brown. Brown opened his outlet — like the Heisers' called The Computer Store — in 1975 along a stretch of Route 128 in Burlington, Massachusetts, the East Coast version of Silicon Valley. Brown originally intended to sell only peripheral equipment like printers and disk drives. But he soon picked up the MITS line. Store personnel did no programming or kit assembly, but they did offer free assistance to customers whose kits failed to work. When Ed Roberts insisted that The Computer Store carry only MITS goods, Brown, like Terrell, decamped. He went to Data General, which had just announced a small and inexpensive minicomputer, and to Apple. Within a year, Brown had won Apple's first East Coast distributorship.

Of course, not every retailer commenced under MITS's auspices. In 1975, Stan Veit had recently been laid off as a technical writer for a Long Island, New York, computer company and realized that he too could sell micros. He called MITS. The company informed him that it had awarded its East Coast distributorship to Dick Brown. Veit would have to deal with Brown and pay him a percentage of the gross. Veit decided such an arrangement was for someone else. He approached Sphere, but after seeing the Sphere in action he changed his plans. Eventually, Veit simply sold whatever he could get—IMSAI, Southwest Tech, Cromemco, Processor Tech, and Apple. "We were selling everything," he said. He called his store the Computer Mart, and soon other Computer Marts—at most only loosely associated with the original—were appearing. Veit was one of the first retailers to sell computers other than MITS's.

In the Midwest, Ray Borill opened Data Domain early in 1976 with the aim of out-Terrelling Terrell. Borill quickly spun off nearly a dozen affiliated stores from his first outlet in Bloomington, Indiana. He also helped start the Chicago-based Itty-Bitty Machine Company, an ill-fated venture that derived from his talks at the World Altair Computer Conference with Ted Nelson.

With computer stores opening all across the country, countertop sales had clearly started to elbow mail order aside. Indeed, at club meetings Terrell used to say, over and over again, "You don't have to buy mail order any more." Rescue from the hazards of mail order was one of the best selling points the new retailers had.

While at the Byte Shop, Terrell began marketing his own brand of computer. Called the Byte 8, it was a private-label product with a profit margin of around 50 percent, twice the retailer's 25 percent. "We were rolling our own," he said. It proved an easy commercial success. "All of a sudden, I realized the power of distribution that Tandy/Radio Shack had. Guaranteed sales." Tandy, a huge electronics distributor, had not yet ventured into computers, though some microcomputer retailers feared Tandy the way microcomputer makers feared Texas Instruments. Neither group had cause to worry, for the moment.

&

My most ambitious hopes were that we might have some store somewhere that might be able to do $50,000 a month. Well, the average store in ComputerLand does $130,000 a month.

Ed Faber

Franchising

IMSAI had been a manufacturing company run by a sales force; it made little effort to adorn its computer with technological breakthroughs. IMSAI thrived on its vigorous sales effort and ultimately failed through its neglect of manufacturing—both production and service. It is fitting, therefore, that IMSAI's most lasting contribution to the field should be a pure sales enterprise, a chain of retail stores, a franchise.

Ed Faber left IMSAI in 1976, with Bill Millard's blessing, to start the new chain for Millard. Faber was an old hand at start-up operations. After graduating from Cornell and serving in the Marine Corps, he had joined IBM as a sales representative in 1957. In 1964, IBM sent him to Holland to set up a European Education Center for the corporation. Suddenly he found himself working at a distance from direct management, and he liked it. In 1966, IBM assigned him to a project he liked even more. He was to help develop a department called New Business Marketing to ease IBM into the small-business area. Faber helped create a business plan for a new sales force and marketing concept within the company. This was his first start-up operation and he relished the challenge. He had to identify problems and devise solutions for them and then deal with the inevitable new problems created by the solutions. By 1967, Faber decided to orient his career toward start-ups, rather than line sales management, the more common path of advancement at IBM at the time.

In 1967, Faber came to the West Coast on another start-up venture for IBM, experimenting with the placement of remote terminals in small businesses. When some of IBM's competitors complained that this activity violated the consent decrees in certain suits, IBM changed the department into a service division. Ed Faber suddenly found himself shunted from the mainstream of data processing into a back eddy, where his career prospects, he thought, were somewhat less promising. In 1969, after 12 years with IBM, he left to join Memorex. There, and later at a minicomputer company, Faber came in to structure the internal marketing organization. A pattern was developing, one Faber did not entirely mind, for, he felt, once he had created and launched a program, running it became mere routine. He liked to work closer to the edge.

In 1975, he was with Omron, a small San Francisco subsidiary of a Japanese electronics firm, when Bill Millard invited him to join IMSAI. Millard described the opportunity in lavish terms, which Faber automatically discounted. The idea of selling kit computers through the mail for buyers to assemble at home seemed preposterous to the IBM man. But Faber couldn't argue with the actual market response. IMSAI was knee-deep in orders. At the end of December 1975, he joined the San Leandro firm as Director of Sales.

Almost immediately Faber found himself in contact with John French, Dick Heiser's competitor in Southern California. French had approached IMSAI with the idea of buying kits in quantity and retailing them in a computer store. Again Faber arched his eyebrows. Sell computers to customers right off the street? It was ludicrous, he thought. Still, Heiser seemed more than solvent, and IMSAI had little to lose. Faber sold French 10 of the kits at a 10 percent discount—not much for a retailer to work with. French soon moved these 10 out the door and was asking for 15 more. Further orders followed. And other retailers were contacting Faber seeking similar deals. By March of 1976, IMSAI had raised its price in order to give retailers a 25 percent margin.

Faber had an excellent reason for courting the dealers. Selling computers to retailers in batches of 10 or 15 was much easier than selling to individuals one-by-one over the telephone. Furthermore, the retail market was wide open. The MITS exclusivity policy was driving dealers to IMSAI like a bullwhip. Not only did Altair dealers have to carry the MITS line and nothing else, but late arrivals were subservient to early ones, who had established "territory." Enterprising dealers like Paul Terrell chafed at the restrictions and often bolted to freedom.

Faber watched the MITS retailing strategy with amazement. Ed Roberts was out to dominate his dealers, Faber thought, and to compel their loyalty. But Faber saw the entrepreneurial spirit balking at such attempts at control and predicted that Roberts's marketing approach would inevitably backfire. So he took a stance diametrically opposed to Roberts's. He encouraged non-exclusivity both in territory and in products. If two dealers wanted to open stores a block away from each other, it was fine with Faber. They would compete. IMSAI products would compete with any others the dealers might want to stock. By the end of June 1976, some 235 independent stores in the United States and Canada were carrying IMSAI products.

Faber kept an eye on these dealers, observing their strengths and weaknesses. Most of them, he realized, were hobbyists with meager backgrounds in business. This inexperience was a good enough reason to fail, he thought. Yet they weren't failing. They were buying more and more merchandise from IMSAI and selling it. In addition, the number of retailers was growing steadily.

Faber and Bill Millard began discussing the phenomenon. They wondered what would happen if someone with a well-recognized name started providing centralized services—product purchasing, education, and accounting systems

—for a network of small retail store owners. They were thinking about a franchise.

There seemed no reason not to start one. Faber talked to John Martin, a former associate of Dick Brown's who knew something about franchising, and attended a seminar on franchising offered under the aegis of Pepperdine University. One day Faber sat down with Millard, and they talked about starting this operation. Millard asked Faber what he would choose to do. Faber sensed the *est* in this question and said he wanted to be president of the franchising operation.

ComputerLand incorporated on September 21, 1976, and opened its pilot store in Hayward, California, on November 10. This store served not only as a retail outlet, but also as a training facility for franchise owners. At first, Gordon French, who had helped start Homebrew, worked there helping to evaluate products and establish the store before moving on to become a consultant. ComputerLand eventually sold this outlet and became a pure franchise operation owning no stores at all.

The first ComputerLand franchise store opened on February 18, 1977, in Morristown, New Jersey. The second appeared soon after in West Los Angeles. The stores initially offered the products of IMSAI, Proc Tech, Polymorphic, Southwest Tech, and Cromemco. Cromemco was one of the first manufacturers to support the new enterprise. Roger Melen and Harry Garland told Faber they thought the idea was important and gave him one of the best discounts then available. Faber soon also developed a strong relationship with Apple, partly because of the market tactics of its rival Commodore. Commodore had recently come out with its PET, which it was selling mainly in Europe. When it did enter the United States market, Commodore demanded that each retail store forecast the monetary value of the machines it expected to sell each month and then lay that amount at Commodore's feet as a deposit. ComputerLand found this demand unreasonable and became very interested in stocking the Apple instead. Apple, in turn, proved highly cooperative and issued much advertising linking the two company names together. Apple became a ComputerLand staple.

But the franchise hadn't been named ComputerLand from the start. The firm had incorporated under the name Computer Shack, which did not enchant the well-entrenched electronics chain Radio Shack. Faber soon received a communication from Radio Shack attorneys alleging that it owned the rights to the word *Shack*. The letter further indicated that if Computer Shack did not change its name, it faced litigation. Faber consulted his own attorneys, who, he said, assured him that the Radio Shack contention was baseless and that he would prevail in court. Great, he would take Radio Shack to court, he decided. He brought suit in California, seeking a judgment on the matter. Radio Shack responded by filing a complaint in New Jersey, where the first Computer Shack franchise had opened. Faber thought he saw Radio Shack's strategy clearly then: litigation would be commenced in every state where the new franchise appeared. Though he might win every case, the expense of the repeated defenses would wear him down. It wasn't worth it, Faber decided. He was already calling one part of the store "ComputerLand," and began asking franchise owners to adopt this new name. Faber recalls that not only was everyone supportive of changing the name, but some said that they had never liked the name *Computer Shack* all along.

Like IMSAI, ComputerLand was the enterprise of Bill Millard. He founded it and poured the initial capital into it. He chaired its board of directors. Even in 1983, about 25 percent of the ComputerLand company was composed of *est* graduates.

When IMSAI began staggering in 1978, ComputerLand faced a new problem. People thought the corporations were tied together. They knew the franchising business had descended from IMSAI. They saw Bill Millard at the top, running both of them, and ex-IMSAI Sales Director Ed Faber as ComputerLand's president. Would ComputerLand be dragged down into the hole after IMSAI? Faber spent much time assuring people that the companies had legally separated. ComputerLand had a buyer-vendor relationship with IMSAI, purchasing the product and paying its bills. IMSAI imposed no formal quota on ComputerLand. And when IMSAI went bankrupt, Faber was proven correct. Creditors were unable to penetrate the gap between IMSAI and ComputerLand to get at the latter's assets. ComputerLand went on to become a spectacular success as the nation's largest chain of computer stores. At the end of 1977, it had only 24 stores. By September 1978, it had 50, and its growth continued rapidly. By November 1979, there were 100 ComputerLand franchises; by December 1981, 241; by December 1982, 382; and by June 1983, 458. ComputerLand outdistanced the Byte Shops, and its competition was instrumental in the demise of the Data Domain chain in the Midwest. In the early 1980s, Faber could reasonably claim that, to the general public, the place where computers were sold was called "ComputerLand."

In 1982 the chain launched plans for a string of software stores called ComputerLand Satellites. ComputerLand intended to license the new software stores to existing franchise owners in its chain.

By 1983 Ed Faber was considering a bucolic semi-retirement within the next five years. He loved to fish and hunt geese and pheasants, and he was looking forward to a little relaxation. But for the moment, he was still seeking out the competition. In order to spur the performance of his own franchise chain, he was trying, whenever he could, to locate a ComputerLand store near his biggest rival, the new Radio Shack Computer Centers.

&

*Not a kit, the TRS-80 comes completely
wired and tested, ready to plug in and use.*
A Tandy Corporation press release

Tandy Enters the Ring

Tandy/Radio Shack was an electronics distributor and did not want to touch computer manufacturing at all. The giant chain, known around its Fort Worth base as "the McDonald's of the electronics world," simply wanted to stock the machines. But when Charles Tandy was unable to reach an agreement with Bill Millard about investing in IMSAI, Tandy was pushed one step closer to making micros himself.

The Tandy Corporation was not always an electronics distributor. It began as a small leather business in 1927, when Dave Tandy and a friend founded the Hinckley-Tandy Leather Company, which soon established a reputation around Fort Worth. In 1950, Tandy's son Charles, a graduate of Harvard Business School, conceived of an expanded business, a chain of leathercraft stores that would sell its goods partly by retail mail order. Co-founder Hinckley balked at this idea and dropped out of the Tandy story. The number of leathercraft stores grew throughout the early 1950s. In 1955, the chain was purchased by another company, which proceeded to buy three more companies, all unrelated to leathercraft, and to amalgamate the lot as General American Industries. The other companies were soon struggling, and Charles Tandy felt himself trapped. He purchased the small conglomerate, and by 1960 had unloaded the albatross companies. The corporation emerged with a new management team, marketing direction, and operating objectives, and 1960 was the last year in which it lost money.

Charles Tandy had an engaging, magnetic personality with a sarcastic sense of humor, and he seemed to influence all about him. He was a perpetual teacher, always engrossed in the daily operations of the company, and when he had nothing else to do on a Friday afternoon, he would sometimes phone the outlets and ask how business was.

Tandy quickly set about building a national retail base. By 1961, he had 125 stores in 105 cities in the United States and Canada. In 1962, Tandy bought a company that represented a fundamental change for the corporation. He had noticed a small, struggling chain of nine mail-order electronics stores based in Boston called Radio Shack. He took control of it in 1963 and at once began reconstructing it, adding hundreds of retail stores throughout the country. Within two years, Radio Shack, which had been losing 4 million dollars annually, was turning a profit. By 1973, when Radio Shack purchased Allied Radio of Chicago, its closest competitor, Radio Shack so dominated the market that the Justice Department brought an antitrust suit against it and compelled Tandy to divest itself of the corporation.

Tandy had begun manufacturing some of its own wares in 1966, but it resisted making microcomputers. The behemoth chain was pushed into the field chiefly by one man: Don French.

French was officially a buyer for Radio Shack in 1975. When the Altair came out, he bought one and studied it. Concluding that it had potential, French began to devise his own machine. Though forbidden to work on the computer on company time, French eventually managed to convince John Roach, then vice-president in charge of marketing at Radio Shack, to take a look at his project. As French recalls, Roach was not particularly impressed. Nonetheless, Radio Shack soon offered to pay Steve Leininger, of National Semiconductor, to examine French's design. Leininger needed no arm-twisting, and by June 1976 he and French were working together on the project, using equipment and software of their own design.

In December of 1976, the two engineers received the official go-ahead to develop a Radio Shack computer, though the company's commitment to their enterprise remained slight. Radio Shack told French to "do it as cheaply as possible." This attitude was nonetheless an improvement over that of a few months earlier, when one Radio Shack executive had telexed French: "Don't waste my time — we can't sell computers."

A month later, in January 1977, French and Leininger demonstrated a working model of the new machine to Charles Tandy in the Radio Shack conference room. The keyboard and display sat on the table, but the computer itself lay hidden beneath it. The two computerists had devised a quick tax accounting program, *H & R Shack*, and offered it to the magnate. Tandy typed in a salary of $150,000 for himself and promptly crashed the program. When French and Leininger explained the limits of integer arithmetic in BASIC, Tandy gracefully cut his simulated salary, but French made a mental note that the machine needed a more powerful arithmetic.

By the spring of 1977, serious work on the machine had begun. The company assigned it a target retail price of $199 and projected sales of 1000 computers per year. French thought the second figure absurd. MITS had sold over 10,000 Altairs in one year without the overwhelming advantage of Radio Shack's retail network. French wasn't too sanguine about the $199 price either. Soon after, in May, Tandy and Roach met with company computer personnel to discuss what to do with the little computer if it failed to sell. Could they use it in internal Radio Shack accounting? French, they knew, was doing some simple record-keeping on his handmade version. The company's own stores could be the back-up customer base and could absorb the first year's projected production of the machines. In the same month, Radio Shack raised its sales projection to 3000 units per year.

In August, at New York City's Warwick Hotel, the company announced the new TRS-80. The machine would cost $399 and come complete and ready-to-use in a black and gray plastic case. By September 1977, while projected sales held firm at 3000 annually, Radio Shack stores had already sold 10,000 TRS-80s.

In June, Radio Shack had assigned French to establish retail stores for the TRS-80. The computer was still an orphan within Radio Shack, French felt. The company wasn't sure of its success, and did not take it seriously. At first, Radio Shack outlets did not even stock the TRS-80. Buyers had to order it.

Tandy/Radio Shack ventured slightly farther in October 1977, when it opened its first all-computer store in Fort Worth. The outlet carried not only the TRS-80, but IMSAIs and other companies' products. It was frankly an experiment. But it too succeeded, and resistance to microcomputers began fading away. Soon Radio Shack outlets were stocking the TRS-80s, and Radio Shack Computer Centers were appearing all over the country, staffed by individuals who knew more about computers than ordinary salespeople did. The backlog of orders was great: Radio Shack President Lewis Kornfeld admitted in June 1978 that only about one-third of the stores had computers in stock, though over half had sold some.

Making his entrance to a party atop an elephant, Charles Tandy celebrated his sixtieth birthday in style. A few months later, on a Saturday afternoon in November 1978, he died in his sleep. The following Monday, Tandy stock dropped 10 percent on Wall Street.

But Tandy Corporation was not a one-man performance, despite the flamboyance of its leader. For Charles Tandy had, in fact, surrounded himself with capable executives, and the company maintained a solid standing.

The original TRS-80 was a limited machine with only 4K of memory, a Z80 processor running at slightly under half-speed, a sketchy BASIC, and very slow tape cassettes for storage. Most of these limitations stemmed from the company's cut-rate approach to the product. The first TRS-80 lacked lowercase letters. It was not an oversight. French and Leininger had deliberately omitted them to save $1.50 on parts, which meant $5.00 on the purchase price.

But Tandy quickly supplemented this machine with a better BASIC and add-on memory kits and soon offered a combination disk and printer. These enhancements were a prelude to Tandy's announcement, on May 30, 1979, of the TRS-80 Model II, a capable business system that overcame many of the drawbacks of the original computer.

The Model II showed that Tandy had learned from the Model I and could make a state-of-the-art business machine. This fact surprised some corporations, and not without reason, given Tandy's torpid entry into the field. Between 1978 and 1980, personal computers and related equipment rose from 1.8 to 12.7 percent of Radio Shack's North American sales.

In 1980, Radio Shack introduced a spate of new machines. Its Pocket Computer cost $229, was slightly larger than an advanced calculator, and contained four times the memory the original Altair computer came with. Its Color Computer, at $399, offered graphics in eight colors and up to 16K of memory. And the TRS-80 Model III was an upgrade of the Model I.

The TRS-80 Model I had been a price breakthrough, and people who knew nothing about computers began buying Model I's. But Tandy was not the only company driving the price down, thereby opening the market for the home computer. Nolan Bushnell's Atari, which initially produced only video game machines, began putting out low-priced machines that could legitimately be called computers. Commodore, with strong distribution channels for its electronics equipment, was doing well with its PET computer and soon added more sophisticated, less hobbyist-oriented machines to its product line. Texas Instruments, the company that so many microcomputer manufacturers feared would announce a bargain-basement computer, did just that with its TI-99/4. And in Britain, a daring and brilliant entrepreneur named Clive Sinclair introduced a computer called the ZX-80, later replaced by the ZX-81, which eventually sold (distributed by Timex) for under $50.

But Tandy's most serious competition during the early 1980s came from a Silicon Valley firm financed by the sale of two calculators and a Volkswagen bus. In 1981, when John Roach, at 42, took the reins of Tandy, he seemed young to those accustomed to Charles Tandy's leadership, but that youth began to look like an advantage as the TRS-80 faced serious competition from the most youthful company of all.

&

American Pie

Chapter 7

The world of computer design had Steve Wozniak for a golden moment.

Chris Espinosa

The Prankster

In 1962 young Stephen G. Wozniak obtained a few transistors from a Fairchild engineer and built an addition-subtraction machine. He did all the work himself, soldering the wires in the backyard of his suburban home in Cupertino, California. And when he entered the machine in a local science fair, no one who knew him was surprised when he won the highest award given for electronics.

Wozniak, known to his friends as "Woz" (or "The Woz"), was bright, and when a problem caught his interest, no one worked any harder at solving it. When he enrolled in Homestead High School two years later, The Woz quickly became a top math student, although electronics remained his strongest intellectual interest. Had it been his only interest, Wozniak would have caused the teachers and administrators of Homestead High less trouble.

But with all respect to Thomas Edison, who thought genius was mostly sweat, genius may be more playing and breaking rules than anything else. Steve Wozniak knew about these little things. The Woz was a prankster. He knew about hard work too, or at least hard play. He brought to his pranks all the ingenuity and determination that he gave to electronics. He spent hours at school trying to dream up the perfect prank. His efforts were clever and well executed, and he usually emerged from them unscathed.

But not always. Once The Woz wired up an electronic metronome and placed it in a friend's locker, where its ticking was audible to anyone standing next to the locker. The friend was to think it was a bomb, but the principal discovered it first, and, falling for the trick, snatched it up bravely and ran out of the building with it. Wozniak thought it was hilarious. The principal, in appreciation of the joke, suspended him for two days.

Soon after, Steve Wozniak's electronics teacher decided to take him in tow. The Woz clearly found high school unstimulating. Teacher John McCullum saw that he needed a genuine challenge, an outrageously difficult problem to play with. Although The Woz loved electronics, electronics class was not enough. McCullum worked out an arrangement with Sylvania Electronics whereby Wozniak could go to its nearby facilities once a week to work with the computers. For the first time, Woz saw the capabilities of a real computer. One of the machines he played with was a DEC minicomputer called the PDP-8. "Play" for Wozniak was an intense and engrossing activity. He read the PDP-8 manual from cover to cover and absorbed its information about instruction sets, registers, bits, and Boolean algebra. He began to read chip manuals as well. Confident of his expertise, Woz was drawing plans for his own version of the PDP-8 within weeks.

Woz was falling in love. He came across other computers at Sylvania one after another, and each time he studied their designs and modeled similar computers after them. He knew that he was going to design computers, real computers, one day. He had not the slightest doubt of it. Only one thing bothered him: he wanted to build them *now*.

During the years Wozniak attended Homestead High, new computers were being conceived and built with the new semiconductor technology that made smaller machines possible. It was the heyday of the minicomputer. The PDP-8 was one of the most popular, but Data General's Nova, which came out in 1969, was one of the most elegant. Woz was enchanted with the Nova. He loved the way its programmers had packed its power into a few simple instructions. The software design was "tight." Writing a flabby program that does a lot is easy, but the svelte Data General software could also do a lot. The Nova's chassis also appealed to him. While his buddies followed rock stars, Woz taped photos of the Nova and brochures from Data General on his bedroom wall. He decided then—and it became his biggest goal in life—that he would one day own his own computer.

The Woz was not the only student in Silicon Valley with this dream. But in some ways, he was a prototype. Many students at Homestead High had parents in the electronics industry, and these kids were not intimidated by new technology. They had grown up with it. They were used to watching their fathers work with oscilloscopes and soldering irons. Homestead High also had teachers who encouraged students' interests in high tech. Woz may have followed his dream more single-mindedly than others, but the dream was not his alone.

The dream was, however, highly unrealistic. In 1969, people did not own their own computers. Even minicomputers like the Nova and the PDP-8 were priced to sell to research laboratories. Woz went on dreaming.

He did well on his college entrance exams, but had not thought much about which college to attend. And his final decision bore little relation to academics. On a visit to the University of Colorado with some friends, this California boy saw snow for the first time and concluded that Colorado would suffice. His father agreed he could go there for a year.

At Colorado, Woz played bridge intensely, designed more computers on paper, and engineered pranks. After creating a device to jam the television in his college dorm, he told trusting hallmates that the television was badly grounded. They would have to move the antenna. When he had one of them on the roof in a sufficiently awkward position, such as holding the antenna while standing crane-like on one leg, he would quietly turn off his jammer and restore reception. His hallmate remained contorted, for the public good, until the prank was revealed.

Academics was not Wozniak's main priority. After his first school year, he returned home and attended a local college. After another year, in the summer of 1971, he found a job with a small computer company and enjoyed it enough to stay with it on into the fall after his friends returned to school.

That summer, with his old high-school friend Bill Fernandez, Woz built his first computer out of parts rejected by local companies, parts with cosmetic defects. Woz and Fernandez stayed up late at night cataloging the parts on the Fernandez living room carpet. Within a week Woz showed up at his friend's house with a cryptic penciled diagram. "This is a computer," Woz told Fernandez. "Let's build it." They worked far into the night, soldering connections and drinking cream soda. Finally they had a computer, which had lights and switches just as the Altair would more than three years later. They called it the Cream Soda Computer.

Woz and Fernandez telephoned the local newspaper to boast about it. A reporter and a photographer came down, sensing a possible boy genius story. But when Woz and Fernandez plugged in the Cream Soda Computer and began to run a program, smoke billowed out of the power supply. The computer literally went up in smoke, and with it went Woz's chance for fame, at least for the moment. More interested in solving the problem than pursuing renown, Woz laughed it off and went back to his paper designs.

Besides assisting with the Cream Soda Computer, Bill Fernandez introduced Woz to another electronics hobbyist, an old friend of his from junior high school. A good number of Silicon Valley students were interested in electronics because their parents were. Woz's father was an engineer; so was Fernandez's. Fernandez's friend, a couple of years behind him in school, was an anomaly in this respect. His foster parents were blue-collar workers not connected with the computer industry. This friend was a quiet, intense, long-haired boy named Steven P. Jobs.

Though Jobs was five years younger than Woz, the two got along at once. In addition to a common fascination with electronics, they shared a certain intensity, though they showed it in different ways. Wozniak's intensity appeared in his willingness and ability to dig deeper into an intellectual problem than anyone else. Jobs lacked this strength, but his intensity was one of ambition.

Jobs was in some ways a very serious young man, but he had been "a terror early on," he confessed. He believed he "would probably have been in jail," but for a teacher, Mrs. Hill, who moved him ahead a year to separate him from a boisterous buddy. Mrs. Hill also bribed Jobs to study. "In just two weeks she figured me out. She said, 'I'll give you five dollars if you finish this workbook.'" Later she bought him a camera kit. He learned a lot that year.

Jobs became interested in electronics, and he acquired an unshakable self-confidence. Although in some respects shy, Jobs was capable of serene chutzpah. For instance, when he ran out of parts for a frequency counter he was building, he simply picked up the phone and called William Hewlett, co-founder of Hewlett-Packard, to ask for aid. Jobs could also be convincing. Not as financially well-padded as some of his classmates, he made money at Homestead High by buying, selling, and trading electrical equipment. He would buy a stereo, fix it, and sell it at a profit.

But for Woz, the cement in the relationship wasn't electronics. It was pranks. Jobs, he discovered, was another prankster. This mutual inclination led to their first, rather shady business enterprise.

&

*I didn't know what I wanted to do with my
life. I knew there was this spirit, but I didn't
know the form of it. I thought: I really want
to go to India.*

Steve Jobs

Blue Boxes and Buddhism

Woz had returned to school, this time the University of California at Berkeley, to study engineering. He had resolved to take school more seriously and even enrolled in several graduate courses. He did well, but by the end of the school year he was spending most of his time building "blue boxes" with Steve Jobs.

Woz first learned about blue boxes in an article in *Esquire* magazine. The story was nominally fiction, but the technical descriptions of the blue box sounded very real to the budding engineer. Before he even finished reading the article he was on the phone to Steve Jobs, reading it to him. The story described a colorful character who used a device called a blue box to make free long-distance phone calls as he crisscrossed the country in his van with the FBI panting in pursuit. In fact the *Esquire* piece was drawn directly from the extraordinary real-life experiences of one John Draper, a.k.a. Captain Crunch.

Draper was the world's premier "phone phreak," that is, someone who uses electronic or other devices to outwit telephone central circuitry and make free calls or otherwise exploit the system. True phreaking, purists say, is motivated solely by the intellectual challenge. The telephone company, however, takes a philistine view of the enterprise and prosecutes phreaks whenever it can catch them.

Draper virtually invented phone phreaking and was for many years its leading practitioner, the legendary "phirst phreaker." He owes his nickname to his discovery that the whistle once distributed as a prize in boxes of Captain Crunch cereal had an interesting capability. Directed into a telephone, its tones caused the central telephone circuitry to release a long-distance trunk line.

A blue box worked in a similar way. Typically an actual blue-colored box, the device allowed its user to gain control of telephone trunk lines. Draper, itinerant champion of the device, traveled around the country showing people how to build and use it.

Woz didn't know the full extent of the Draper saga at the time, but he was intrigued and began researching the technology. At about the same time, he came across another magazine article and some information in a book by political gadfly Abbie Hoffman that taught the reader how to construct a device that prevented incoming calls from being billed.

With his customary thoroughness Wozniak collected articles on phone phreaking devices of all kinds. In a few months, he had become a phone phreaking expert himself. It was inevitable that his modest fame would get back to the man who had inspired him. One night a van pulled up outside his dorm.

Wozniak was thrilled to meet John Draper, though Captain Crunch's famous van disappointed him a bit. He had expected it to look like something from *Mission: Impossible*, but it was just an ordinary vehicle. Despite this setback, the two became good friends. Together they used phone phreak techniques to tap information on computers all over the U.S. At least once they listened in on an FBI phone conversation, according to Wozniak.

But it was Jobs who made this pastime turn a profit. Jobs enjoyed phone phreaking too, claiming that he and Woz had called around the world several times and once "woke up the Pope" with a blue box call. Soon Wozniak and Jobs had a tight little business marketing the various phone phreaking boxes. "We sold a ton of 'em," Woz would later confess. Since Jobs was still in high school, Woz made most of the sales to students in the Berkeley dorms. Later, when Jobs entered Reed College in Oregon in the fall of 1972, he was able to broaden their market.

Even at college, Jobs remained a recluse. As the son of working-class parents, he may have felt out of place in a school populated primarily by renegade upper-class youths. Tall and thin, with long straggly hair that fell below his shoulders, he certainly looked like a product of the rebellious 1960s. Philosophically, if not socially, he was at home at Reed. Jobs had considered going to Stanford, where he had attended some classes during high school. "But everyone there knew what they wanted to do with their lives," he said. "And I didn't know what I wanted to do with my life at all." On a visit to Reed he had fallen in love with the school, seeing it as a place where "nobody knew what they were going to do. They were trying to find out about life." He was visiting Woz at Cal Berkeley when his father called to say that Reed had accepted him. He was ecstatic.

It was at Reed that Jobs began investigating Eastern religions. More and more often, he stayed up late at night with his friend Dan Kottke to discuss Buddhism. They devoured dozens of books on philosophy and religion, although at one point Jobs became interested in primal therapy.

Although he spent a year at Reed, Jobs seldom attended class. After six months he dropped out but managed to remain in the dorm. "The school sort of gave me an unofficial scholarship. They let me live on campus and looked the other way." He remained for over a year, attending classes when he felt like it, studying philosophy, and meditating. He ate little, converted to vegetarianism, and lived on Roman Meal cereal, partly, he remembers, because a box costing less than 50 cents could last a week. At parties he tended to sit quietly in a corner. Jobs seemed to be clearing things out of his life, searching for some simplicity.

Although Woz was uninterested in the non-scientific pursuits of his friend, their friendship remained unaltered. Woz frequently drove up to Oregon to visit Jobs on weekends.

Woz had taken a summer job in 1973, joining Bill Fernandez at Hewlett-Packard. Woz had just finished his junior year, and soon found HP clearly preferable. College would have to be delayed once again as Woz pursued his education in the firm's calculator division. HP was then manufacturing the HP-35 programmable calculator, and Wozniak realized how much this device resembled a computer. "It's got this little chip and serial registers and an instruction set," he thought. "Except for its I/O, it's a computer, the love of my life." He studied the calculator design with the same intensity he had brought to the minicomputers he had seen in high school.

After his year at Reed, Jobs returned to Silicon Valley and took a job with a young video game company, Atari. He stayed until he had saved enough money for a trip to India that he and Dan Kottke had planned. The two had had long discussions about the Kainchi ashram and its famous inhabitant, Neem Karoli Baba, a holy man described in the popular book *Be Here Now*. Though they embarked for India at different times, they met there and went searching for the ashram. When they found Neem Karoli had died, they drifted around India, talking and reading about philosophy. "We both took it very seriously," Kottke later said. When Kottke ran out of money, Jobs gave him several hundred dollars. Kottke went to a meditation retreat for a month. Jobs didn't go with him, but rather wandered the subcontinent for a few months, then returned to California, went back to work for Atari, and contacted his friend The Woz.

Jobs had worked at HP one summer years before. He had been 13, needed parts, and phoned Hewlett. "I'm Steve Jobs," he explained, "and I was wondering if you had any spare parts I could build a frequency counter out of." Hewlett was taken aback by the call but Jobs got his parts, and that summer Hewlett gave him a job working on the line at HP. Jobs loved it. Now he was at Atari, and he had changed. He was still brash, but the year at Reed and the Indian trip had had an effect.

Meanwhile, Woz had started Dial-A-Joke. Every morning before he left for work he would turn on the telephone answering machine in his apartment, and, in a gravelly voice and a thick accent, tell a Polish joke. His phone number became the most frequently called in the San Francisco Bay Area, and he had to argue more than once with the telephone company in order to keep it going. The nature of his jokes also caused trouble. The Polish American Congress sent him a letter asking him to desist. So Wozniak, of Polish extraction, made Italians the butt of his jokes instead. When the attention faded, he went back to Polish jokes.

In the early 1970s computer arcade games were becoming popular. One day Woz spotted *Pong* in a bowling alley and was inspired. "I can make one of those," he thought, and immediately went home and designed a game. It probably wasn't marketable: when the player missed the blip, "OH SHIT" flashed on the screen. The programming was good though. When Woz demonstrated his game for Atari, the company offered him a job, which he, comfortable at HP, turned down. Woz was devoting much time to Atari nonetheless. He had been dropping a lot of quarters into arcade games when Jobs, who often worked nights, invited him to come to the factory while he worked so Woz could play for free. Jobs sneaked him in, and Woz sometimes played for eight hours at a stretch. It worked out well for Jobs, too. "If I had a problem, I'd say, 'Hey, Woz,' and he'd come and help me."

But Atari was looking for a new game, and company founder Nolan Bushnell gave Jobs his ideas for *Breakout*. Jobs boasted that he could design it in four days, meaning that he and Woz could design it in four days. Jobs was always very persuasive, but he hardly had to bring out the thumbscrews to get his friend to help him. Working at Hewlett-Packard by day, Woz stayed up for four straight nights designing the game. In the daytime, Jobs would work at putting the device together, and at night Woz would look over his efforts and perfect the design. They finished it in four days and were paid $700. The experience told them something: not that they could do the job—they knew that beforehand —but that they could work well together on a tough project with a tight deadline and succeed.

I met the two Steves. They showed me the
Apple I. I thought they were really right on.
Mike Markkula

Apple

Breakout wasn't Woz's only extracurricular project at HP. He also designed and built a computer terminal. Jobs had heard that a local company that rented computer time needed an inexpensive home terminal to access the company's large computer. He told Woz about it and Woz designed a small device that used a television set for a display. About the same time, Woz began attending the Homebrew Computer Club meetings.

Homebrew was a revelation for Steve Wozniak. For the first time he found himself surrounded by people who shared his love for computers, people more knowledgeable about them than any of his friends—than himself, in many ways. Woz hadn't even heard of the Altair. He had only attended the meeting because a friend of his at HP told him that a new club was forming that was for people interested in computer terminals. When he arrived in Gordon French's suburban garage, he felt a little out of place. The others were talking about the latest chips: the 8008 and the 8080. Woz felt lost. He hadn't heard of them. But he had designed a video terminal and the club was interested. Woz was encouraged. He went home and began studying the latest microprocessor chips. He bought the first issue of *Byte*. And every two weeks he went to the meeting of the Homebrew Computer Club.

"It changed my life," Woz would later recall. "My interest was renewed, and every two weeks the club meeting was the big thing in my life." And Woz reciprocated. If the club encouraged him, he encouraged it. His technical expertise and innocent, friendly manner gave him a sort of magnetism. For two younger club members—Randy Wigginton and Chris Espinosa—Woz became the prime source of technical information, as well as their ride to meetings.

Woz couldn't afford an Altair, but he watched with fascination as others brought theirs to the gatherings. He was impressed by the smooth tact with which Lee Felsenstein chaired the meetings. He realized that many of the home-built machines that were shown at the club resembled the Cream Soda Computer, and he began to feel that he could improve on the design.

He soon saw his chance. MOS Technology had advertised that it would sell its new 6502 microprocessor chip at the upcoming Wescon computer show in San Francisco for only $20. At that time microprocessors were generally sold only to companies that had established accounts with the semiconductor houses, and they cost hundreds of dollars apiece. Chuck Peddle was going to sell these things over the counter for $20—well, almost over the counter. The show did not permit sales on the exhibit floor, so Peddle had rented a hotel room. Woz went for it. He gave Chuck Peddle's wife, who was handling the sales when he walked in, his $20, and he went to work.

Before designing the computer, Woz wrote his programming language. BASIC was the hit of the Homebrew Computer Club, and he knew he could impress his friends if he could get it working on his machine. "I'm going to be the first one to have BASIC for the 6502," he thought. "I can whip it out in a few weeks and I'll zap the world with it." He did exactly that, and when he finished, he set to work making a computer for it to run on. That was the easy part, he felt, since he had already built a computer. Woz designed a board with a processor (the 6502) and interfaces that connected it to a keyboard and a video monitor. Within a few weeks, he brought his computer to Homebrew and passed out photocopies of his design so that others could duplicate it. Like a perfect hobbyist, Woz believed in sharing information. The other hobbyists were indeed impressed. Some questioned his choice of processor, but no one argued with its $20 price. He called the machine an Apple.

The origin of the name "Apple" is unclear. Jobs claims it was a random decision. He was sitting around with Woz and a few friends and suggested calling it Apple unless someone had a better idea. Friends of Jobs say that he named it after the Beatles's record label Apple. Jobs was a serious Beatles fan. Still others say that Jobs's work in the Oregon apple orchards led him to the designation.

The Apple I had only the essentials. It lacked a case, a keyboard, and a power supply. The hobbyist owner had to connect a transformer to it in order to get it to work. It also required laborious hand-assembly. Woz spent a lot of time helping friends implement his design.

Steve Jobs saw an opportunity in this skeletal machine. He suggested that they start a company. Woz reluctantly agreed. The idea of turning his hobby into a business bothered him a little. But Jobs persisted. "Look, there's a lot of interest in what you've done at the club," he argued. Since he wouldn't have to leave his job at Hewlett-Packard, Wozniak conceded.

The two soon sold their most valuable possessions—Jobs, his Volkswagen microbus, and Wozniak, his two HP calculators—to pay for someone to create a printed circuit board. The PC board would save them the trouble of assembling and wiring each computer—a task that was driving them to 60-hour weeks. Jobs figured they would be able to sell the boards at Homebrew.

But Jobs set out to do more than sell them to hobbyists. He also began trying to interest retailers in the Apple. At a Homebrew meeting in July 1976, Woz gave a demonstration of the Apple I. Paul Terrell, one of the industry's earliest retailers, was in attendance. Jobs gave Terrell a personal demonstration of the machine. "Take a look at this," Jobs told Terrell. "You're going to like what you see."

Jobs was right. Terrell did like the machine. He told Jobs that it showed promise and that he should keep in touch. Terrell meant what he said. The machine was interesting, but there were a lot of sharp engineers at Homebrew.

This computer might be a winner, or some other machine might. If Jobs and Wozniak really had something, he figured, they'd keep in touch.

The next day Jobs appeared, barefoot, at the Byte Shop. "I'm keeping in touch," he said. Terrell was impressed by this confident perseverance. He ordered 50 Apples. Visions of wealth flashed before Jobs's eyes. But Terrell added a condition. He wanted the computers fully assembled. Woz and Jobs were back to 60-hour workweeks.

They had no parts and no money to get them with, but with a purchase order from Terrell for 50 Apple I's, Jobs and Woz were able to obtain net 30 days credit. Jobs didn't even know what net 30 days credit was at first. Terrell later received several calls from suppliers who wondered whether the long-haired kids really had the guarantee from Terrell that they claimed.

They were in business. But though they knew they could work together under time pressure, they also knew they couldn't do this task alone. The parts had to be paid for in 30 days. Thus they had to build 50 computers and deliver them to Paul Terrell in 30 days. Jobs paid his sister to plug chips into the Apple I board. He also hired Dan Kottke, who was in town for the summer from college, telling him, "You've got to come out here this summer. I'll give you a job. We've got this amazing thing called 30 days net."

Terrell got his 50 Apple I's on the 29th day. The 200 or so Apple I's that were eventually built were sold through a handful of computer stores in the Bay Area and through United Parcel from Jobs's garage for $666. Jobs ran the business.

By the end of the summer Wozniak had begun work on another computer. The Apple II would have several advantages over the Apple I. Like Processor Technology's Sol, which had not yet appeared, it would be a complete computer with a keyboard and power supply, BASIC, and color graphics all built into an attractive case. Jobs and Woz made provisions to sell just the circuit board to hobbyists who wanted to customize the machine. For output, the user would hook it up to a television set. They agreed it was going to be the hit of Homebrew. Jobs hoped it would have a much broader appeal.

When the features of the Apple II became clear, Woz and Jobs argued over its price. Jobs wanted to sell the board alone for $1200. Woz said that if the price were that high, he wanted nothing to do with it. They finally decided to charge $1200 for the board and the case.

Now they had at least the outline of a real commercial product, and Jobs's ambition flowered. "Steve was the hustler, entrepreneur type," said Woz. Jobs wanted to create a large company. He sought advice from Atari founder Nolan Bushnell, who introduced him to Don Valentine, a successful venture capitalist in Silicon Valley. Valentine suggested that he speak to a friend of his. Although Mike Markkula was now retired, Valentine had a hunch that this former Intel executive would be interested in Jobs and Wozniak's machine.

In the busy two years after the introduction of the Altair, the microcomputer industry had reached a critical turning point. Dozens of companies had come and gone. Most notably, MITS, the industry pioneer, was thrashing about. IMSAI, Processor Technology, and a few other companies were jockeying for control of the market even as they wobbled. All of these companies failed. In some cases, their failure stemmed from technical problems with the computers. But more serious was the lack of expertise in marketing, distributing, and selling the products. The corporate leaders were primarily engineers, not managers. They alienated their customers and dealers. At MITS they drove retailers away by forbidding them to sell other companies' products. At IMSAI they ignored dealer and customer complaints about defects in the machines. At Processor Technology they responded to design problems with a bewildering series of slightly different versions, failed to advance with the technology, and boxed themselves in by refusing the venture capital needed for growth. Computer dealers grew tired of these practices.

At the same time, the market was changing. Hobbyists had organized into clubs and users' groups that met regularly in garages, basements, and school auditoriums around the country. The number of people who wanted to own computers was growing. And the ranks of knowledgeable hobbyists who wanted a better computer were also growing. The manufacturers wanted that "better computer" too. But they all faced one seemingly insurmountable problem. They didn't have the money. The manufacturers were garage enterprises, growing, like MITS had since January of 1975, on prepaid mail orders. They needed investment capital, and there were strong arguments against giving it to them: the high failure rate among microcomputer companies, the lack of managerial experience among their leaders, and—the ultimate puzzle—the absence of IBM from the field. Investors had to ask: If this area has any promise, why hasn't IBM preempted it? In addition, some of the founders of the early companies looked unfavorably upon the notion of taking money from an outside source. That could mean losing some control of the company.

What was needed was an individual with a special perspective to see through the basic risks, the bad management, the poor dealer relations, and the sometimes slipshod workmanship to the enormous possibilities of these garage entrepreneurships.

In 1976 A. C. "Mike" Markkula had been out of work for over a year. His unemployment was deliberate, self-imposed, and rather pleasant. Markkula had done well for himself during his tenure with two of the most successful chip manufacturers in the country: Fairchild and Intel. He was uniquely suited to the work. Though a trained electrical engineer who understood the possibilities of the microprocessor, at Intel he worked in marketing, and friends said he was a marketing wizard. He certainly loved the job. Beyond the excitement of the technology, Markkula enjoyed forging a large company in a competitive environment. Outside the hobbyist community few people understood the potential of microprocessor-based technology as well as Mike Markkula. No microcomputer company had anyone like Markkula. No microcomputer company could afford him.

In 1976 Mike Markkula had retired. Intel stock options had made him a millionaire, and he had no financial prod to work any longer. He was a dedicated family man and wanted to spend more time at home. He planned a leisurely existence, and he convinced himself that after the breakneck pace of life in the semiconductor industry, he could be happy learning to play the guitar and taking skiing vacations at his cabin near Lake Tahoe. Friends might have observed that his investments in wildcat oil wells did not bespeak a full commitment to the idle life, but Markkula was adamant. He was out of the rat race for good.

In October 1976 Markkula visited Jobs's garage. Like Terrell, he liked what he saw. He wasn't violating his resolve to stay retired, he thought. He was just giving advice to two sharp kids. One couldn't even call it business, since they couldn't afford to pay him what a consultant with his experience would normally get. But Markkula was interested in their project. It made sense to provide computing power to individuals in the home and workplace. He offered to help the pair draw up a business plan.

Within a few months, Markkula decided to join the corporation. He assessed Jobs and Woz's equity in it at about $5000 and added $91,000 of his own money, telling the pair a one-third interest in their company was now worth that amount. Why did this 34-year-old retired executive throw in his lot with two long-haired kids in jeans? Even Markkula couldn't answer the question precisely, but by this time he had become convinced that Apple could make the Fortune 500 list in less than five years, a feat never before accomplished. The idea hooked him. He couldn't stay out.

Thereafter, Markkula set the tone for the company. He helped Jobs with the business plan. He obtained a line of credit for Apple at the Bank of America. He told Woz and Jobs that neither of them had the experience to run a company and hired Mike Scott as its president. Scott, known as Scotty, was a seasoned executive who had worked for Markkula in product marketing at Fairchild. He was accustomed to a traditional business environment, and for this reason would later have problems with Woz's work habits.

The first decision Markkula made was to retain the name Apple. He recognized the simple marketing advantage of being first in the phone book. He also believed that the word *Apple*, unlike the word *computer*, had a positive connotation. "Very few people don't like apples," he said. Furthermore, he liked the incongruous pairing of the words *apple* and *computer*. It would be good for name recognition, he realized.

&

I try to get people to see what I see....
When you run a company, you have to get
people to buy into your dreams.

Steve Jobs

Woz was fortunate to hook up with an
evangelist.

Regis McKenna

The Evangelist

By the fall of 1976 Woz had already made progress on the design of his new computer. The Apple II would embody all the engineering savvy he could bring to it. He had made it considerably faster than the Apple I. There was a clever trick he wanted to try involving color too. The Apple II would be the computer Steve Wozniak would like to own.

As Wozniak had worried about forming his own company, he worried about working full-time for it. He always enjoyed his job at Hewlett-Packard. In particular, he admired the company's emphasis on quality design. He was having a good time. Woz had shown his Apple I design to the managers at Hewlett-Packard with the hope that he could convince the company to build it. But they told him that the Apple was not a viable product for HP. It made more sense for a start-up company to sell it. HP eventually gave Woz a release that permitted him to build the machine on his own. But Wozniak made two more attempts to join computer development projects at HP and was turned down for the project that eventually developed into the HP 75 computer and for work on a hand-held BASIC machine.

As good an engineer as he was, Woz could only work on projects that interested him, and then only for as long as they interested him. Jobs understood his friend's genius better than anyone. He constantly urged Woz on, and this pressure sometimes led to arguments.

One thing that Woz did not want to design, and perhaps could not design, was the device to connect the computer to a television set. Another was the power supply. Both devices required skill in analog electronics and differed from the digital electronics that Woz and Jobs had been working with. The internal circuitry of the computer was basically on/off: one thought of voltages as high or low, present or absent, 1 or 0. To design a power supply or send a signal to a television set, one had to consider actual voltages and interference effects. Woz didn't know or care about these things.

Again Jobs turned to one of his former superiors at Atari, Al Alcorn, for advice. Alcorn suggested that Jobs consult with Rod Holt, a sharp analog engineer at Atari.

At the time Jobs phoned Rod Holt in the fall of 1976, Holt was dissatisfied with his position at Atari. "I was a second-string quarterback," he later said. Holt thought he had been hired just in case his manager, whose hobby was racing motorcycles, got hurt. Holt was notably different from Wozniak and Jobs, except for his love of electronics. A man of contrasts, Holt was born in the Midwest, had strong leftist political leanings, and had a daughter older than Steve Jobs; he had trouble understanding the West Coast culture that shaped Apple's founders.

Holt told Jobs that as an Atari engineer, he felt helping Apple represented an obvious conflict of interest. Besides, he added, he was expensive, at least $200 a day. But that didn't worry Jobs. "We can afford you," Jobs said. "Absolutely."

Holt liked the brash kid at once. Regarding the conflict of interest, Jobs told him to check with his boss and that it would be all right. "Steve is a nice guy. Help the kids out," Holt recalled Al Alcorn telling him. He started working in the evening at Atari on the television interface and the power supply, concentrating on the latter. He also persuaded Jobs not to challenge FCC regulations by trying to build an interface for a television set. Holt knew that the FCC could cause them distress over the interface issue and told Jobs so. Jobs was frustrated at first, but then hit upon a clever way out of the problem. He made it a simple task for *others* to design the modulators to link the computer to a television set. If laws were broken or regulations bent, the malefactor wouldn't be Apple—at least technically.

Holt could have named his job back in the Midwest, and he was building a reputation in the Valley. But he went to work for Apple. He went to work for Jobs. Jobs had pulled in Markkula, he had lived at Reed College for free, he had gotten himself a job at HP—from one of the founders—when he was 13. All his life, it seemed, Jobs had gotten what he wanted. He was a very convincing man with big dreams and a gift for communicating them.

After a few months Holt came on full-time. He handled all kinds of tasks at Apple. When no one else had the technical or managerial expertise to solve a problem, Holt did it. "I was the everything-else guy," he said. As the company began growing faster than even Markkula had hoped for, Holt found that he was overseeing the quality control department, the service department, the production engineering department, and the documentation department. Things got so hectic that several times Holt threatened to resign.

Rod Holt was not the first employee Woz and Jobs hired. That honor went to the friend who had introduced them to each other several years earlier, Bill Fernandez. As a formality, Jobs gave Fernandez a test before officially hiring him. Fernandez answered a series of questions about digital electronics before going to work in Jobs's garage manufacturing the Apple I's. Fernandez practiced the Bahai faith, and he spent many hours discussing religion with Jobs in the garage.

Other early employees were high-school students Chris Espinosa and Randy Wigginton, Woz's friends from the Homebrew meetings. After the meetings the trio would often return to Woz's house and continue discussing means of improving the capabilities of the Apple I to turn it into something more.

Espinosa and Wigginton were hobbyists, but of a different sort than either Jobs or Woz. They had no special expertise in designing a machine. Rather, they enjoyed writing programs. When Woz brought the Apple I to Homebrew, they would quickly write some programs to demonstrate the machine to club members. Woz had built a working prototype of the Apple II by August of 1976 and he loaned one to Espinosa, who began developing games and demonstration software. By actually using the new computer, the self-confident teenager was able to suggest ways to better its design.

Espinosa also spent a lot of time at Paul Terrell's Byte Shop. Espinosa recalls how a "tall, scraggly looking guy would come in every day and say, 'We got a new version of the BASIC!'" That's how he met Steve Jobs. Later, at one of the few Homebrew meetings that he attended, Jobs noticed a demo program running on the Apple I. He asked Espinosa, "Did you do that?" Shortly thereafter Espinosa was working for Apple.

Espinosa spent Christmas vacation of his high-school sophomore year in Jobs's garage helping debug the BASIC that would be sold with the Apple II. Jobs seemed to take him under his wing, although Espinosa's early impression of Jobs was less than filial. "I thought he was dangerous," he said. "Quiet, enigmatic, almost sullen, a fierce look in his eyes. His powers of persuasion are something to be reckoned with. I always had this feeling that he was shaping me."

Jobs was just then facing his biggest challenge in persuasion. By that time the company had coalesced. Markkula had agreed to join Jobs and Woz. The final obstacle was convincing Woz to leave his job at Hewlett-Packard to work full-time for Apple. Markkula would have it no other way.

In October of 1976 Woz wasn't sure he wanted to make this move. Steve Jobs was panicking. All of his carefully wrought plans depended on Woz. Then, one day in October, Woz said that he would not do it. "Steve went into fits and started crying," said Woz. But Jobs's self-control wasn't lost for long. He began lobbying with Woz's friends, having them call Woz to get him to change his mind. The effort was successful. Woz had been afraid that designing computers full-time might not be as much fun as it had been in Homebrew. Somehow his friends helped him overcome this fear. At the time Woz believed, at his most optimistic, that they would sell no more than 1000 Apple IIs.

But Jobs was more ambitious and he aggressively set out to get people who could help him—people like Regis McKenna, owner of one of the most successful public relations and advertising firms in Silicon Valley.

Jobs had already placed an ad in the computer magazine *Interface Age*. But he had also seen the Intel ads and was impressed enough to call the semiconductor company and ask who had done them. Regis McKenna, he had been told. Jobs wanted the best for Apple, and he decided that McKenna was the best. He was going to get McKenna.

McKenna's ads had indeed been very good for Intel. McKenna wore suits and had a large desk and photographs of his favorite Intel ads on his walls. He spoke softly and reflectively and appeared the antithesis of the unkempt and pushy kid who had walked into his office that afternoon in cutoffs, sandals, and what McKenna called a "Ho Chi Minh beard." But since McKenna normally took start-up companies as clients, Jobs's garb did not frighten him off although he took note of it. "Inventions come from individuals," he reminded himself, "not from companies." Jobs was certainly an individual, McKenna thought.

At first McKenna turned Apple down. But Jobs had never taken rejection passively and he persisted in his efforts. "I don't deny that Woz designed a good machine," said McKenna. "But that machine would be sitting in hobby shops today were it not for Steve Jobs. Woz was fortunate to hook up with an evangelist."

McKenna eventually agreed to take Apple on, and right away his firm made two important contributions. The first was a colorful design that has served as the company logo ever since. Initially, Jobs feared that the multicolored picture of an apple wouldn't work, that the colors would run together. But when the first metallic labels arrived for the Apple II, he loved them.

McKenna also decided to run a color ad in *Playboy* magazine. It was a bold, expensive grab for publicity when a cheaper ad in *Byte* would have reached virtually all the microcomputer buyers of that time. "It was done to get national attention," said McKenna, "to popularize this idea of low-cost computers." Other companies had been selling microcomputers for two years, but no one had yet tried to excite the general public's imagination in this way. Apple's publicity campaign resulted in articles in national publications, articles not just about Apple but about small computers generally.

Jobs's persistence persuaded McKenna as it had Woz, Markkula, and Holt. Woz made the machine, Markkula had the business sense, and Scotty ran the shop, but the pushy kid with the Ho Chi Minh beard was the driving force. Jobs was building a company.

By February 1977 Apple Computer had established its first office in two large rooms a few miles from Homestead High School in Cupertino. Desks were brought in, and lab benches were trundled over from Jobs's garage. The night before they were to begin working in the new suite, Woz, Jobs, Wigginton, and Espinosa sat in different parts of the 2000-square-foot office playing a game with the telephones, each trying to buzz one of the others' phones first. "We never thought that we'd grow up to be battling one-on-one with IBM," said Espinosa.

In early 1977 the young company faced more modest tasks: to finish the Apple II design by the time of Jim Warren's First West Coast Computer Faire in April and then ready it for production shortly thereafter. Markkula was already signing up distributors nationwide, many of whom were eager to work with a company that would give them greater freedom than MITS had and also functional products.

Steve Wozniak is justly credited with the technical design of the Apple I and Apple II. However, an essential contribution in making the Apple II a commercial success came from Jobs.

Most early microcomputers were far from attractive as consumer fare. Typically they were ugly, drab, blue metal boxes. Steve Jobs decided to pick up the look of the product. He covered it with a lightweight beige plastic case that brought the keyboard and computer together in a modular design. Woz could design an efficient computer, but he cheerfully admitted that he didn't care whether wires dangled from the side or not. Jobs realized that the Apple had to look presentable.

It took much travail to ready the Apple II for the West Coast Computer Faire. Woz worked, typically, day and night until it was done. Jobs made sure that it would be seen. He arranged to have the biggest and most elegant booth at the Faire. He brought in a large projection screen to demonstrate programs and placed Apple IIs on either side of the booth.

The First West Coast Computer Faire was a big success for Apple. Everyone seemed to like its computer, although *Computer Lib* author Ted Nelson complained that it displayed only uppercase letters. Jobs, Mike Scott, Chris Espinosa, and Randy Wigginton manned the booth while Mike Markkula toured the auditorium signing up dealers for the company. Woz walked around checking out other machines. He also played one of his favorite practical jokes. He decided to advertise a product that did not exist. To avoid immediate disavowals, he had to play the prank on a company not at the show. MITS was not at the show. With the help of Randy Wigginton, Woz whipped up a brochure on the "Zaltair," supposedly an enhanced Altair computer. "Imagine a dream machine. Imagine the computer surprise of the century, here today. Imagine BAZIC in ROM, the most complete and powerful language ever developed," the fake advertisement purred. Woz was satirizing marketing hype as he had learned it from Jobs. "A computer engineer's dream, all electronics are on a single PC card, even the 18-slot motherboard. And what a motherboard..." On the back of the brochure was a mock performance chart comparing the Zaltair to other microcomputers including the Apple. Jobs, who knew nothing of the joke, obtained one of the brochures at the show and read it in dismay. But after a quick, nervous scan of the performance chart, he looked relieved. "Hey," he said, "We came out OK on this."

&

After the Faire we had a sense of exhilaration for having pulled off something so well, not just for Apple, but for the whole computer movement.

Chris Espinosa

Magic Times

In 1977, Apple could do no wrong. It was a magic time for the tiny company, which radiated an innocent confidence. Hobbyists praised Woz's design, dealers requested the new computer, and investors sought to sink money into the company.

Right away Woz and Jobs had offered work to their friends in the Valley. Chris Espinosa and Randy Wigginton frequently came by the Apple offices after school to help develop software for the new machine. They were paid a modest hourly wage, but mostly it was fun. They enjoyed working with Woz because he was their technical mentor, the "extremely brilliant" computer genius, according to Wigginton.

In May Woz reviewed Wigginton's performance to see if he deserved a raise. His work was fine, but Woz—ever the stern taskmaster—demanded something more. He was irritated that he had to walk around the block to get to a nearby 7-Eleven Store. A large fence prevented his direct access. But if Wigginton would remove a big board from below a section of the fence, Woz could pass under it and Wigginton would get his raise. The next day Woz found the board on his desk, and Wigginton started earning $3.50 an hour.

Each Tuesday and Thursday the company opened its doors to the public for a demonstration of the product. Chris Espinosa was completing his final semester at Homestead High. Each Tuesday and Thursday he drove his moped, the "first sign of [his] entering the business world," to the Apple offices and supervised the demos. Once when representatives of the Bank of America came by, Espinosa acted quickly to remove "OH SHIT" from Woz's *Breakout* game and replace it with "THAT'S TERRIBLE." Though boyish in appearance, Espinosa had a serious, responsible, scholarly air that impressed everyone. Jobs and Markkula were thankful that he kept the visitors engaged so they could attend to the more important task of signing up new dealers. "For about six months I was the sole means by which people off the street in the Bay Area would learn about Apple Computer," Espinosa said.

But there were also indications that Apple meant business. Markkula and Scott were growing tired of the youthful crowd that frequently dropped in to check out Woz's progress. Alan Baum, a close friend of Wozniak's from Hewlett-Packard, had even contributed ideas to the design. But Mike Scott finally decreed that some confidentiality was essential. Scott felt obliged to instill a professional atmosphere at Apple. Baum visited less and less frequently as the year wore on.

On the other hand Scott appreciated the contributions of some of the youthful employees. He convinced Randy Wigginton to stay by offering to have Apple pay for his college education.

Mike Scott was a complex individual who was vital to Apple's success. Scott was not a smooth-talking, dapper individual like Mike Markkula. His management style was less formal, more abrupt. He liked to stroll through the company and chat with employees. He often alluded to his role in maritime metaphors. He was a ship captain, standing at the helm. "Welcome aboard," he would say to a new employee. Scott didn't hide his moods. When he was happy, he would make other employees happy too. Around Christmas time in Apple's first year, he dressed up in a Santa Claus suit and walked through the company handing out presents. But if he was displeased with someone's performance, he could let that person know it.

Scotty's bedrock goal was a desire to build a big company. But he could be flamboyant too. According to Rod Holt he had a "slush fund" for special expenses, such as an enormous hot air balloon and a large sail for Holt's yacht, each beautifully decorated with Apple's logo.

Scott quickly grew impatient when projects were delayed. At least once Woz's generosity to his friends caused friction with Scotty, who was less tolerant than Markkula of corporate eccentricity. He couldn't understand Wozniak's irregular work habits, which swung from total dedication to headstrong avoidance, depending on his interest in the task at hand. Scotty also failed to understand some of Woz's friends.

Woz had kept in touch with John Draper. In the fall of 1977 Draper was visiting Woz at Apple and expressed interest in helping design a digital telephone card for the Apple. No one understood telephone lines better than Captain Crunch. Scott had granted Woz a separate office in which to work, hoping that it might encourage his creativity. John Draper went to work there too. But many of the other employees disliked Draper. He was an awkward young man with strange interests, and he made them feel uncomfortable.

Draper and Woz constructed a device that could, among other things, dial numbers automatically and function much like a telephone answering machine. But Draper also built a blue box capability into the card. The cards were powerful. According to Espinosa, a network of a dozen Apples equipped with Draper's cards could bring down the nation's entire phone system. When Scott learned that the device could be used illegally, he stalked the deck in rage. The phone card didn't last long after that, although, without Draper's knowledge, modifications were being designed into the card by other engineers to nullify most of its phone phreak capabilities. According to one Apple board member, Scott almost tried to fire Woz during that time. Would Scott actually have made one of the company's founders walk the plank? "Scotty is the only guy that could [dare] fire me," said Woz. "That guy could do anything." Rod Holt agrees: "Scotty could fire anybody. All he needed was one excuse."

When John Draper was later arrested for phone phreaking he had an Apple with him. The machine was confiscated and Scotty cursed Woz again.

At the same time that Woz took on Draper, Scotty hired two other key employees. Gene Carter became Apple's sales manager in August, and Wendell Sander came in to work under Rod Holt. An electrical engineer with a PhD from Iowa State University, Sander had years of experience in the semiconductor field. But it wasn't his high-technology experience that convinced Apple to hire him.

Sander had bought an Apple I a year earlier and had written a version of *Star Trek* for his teenage children to play. While devising this program he had met Steve Jobs, since Sander wanted to get updated versions of the integer BASIC. Jobs gave him updates and in the process learned of the *Star Trek* program. When Jobs was getting ready to ship the first Apple IIs, he invited Sander to the company's office and asked him to transfer the program so that it would run on the new machine. Sander also met Mike Markkula at the time and decided that he wanted to work for the young firm. After he was hired, he took a loan on his San Jose home in order to buy stock in the company. Woz, Rod Holt, and Sander made up the core of Apple's engineering department for the rest of 1977.

During 1977 and 1978 Woz worked on a number of accessory products that were necessary to keep Apple from falling to earth as soon as it ripened. To make the Apple II appeal to customers outside the hobbyist world, add-on peripherals were needed so the machine could work with different kinds of printers and connect with the modems that allowed users to transfer information from one machine to another over a telephone line.

Thanks to its small size and well-oiled internal mechanism, the company could choose and build new products more easily than many other firms. Among the most important of these items were the peripheral cards: a printer card, a serial card, a communications card, and a ROM card. Woz worked on most of these. But Wendell Sander contributed a great deal too, as did Rod Holt.

Business was promising. More and more dealers signed on and Apple began manufacturing the Apple II. By the end of 1977 the company was making a profit and doubling production every three to four months. An article in *Byte* popularized the Apple II further. Mike Markkula had also attracted investment capital from the successful New York-based firm of Venrock Associates, a firm formed by the Rockefeller family to invest in high-tech enterprises. Arthur Rock became a member of Apple's board of directors.

By year's end the company moved into a larger office on nearby Bandley Drive in Cupertino. The structure was huge and it gave the Apple employees a feeling that the firm was going to get big. They were right. Apple soon outgrew the building and added another on the same street.

Perhaps the most significant accomplishment of this time came out of Woz's 1977 Christmas vacation.

It was a brilliant execution by Woz.

Rod Holt

The Disk

Before the end of the year Woz had started working on his next big project. The idea arose from an executive board meeting in December 1977. Present at the meeting were Mike Markkula, Mike Scott, Rod Holt, Jobs, and Woz. Markkula stepped forward and wrote on a board a list of goals for the company. At the top of the list Woz saw the words "floppy disk."

"I don't know how floppy disks work," Woz thought.

Nevertheless he knew Markkula was right. Cassette tape storage of data was utterly unreliable. Dealers were complaining about it. Markkula had decided that the disk drive was essential while he and Randy Wigginton were writing the checkbook program. Markkula was fed up with the laborious task of reading data off cassette tapes and realized just how much a disk drive would facilitate the use of his program. He told Woz that he wanted the disk ready for the Consumer Electronics Show that Apple would attend in January.

Markkula knew the effect his words would have. They would take away Woz's Christmas vacation. It was entirely unreasonable to expect anyone to devise a functioning disk drive in a month. But that was the kind of challenge Woz thrived on. No one had to tell him to work long hours over the vacation. He drove himself.

In fact, Woz was not ignorant about disk drives. He had, until then, never read a book on the subject or worked on disk drives professionally, but while at HP he had examined a manual from Shugart, the Silicon Valley disk drive manufacturer. As an experiment Woz had conceived a circuit that would do much of what the Shugart manual said was needed to control a disk drive. Woz didn't know how computers actually controlled drives, but his method had seemed to him particularly simple and clever. When Markkula challenged him to put a disk drive on the Apple, he recalled that circuit and began considering its feasibility. He looked at the way other computer companies—including IBM—controlled drives. He also began to examine disk drives—particularly North Star's. After reading the North Star manual, Woz knew that his circuit would do what theirs did and more. He knew he really had a clever design.

But the clever circuit was only part of the disk control problem. The puzzle had other pieces—synchronization. A disk drive presents tricky problems of timing. IBM's technique involved complex circuitry, which Woz studied until he understood it. But that circuitry was unnecessary, he saw, if the way the data were written to the disk was altered. Since this was his machine, he could redefine anything he wanted, so he eliminated the synchronization circuitry completely. The drive would synchronize itself automatically with no hardware circuitry at all, and this "self-sync" technique scored a point against IBM. Woz knew that because the mammoth corporation lacked this kind of flexibility, it *couldn't* do what he had done, and he also knew that whatever economies of scale IBM could bring to bear, no circuitry is still less expensive than some.

Wozniak could now write the software to read from and write to the disk. At this point he called in Randy Wigginton to help. Woz wanted a formatter, a program that would write special non-data to the disk, essentially wiping it clean to set it up for use. Woz gave Wigginton just the essentials, such as how to make the drive motor move through software. Wigginton took it from there.

Woz and Wigginton worked day and night throughout December, even laboring for ten hours on Christmas Day. They knew they couldn't get a complete disk operating system running for the show, so they spent time developing a demo operating system. They wanted to be able to type in one-letter file names and read files stored in fixed locations on the disk. When they left for the Consumer Electronics Show in Las Vegas, however, they weren't even able to do that.

Wigginton and Woz arrived in Las Vegas the night before the event. The Consumer Electronics Show was not a hobby computer show. Many of the exhibitors were established consumer electronics firms producing stereo equipment and calculators. The buyers of such items were general consumers, not electronics hobbyists. But Markkula wanted Apple to pursue a broader market, and he regarded this show as vital for Apple's growth. For Woz and Wigginton, it was an adventure outside time.

They helped set up the booth that night and went back to work on the drive, planning to have it done when the show opened in the morning even if they had to go without sleep. Staying up all night is no novelty in Las Vegas, and that's what they did, taking periodic breaks from programming to inspect the craps tables. Wigginton, 17, was elated when he won $35 at craps, and then he accidentally erased a disk they had been working on. Woz patiently helped him reconstruct the information on the disk. They tried to take a nap at 7:30 that morning, but were both too keyed up.

After the show, Woz completed the disk drive, consulting Rod Holt on what he could really expect the drives to do. Woz himself laid out the circuit board that was to control the drive. Normally the layout work was sent to a contracting firm, but the contractor was busy and Woz wasn't. He worked on it every night until two in the morning for two weeks. When he was finished, he saw a way to cut down on feedthroughs — signal lines crossing on the board — by moving a connector. The improvement meant redoing the entire layout, but this time he completed this task in only 20 hours. He then saw a way to eliminate one more feedthrough by reversing the order of the bits of data transmitted by the board. So he laid out the board again. The final design was generally recognized by computer engineers as brilliant and was by engineering aesthetics beautiful. Woz later said, "It's something you can *only* do if you're the engineer and the PC board layout person yourself. That was an artistic layout. The board has virtually no feedthroughs."

The disk drive, which Apple began shipping in June 1978, was vital for the company, second in importance only to the computer itself. The drive made possible the development of serious software such as word processors and data base packages. Like most early successes at Apple, it represented an enormous amount of unconstrained individual effort, as did the early achievements of the Altair and the Sol. But at Apple, the hobbyist spirit was being channeled by a few sharp executives who understood how to build a company.

However, some of the development of the Apple market was being undertaken by people with no connection to the company.

For instance, the Apple II needed a good technical reference manual. When the company started shipping the computer in 1977, the instruction manual, or documentation, was not much better than documentation in the industry overall; that is, it was unspeakable. Documentation was the last thing a microcomputer company worried about in 1977. Customers were still hobbyists and would tolerate abominable documentation because, as often as not, they *wanted* the challenge of assembling or troubleshooting their machines. Hobbyists learned about computers as they put them together and used them, and while inadequate instructions and information didn't aid the learning process, overcoming the poor documentation sometimes did. Apple could not neglect the documentation if it wanted to bring a broader spectrum of customers into personal computing.

Jeff Raskin had left a writing job at *Dr. Dobb's* to run Apple's documentation effort, and he encouraged Chris Espinosa, who had planned on attending college full-time, to write something to explain the Apple to its users.

While a freshman living in the dorms of the University of California at Berkeley — as Lee Felsenstein and Bob Marsh had done years earlier — Chris Espinosa worked on the "red book," a manual that explained, in a clear and organized fashion, the technical details of the Apple II. The book's genesis is a true hobbyist's story. Espinosa wasn't quite finished with it when he had to leave his dorm, and for a week he slept in parks and the computer rooms on campus, living out of his backpack, working 18-hour days to complete the book. He typeset it on university equipment and turned it in to Apple. The manual provided the kind of information that mattered to people who wanted to develop software or add-on products for the Apple II; it was a great success and unquestionably aided Apple.

In fact, it would be hard to overestimate the contribution of third-party developers to Apple. If the public was to buy personal computers, it had to believe that the machines served a practical purpose. Gary Kildall's CP/M operating system and the subsequent development of business applications software helped some companies, such as Vector Graphic, sell machines. But

Apple's operating system was different from CP/M, and the machine needed different software.

Several programmers started writing games and business applications for the Apple, but while some of these were impressive, none was good enough to induce people to buy the computer just to use the program. Not until VisiCalc.

Without VisiCalc things would have been tougher for them. But without Apple things would have been tougher for VisiCalc.

Daniel Fylstra

VisiCalc

While an associate editor for *Byte* in its early days, Daniel Fylstra, a Californian who had gone East to learn computers and electronics at MIT, had been impressed with the chess program designed by Peter Jennings. But soon after reviewing it in *Byte*, Fylstra left for Europe to work as an engineer in the European Space Agency. He quickly grew frustrated with management problems in the intragovernmental bureaucracy and decided to return to the States to get an MBA degree at Harvard Business School. Bill Gates was attending Harvard as a freshman.

By the time he received his MBA in 1978, Fylstra had already started a small software marketing company, called Personal Software, that was marketing Jennings's *Micro Chess*. By this time Tandy had entered the microcomputer field, and the first version of the program he sold ran on the TRS-80 Model I. But soon he was offering it for the Apple II also. Fylstra liked the Apple's graphics.

Meanwhile, another Harvard MBA candidate, a quiet, unassuming student named Dan Bricklin, conceived an idea for a computer program to do financial forecasting. He thought it would work well in the real estate business. Bricklin had been a software engineer with DEC and had worked on its first word processing system. He thought he could sell his program to users of DEC minicomputers, or perhaps he might even sell into the new microcomputer market. Bricklin approached a Harvard finance professor with the idea. The academician ridiculed him: *Another* financial forecasting program? He better not expect the business world to carry him down Wall Street on its shoulders. Bricklin might want to talk to an ex-student of his, Dan Fylstra, who had researched the market for personal computer software, the professor added, but he frankly advised Bricklin not to waste his time. As he had warned Fylstra earlier, because of the availability of timesharing systems, microcomputer software would never sell.

But Fylstra liked Bricklin's idea. The only machine he had available at the time was an Apple and he loaned it to Bricklin, who began designing the program with a friend of his, Bob Frankston. Frankston, something of a mathematics genius, had been involved with computers since he was 13. And he had done some programming for Fylstra's company, converting a bridge program to run on the Apple.

Frankston and Bricklin soon founded a company, Software Arts, and commenced coding the financial analysis program. Throughout the winter Frankston worked on it at night in an attic. During the day he consulted with his partner on his progress. Occasionally the two got together with Dan Fylstra to dream of a lucrative future.

A prototype of the program was ready by the spring of 1979, and they called it VisiCalc. VisiCalc was a novelty in computer software. Nothing like it existed on any computer, large or small, and in fact there were reasons why it had not appeared on mainframe computers. In many ways it was a purely personal computer program. VisiCalc kept track of tabular data, like financial spreadsheets, using the computer's screen like a window through which a large table of data was seen. The window could slide across the table showing different parts of it. It simulated paper-and-pencil operations very well, but also went dramatically beyond them. Rows and columns in the chart could be made to depend on one another, so that changing one value in a table caused dependent values to change. This "what-if" ability made VisiCalc very appealing: one could enter a budget and see at once what would happen to other values if *this* value were changed by *that* much.

When Bricklin and Fylstra began showing the product around, not everyone responded as well as they had anticipated. Fylstra recalls demonstrating VisiCalc to Apple chairman Mike Markkula, who was unimpressed and proceeded to show him his own checkbook balancing program. But when VisiCalc was released through Personal Software in October of 1979, it was an immediate success. By this time Fylstra had moved his company to Silicon Valley.

Fylstra asked his dealers to estimate a proper price for VisiCalc, and they suggested between $35 and $100. Initially Fylstra offered the package for $100, but it sold so fast that he quickly raised the price to $150. Serious business software was rare on a personal computer and no one was sure how to price it. And VisiCalc had new capabilities. Year after year, even as VisiCalc increased in price, the volume of sales rose dramatically. At first release in 1979 Personal Software shipped 500 copies per month. By 1981 it was shipping 12,000.

Not only did VisiCalc sell, but it helped sell Apples. During its first year, VisiCalc was available only on an Apple disk, and it provided a compelling reason to buy an Apple. In fact, the Apple II and VisiCalc were an impressive symbiotic combination, and it's difficult to say which contributed more to the other. Together they did much to help legitimize both the hardware and the software industries.

Another early applications program for the Apple was a simple word processor called EasyWriter, a program similar to Electric Pencil. The EasyWriter program was written by John Draper. Eventually Draper marketed his program through Information Unlimited Software of Berkeley, California, the same company that was selling the early data base management program, WHATSIT.

&

> *Committee marketing decisions — that was*
> *the major source of all the problems.*
>
> **Dan Kottke**

The Apple III Fiasco

During Apple's third fiscal year, which ended on September 30, 1979, sales of the Apple II increased to 35,100, more than quadruple those of the previous year. Nevertheless, the company recognized a need to develop another product soon. No one believed that the Apple II could remain a best-seller for more than another year or two.

In 1978 Apple took several steps to gear up for the challenge. Chuck Peddle was hired in the summer although his responsibilities were unclear. As the designer of both the 6502 microprocessor and Commodore's PET computer, which was competing with the Apple, he seemed like a good person to have around. Before Apple had emerged from the garage, Peddle had tried to convince Commodore to purchase the small operation. But Apple and Commodore were unable to come to terms. Peddle's PET (said to stand for Personal Electronic Transactor or Peddle's Ego Trip, but actually named after the pet rock phenomenon of the day) was introduced at the same time as the Apple II at the First West Coast Computer Faire in 1977. The PET did not greatly influence the development of the American personal computer industry because company president Jack Tramiel opted to concentrate on European sales and because Commodore was slow to provide a disk drive. Eventually, Apple executives failed to agree with Peddle on his role, and he returned to Commodore at the end of 1978.

By that time Tom Whitney, Woz's former boss at Hewlett-Packard and a student at Iowa State University with Wendell Sander, was hired to supervise and enlarge the engineering department in order to begin designing new products.

In late 1978 several new computer projects were started. The first, an enhanced version of the Apple II with custom chips, was code-named Annie. Woz worked with another engineer on it but didn't complete the project. Moreover, he didn't pursue it with the intensity he had given his previous computer designs or the disk drive. Executives also discussed having Woz design a supercomputer utilizing bit-sliced architecture, which would spread the capabilities of the microprocessor over several identical chips. Its chief advantages were speed and variable precision, that is, high precision for scientific data and low precision for integer and character data. An engineering staff was put together for this computer, code-named Lisa. The Lisa project started slowly and passed through many incarnations over several years. Eventually a former Hewlett-Packard engineer hired by Tom Whitney took over as its project director.

Meanwhile, Wendell Sander took charge of designing the next Apple computer, the Apple III. Sander, one of Apple's most trusted employees, was being asked to design a machine that would equal the success of all the other Apple products. When he commenced work, the company told him that it hoped he could finish it within a year.

Woz had designed the Apple II to be what *he* wanted in a computer. But Sander had constraints from the outset. They derived from a meeting of the executive staff that at the time still included Chuck Peddle. The staff compiled a general and somewhat vague list of guidelines, mentioning such desiderata as enhanced graphics and more memory. There were a few detailed, specific concepts as well. For instance, executives said, the machine should be able to display 80 columns rather than 40, and it should have both upper- and lowercase characters.

Sander was told that the new machine should be able to run software designed for the Apple II. Although this compatibility was desirable considering the large pool of software being developed for the Apple II by outside programmers, it posed a problem. Designing a computer that is significantly different from another machine but that can still run the other's software is not an easy task. The hardware itself determines, at bottom, what the software must do. The microprocessor chip determines the possible machine language operations, and the disk drive determines the features of the operating system software. When this hardware differs between two machines, the computers can only run the same applications software through an intermediate layer of software built into the machine to permit an "emulation mode." The intermediate layer intercepts commands from the applications program and translates them into corresponding commands—or sequences of commands—for the underlying hardware. The process is inherently inefficient and the inefficiency shows most in programs where timing is vital. The most critical hardware feature in the emulation problem is the microprocessor, and Apple decided to simplify this aspect of it by using the Apple II's processor, the 6502.

The emulation edict was not without controversy. Apple engineers and programmers felt that emulation would limit the capabilities of the breakthrough machine they were supposed to create. *They* wouldn't want this kind of machine, they felt. But the marketing staff saw emulation as a stimulus to sales. First, an existing body of software could run on it immediately. Second, Apple could claim it was designing a family of computers. The decree was not rescinded.

In a sense, emulation boxed Sander in, limiting his creativity. The most important decision in the design of a computer—selection of a microprocessor —had been made by others. In fact, designers of the 6502 hadn't intended it to be used as the central processor in a computer. Apple considered adding an additional processor, a second brain, with some capacity to switch from one to the other. But a dual-processor machine would have been more expensive than the company wanted. Sander wasn't a person to protest. He liked computer designing, and he took the guidelines and set out to implement them. Dan Kottke worked as Sander's technician on the project. Each day Sander would hand him a drawing of a new part of the computer, and each day Kottke would copy over the schematic to make it more legible, and then put his stereo headphones on and wire-wrap the computer to music. Within a few months Sander had laid out a prototype of the main board.

About that time the company assembled a software team to design an operating system and a few applications for the new computer. Management wanted the Apple III to have a better operating system than the simple one that Woz had created for the Apple II. Indeed, the Apple III required a more complex system to handle its extra memory. Although the 6502 microprocessor could normally handle only 64K of memory, Sander was sidestepping that limitation by a technique known as bank switching. The computer would have several banks of 64K, and the operating system would keep track of which bank was currently active and what information was in each bank. The operating system would move from bank to bank as necessary. The microprocessor would act just as though the machine had only 64K. But the applications software could act as though the machine were handling 128K or 256K directly. Sander labored on the computer throughout 1979. He discovered that the emulation requirement also limited the extent to which he could improve the new computer's graphics. In the Apple II, a chunk of memory was reserved for symbols representing the colors of pixels (small squares) on the screen. Apple II software went to this graphics screen map whenever it needed to update the screen with lines and pictures. The Apple III had to have the *same* map: the same size, the same location in memory, and the same means of access. This need foreclosed many possibilities for enhancing graphics on the Apple III.

Woz occasionally consulted with Sander on the project but he trusted his colleague, who was "an incredible engineer." Nevertheless, Woz later complained about emulation. He would have done it differently. "Apple claims they've got it and they don't," he said.

Since no project had completely captured his attention, Woz was in a joking mood. One day he sneaked into a programmer's cubicle and placed a mouse inside his computer. When the programmer returned it took him more than a few minutes to figure out why his Apple was squeaking.

Delays in the Apple III were soon causing concern in the marketing department. The growing pains of the young company were beginning to show at last. The Apple III was, in fact, the first computer that Apple — as a company — had built from scratch. When the company formed, the Apple II was already near completion. The III was also the first Apple not built by Steve Wozniak in pursuit of his dream machine. Instead it was an awkward collage, pasted together by the many hands of a committee. Often the left hand didn't like what the right hand was doing.

Moreover, the pressure put on the Apple III project group for a swift completion probably wasn't even necessary. Although new companies were entering the personal computer market, Apple had erased the gap with Radio Shack and had become the leading personal computer company. In 1980, Apple II sales doubled to more than 78,000. Nevertheless the marketing people were worried. The Apple III must be announced.

Sander consented to introduce the new machine at the National Computer Conference in May 1980 in Anaheim, California. He felt that curtain raising was a bit premature. Nonetheless, there were a few working prototypes and the operating system software was "in workable shape." Perhaps it could be managed.

At the NCC the Apple III was well received by the industry and the press. The glamor story was continuing. In addition to unveiling the computer, Apple also announced the software it intended to have for the machine when shipping began a few months later: a word processor, a spreadsheet program, an enhanced BASIC, and a "sophisticated" operating system. The marketing plan was to portray the III as a serious computer that could be used in the office. It seemed likely to succeed.

A few months later, continuing to ride the tide of acclaim, Apple announced its first public stock offering. The *Wall Street Journal* wrote, "Not since Eve has an apple posed such temptation." When Apple was first formed, Mike Markkula dreamed of building the largest privately-held company in the nation, a company fully owned by its employees. But the industry was growing faster than anyone had foreseen. To keep pace, investment for research and development as well as advertising and marketing was essential. On November 7, 1980, when the company filed its registration with the Securities and Exchange Commission for an initial public offering, Apple revealed that its advertising budget for the year had doubled to $4.5 million.

Once shipments of the Apple III commenced in the fall of 1980, it became apparent that the machines were defective. Users brought the computers back to their dealers complaining that programs were crashing inexplicably. The dealers started complaining to Apple.

The Apple III staff began attempting to isolate the problem, carrying out the diagnostic tests they should have done before the computer was announced, or at least before it was released. As mishaps with the III became public knowledge, Apple slowed its promotion of the new computer and called a temporary halt to production. Soon the staff had identified one problem: a loose connector. While working on the Apple III, Dan Kottke had noticed that on occasion the machine would die. When he picked it up a half inch off the table and let it drop, it would turn on again. Kottke suspected a faulty connector. But he had hesitated, as a lowly technician, to broach his doubts to his superiors. And Sander, an engineer, was not involved with mechanical details like connectors. The problem had fallen through the cracks.

Another shortcoming stemmed from a bad break. Sander had counted on having a special National Semiconductor chip to use as an internal electronic clock. National finally informed him that the chip would not be available. Apple considered other chips and finally scrapped the entire idea. But since the Apple III had been advertised as having an internal electronic clock, the price had to be lowered since a promised feature was absent.

The problems were identified by January 1981, but selling a defective computer for several months had hurt Apple's reputation. Until then the company had done no wrong, and a certain overconfidence led Jobs, Markkula, and Scott to release the computer without proper testing.

&

I have always loved and cared for those at
Apple. That responsibility will never end.
Mike Scott

Black Wednesday

On February 7, 1981, Woz crashed his four-seater single-engine airplane at the Scotts Valley Airport, just a short drive from Apple. He had been practicing touch-and-go landings with two friends and his fiancee. Woz and his sweetheart were injured, but he was lucky not to have smashed into a skating rink just 200 feet away where hundreds of children were playing.

Woz suffered cuts on his face but was considered in good condition otherwise. No one realized, not even Woz, that he had hit his head badly enough to bring on a serious case of amnesia. Soon he found he could remember everything up to the day before the accident, but could form no new long-term memories. At the time Woz's family and friends didn't understand the problem. They just thought he seemed a bit slow.

"I didn't know I had had a crash," said Woz. "I didn't know I had been in the hospital. I didn't know I had played games on my computer in the hospital. I thought I was just resting on a weekend and after the weekend I would go back to work at Apple."

It took Woz over a month to snap out of his amnesia. He says that he talked himself out of it. As the image of a plane crash passed repeatedly through his mind, he finally realized that he had had an accident. "I went from zero to a one state in my head."

Woz didn't want to return to Apple right away. He had already gradually phased himself out of major decision-making there. He wasn't interested in it. He didn't understand business. He was an engineer and he had continued to work on the engineering projects assigned to him. "I'm not a manager type. I just love instruction sets," he said.

One of his last projects before the crash involved creating math routines for a new software program that Randy Wigginton was developing. The program itself was Mike Scott's idea. Frustrated with the long project delays at Apple, Scott had ignored the company bureaucracy and assigned Wigginton to develop a spreadsheet program similar to VisiCalc.

Wigginton worked faster than Woz had anticipated and was ready for the routines almost before Woz had begun. Mike Scott, angered by Woz's inconsistent work habits and by delays in shipping of the Apple III, began pressuring him. Woz worked night and day, suffering Scotty's daily complaints about his slow progress.

At one point, in order to get his boss off his back, Woz dreamed up one of his practical jokes. Woz knew that Scotty was a fan of movie director George

Lucas, and he had told Woz that he hoped the director might join Apple's board of directors. So Woz had a friend phone Scott's secretary saying that he was Lucas and would call again. Scott, anxiously anticipating the Lucas call, left Woz alone for the next few days.

Woz still isn't sure, but he believes he may have had the final spreadsheet routines with him when he crashed the plane. But subsequent events at Apple wiped out more than this program.

Just three weeks after Woz's accident, Mike Scott decided that Apple needed a good healthy shakeup. The ship he was trying to steer had sunk a bit in his estimation. It was time to jettison the dead weight. And so on a day referred to as Black Wednesday he fired 40 Apple employees. In addition, he terminated several hardware projects that he believed were taking too long. The move stunned the company at every level.

Mike Scott had never hidden his volatile personality. He had had a number of arguments with both Woz and Jobs. "I've never yelled with anybody more in my life," Jobs recalled. Sometimes Jobs would leave the president's office in tears after a long altercation. Scott was known for his flamboyance. He was a familiar figure walking about the company, visiting line employees regularly to keep in touch with what was happening. Scott also knew how to promote the company's morale, as evidenced by his suggestion that the company pay for a trip to Hawaii for the entire staff.

But the Apple III exhausted Scotty's limited patience. Since the actual need for the firings was unclear, the young company was shocked. At first remaining employees wondered who would be next. Simultaneously, they mounted an effort to hire back some of the people Scotty had fired. Even those who agreed that a shakeup was necessary felt that Scott had fired some good employees unfairly.

Chris Espinosa visited Jobs in his office the day after the firings and told him, "This is a helluva way to run a company." Jobs defended the mass ejection, but Espinosa nonetheless found him demoralized too. In fact, Scotty had acted too arbitrarily for the taste of either Jobs or Markkula. A month later, they demoted him to a lesser rank. He was no longer at the helm. By July Scott decided this state of affairs was intolerable. In his bitter letter of resignation, dated July 17, he announced that he was fed up with "hypocrisy, yes-men, foolhardy plans, a 'cover your ass' attitude and empire builders." Perhaps his most significant allegation, one which epitomized his approach to management, was that "A company's quality of life is not and cannot be set by a committee." The next day he flew to Germany to attend the Bayreuth opera festival, something he had wanted to do all his life.

Despite the problems with the Apple III, Woz's amnesia, Black Wednesday and its aftermath, and Scotty's resignation, Apple prospered. As always, Woz's labor of love, the Apple II, carried the company. Net sales of Apple IIs had more than doubled during fiscal 1980 and continued to boom through the first half of 1981. By April 1981, Apple employed more than 1500 people. The company had opened domestic manufacturing facilities in San Jose, Los Angeles, and Dallas, in addition to Cupertino. To meet the growing demand in Europe, a facility was opened in Cork, Ireland. Worldwide sales of Apple products were increasing at a pace of 186 percent above the previous year to more than $300 million. The number of Apple dealers had risen to 3000.

Mike Markkula took over as president of Apple, a position he believed to be a temporary one, and at age 26 Steve Jobs became chairman of the board. Apple was investing millions of dollars in research and development to create a product that would stun the world. They wanted to prove that they had learned the lessons of the Apple III, that Apple could indeed introduce a new product successfully.

By the fall of 1981, rumors abounded in the trade journals about new products Apple was developing. Leaks about Apple's secret projects angered Jobs.

Nevertheless the continued publicity helped to promote the Apple mystique. The company commenced its first national television advertising campaign with talk show host Dick Cavett as its advocate. Jobs was becoming a Silicon Valley celebrity, and thanks in part to its advertising, the name "Apple" had become virtually synonymous with "personal computer."

When you have nothing to lose you can shoot for the moon. So we shot for the moon, and we knew if we were successful that it would come down to Apple and IBM. And that's exactly what's going to happen.

Steve Jobs

The Big Leagues

In the fall of 1981 Steve Wozniak returned to school to finish his undergraduate work at UC Berkeley. He enrolled under an assumed name to avoid any special attention from students or faculty. Woz had gotten remarried in the June following his plane crash, and he wanted to take at least a year off from Apple. Although he worked late into the night finishing up his scholastic assignments, he also found time for a new project: a rock music festival called US.

Apple was taking the final steps to correct the damage from the Apple III snafu. Late in the fall Apple officially reintroduced the Apple III. This time the machine included increased memory storage in the form of a hard disk and improved software.

But two other projects were consuming most of Steve Jobs's time. In the spring of 1979 Jobs had paid a visit to Xerox's Palo Alto Research Center (PARC), a laboratory funded by Xerox with millions of dollars to carry out high-tech experiments. PARC scientists frequently foresaw advances in computer technology years before anyone else. Jobs wanted to see what the Xerox researchers were working on now.

He was welcome. "The year before," Jobs said, "I went down to Xerox Development Corporation, which made all of Xerox's venture investments, and I said, 'Look. I will let you invest a million dollars in Apple if you will sort of open the kimono at Xerox PARC.'"

During his tour of PARC, Jobs saw a demonstration of a new computer language, Smalltalk, which emphasized graphics and a new mouse-controlled user interface. The graphics resolution was good enough to allow all sorts of tricks that Jobs knew were impossible on the Apple II or III. The mouse could be used to select options by pointing at things on the screen. It was an input device conceptually distinct from anything then in use on personal computers. The language could lead to a new kind of computer system, one much easier to use.

"I was blown away," Jobs said.

Jobs was so impressed that he decided that Apple should do a similar system. He met resistance. Many people within Apple were not enthusiastic about the idea. "They thought that whatever their own religion was was the way to go," Jobs recalled. So he began to convert people.

Jobs made a second trip to PARC, this time with Bill Atkinson. Bill had been instrumental in getting the Pascal language for the Apple and had substituted for Woz on the Lisa project. Bill was as excited as Jobs about the PARC innovation. Over a few months, Lisa had changed from Woz's multi-chip design to one based on a new, powerful microprocessor from Motorola, the 68000, and this goal in turn changed into Apple's version of the PARC system. Atkinson would create a revolutionary graphics package for it. Not everyone was happy about these transformations, but Jobs had his way.

Jobs even hired one of the principal scientists away from Xerox PARC and assigned him to Lisa. Larry Tessler's task was to design the most advanced personal computer system available and to make Apple the technological leader in an increasingly competitive industry. Former HP engineer John Couch, hired in 1978, was in charge of Lisa. Meanwhile Jobs took control of another independent research project at Apple code-named Macintosh. The Macintosh team was also to use advanced software technology, but was to put it in an economical personal computer.

In 1981 Apple tripled its investments, spending $21 million on new product research and development. Jobs toured the world's leading automated factories and then commissioned one for Apple in Fremont, California, to build the Macintosh. "We have designed the machine to build the machine," Jobs said. "The Apple II was designed in a garage to be built in a garage. Macintosh has been designed from Day One to be highly automated."

Jobs and others at Apple wanted to continue the company's rapid growth and to establish it as the technology leader for several reasons. One was the likelihood of a late-1981 entry into the personal computer market by a company called International Business Machines Corporation.

Apple was not surprised by rumors that IBM planned a personal computer. The company had considered the possibility for several years. Jobs described it as a gate coming slowly down, and Apple had been running at top speed for four years to get through before it shut. In fact Apple made this concern public knowledge in its prospectus for its initial stock offering in December 1980. Apple also expected competition soon from Hewlett-Packard and various Japanese firms. But the greatest challenge by far was IBM, the chrome colossus whose name meant "real" computers to most people, a multinational corporation richer than many individual countries were. Whatever IBM had to offer, Apple would be meeting it with its Lisa and Macintosh.

There was no looking back.

&

John Draper, alias Captain Crunch
(Photo courtesy of Bill Baker)

Steve Jobs, co-founder of Apple
Computer, when Apple was still a garage
operation
(Photo courtesy of Margaret Wozniak)

Rod Holt, Apple's "everything-else guy"
(Photo courtesy of Apple Computer)

Following page, top,
The original Apple I circuit board, framed and hung in the Apple offices with the legend "Our Founder"
(Photo courtesy of Apple Computer)

Following page, bottom,
Wozniak and Jobs's creation: the Apple II
(Photo courtesy of Apple Computer)

Steve Wozniak scrambles for a phone in one of Apple's original offices
(Photo courtesy of Margaret Wozniak)

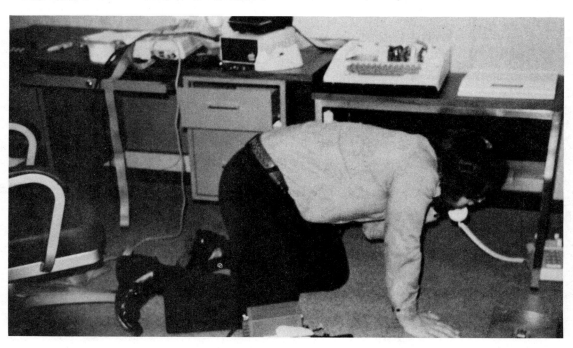

OUR FOUNDER

244

Steve Jobs (*right*) with Dan Kottke at the
Apple booth at an early computer show
(Photo courtesy of Dan Kottke)

Apple's original logo
(Photo courtesy of Dan Kottke)

An early Apple ad with its current logo
(Photo courtesy of Apple Computer)

Steve Wozniak (*left*), Steve Jobs, and
Dan Kottke with the Apple I at the PC-76
show in Atlantic City, New Jersey
(Photo courtesy of Dan Kottke)

One of Steve Wozniak's practical jokes,
a brochure describing the Zaltair
(Courtesy of Steve Wozniak)

from altair™ to zaltair™

Predictable refinement of computer equipment should suggest online reliability. The elite computer hobbiest needs one logical optionless guarantee, yet.

Ed Roberts
President, MITS, Inc.

Imagine a dream machine. **Imagine** the computer surprise of the century, here today. **Imagine** Z80 performance plus. **Imagine** BAZIC in ROM, the most complete and powerful language ever developed. **Imagine** raw video, plenty of it. **Imagine** autoscroll text, a full 16 lines of 64 characters. **Imagine** eye-dazzling color graphics. **Imagine** a blitz fast 1200 baud cassette port. **Imagine** an unparalleled I/O system with full **ALTAIR-100** and **ZALTAIR-150** bus compatibility. **Imagine** an exquisitely designed cabinet that will add to the decor of any living room. **Imagine** the fun you'll have. **Imagine ZALTAIR**, available now from MITS, the company where microcomputer technology was born.

bazic™

Without software a computer is no more than a racing car without wheels, a turntable without records, or a banjo without strings. BAZIC is the language that puts ZALTAIR's powerful hardware at your fingertips. For example, you can test the entire memory with the MEMTEST statement. Or read the keyboard directly with the KBD function. If you like to keep time the CLCK function will really please you. And in case you're in a hurry, you'll be glad to know that BAZIC runs twice as fast as any BASIC around. The best thing of all about BAZIC is the ability to define your own language . . . a feature we call perZonality.™ And ZALTAIR's BAZIC language comes standard in ROM, to insure 'rip-off' security.

hardware

We really thought this baby out before we built it. Two years of dedicated research and development at the number ONE microcomputer company had to pay off, and it did. A computer engineer's dream, all electronics are on a single pc card, **EVEN THE 18-SLOT MOTHERBOARD**. And what a motherboard. The ZALTAIR-150 bus is fully ALTAIR-100 compatible with 50 extra connectors. In addition, with ZALTAIR's advanced I/O structure called verZatility,™ access to peripherals is easier than ever before. And of course, our complete line of ALTAIR peripherals is directly compatible with the ZALTAIR 8800.

don't miss out

Weighing just 16 pounds, the ZALTAIR 8800 is a **portable** computer. The highly attractive enclosure was designed by an award winning team, and is fabricated from high-impact, durable ABS Cycolac® plastic. In the MITS tradition, nothing is compromised. Because of its superior design we were able to price the ZALTAIR 8800 far below the competition for this special introductory offer only. **You will not find the ZALTAIR in any store.** We want to bring this incredible offer to you directly, and avoid the retail mark-up of a middle man. Already, over 100 ZALTAIR's have been delivered to 75 satisfied customers. Don't miss out, order your ZALTAIR before April 30, 1977, and get immediate delivery.

Dan Fylstra of Personal Software
(later VisiCorp)
(Photo by Liane Enkelis)

Michael Scott (*left*), Apple president, and
Chuck Peddle at a computer show in 1978
(Photo courtesy of David Ahl)

Wendell Sander, designer of the Apple III
(Photo courtesy of Apple Computer)

Opposite page, top,
Steve Jobs and Steve Wozniak at an
Apple computer show in Boston in 1982
(Photo by Russell Fine)

Opposite page, bottom,
The Apple III in an early stage of
development (notice the code name SARA
on the disk drive)
(Photo courtesy of Dan Kottke)

The Apple III
(Photo courtesy of Apple Computer)

Steve Jobs showing off the Apple I
(Photo by Maggie Canon)

Following page, top,
Adam Osborne (in jacket and tie) at his book publishing company's booth at an early West Coast Computer Faire
(Photo courtesy of David Ahl, *Creative Computing*)

Following page, bottom,
Lee Felsenstein with his inventions, *clockwise from top left:* VDM video circuit board, Pennywhistle modem, Osborne 1 computer, Expander computer, Sol computer
(Photo by Levi Thomas)

Apple's Lisa, which broke new technological ground by employing a mouse interface and integrated software
(Photo courtesy of Apple Computer)

A later photo of Bill Gates of Microsoft
(Photo courtesy of Microsoft)

Following page, top,
Charles Simonyi and Bill Gates of
Microsoft
(Photo courtesy of Microsoft)

Following page, bottom,
The Digital Research booth at a recent
computer show
(Photo courtesy of Digital Research)

Bill Gates (*seated*) and Paul Allen,
co-founders of Microsoft
(Photo courtesy of Microsoft)

Clive Sinclair, British inventor, who brought the price of computers below $100 (Photo courtesy of David Ahl, *Creative Computing*)

Following page, top,
An early prototype of the Apple Macintosh
(Photo by Richard Cash)

Following page, bottom,
Two prototypes and the final design for the Apple Macintosh
(Photo by Richard Cash)

The IBM PC
(Photo courtesy of IBM)

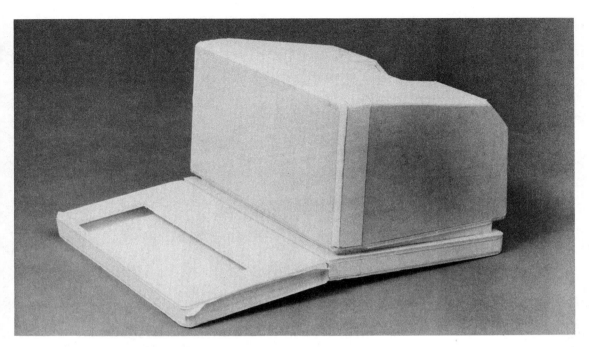

Members of the Macintosh design team
(Photo courtesy of Apple Computer)

The Apple Macintosh
(Photo by Richard Cash)

Big Companies

Chapter 8

We wanted to be able to pick it up and move it about.

Adam Osborne

Osborne's Portable Computer

In the years since they had left Albuquerque for their native Bellevue, Washington, Bill Gates and Paul Allen had established a successful software business specializing in programming languages for personal computers. The BASIC they had written for the MITS Altair was still their most popular product, a standard in an industry with few of them. In addition, Gates and Allen had introduced other programming languages such as FORTRAN and COBOL for personal computers.

Gates, 24, and Allen, 27, were pleased with their accomplishment. Microsoft was racking up $8 million in annual sales and it employed 32 people, most of them programmers. But in July 1980 Gates became involved in a project that would jolt and transform not only his company, but the entire personal computer industry.

By 1980 there were dozens of personal computer hardware and software companies. But the success of Apple had notified the world that personal computers were serious business. The growth of the garage operation into a large company, the enormous annual sales increases, and the proliferation of smaller companies writing software and making add-on hardware for the Apple convinced skeptics that the personal computer was not another hula hoop.

The biggest doubters of the personal computer were the large minicomputer and mainframe corporations. Some of them, such as Digital Equipment Corporation and Hewlett-Packard, had rejected employee proposals to build a personal computer in the early 1970s. Nor did IBM take the initiative, perhaps partly because of the federal antitrust suit that harried the company throughout the 1970s.

There were many reasons for the large corporations' hesitation about the new technology. Prior to Apple's success, they could still question the existence of a market for personal computers. And for the non-IBM companies, the established markets already offered sufficient risks. Launching an unproven product can be perilous, and while a start-up company has relatively little to lose, an established firm can badly damage its reputation by plunging into untested waters. The expense was higher for the established companies too. Their engineers' salaries for assessing the feasibility of a personal computer alone could cost a big company more than MITS and Proc Tech spent on research and development in their entire corporate histories. The company would also need prototypes and market research, which cost more money. Finally, there was the seemingly intractable problem of the sales force. Large computers were sold one at a time by engineers who understood their workings. The transaction often involved several visits and phone calls and many hours of a highly trained professional's time, and the cost to a company of selling a mainframe could easily exceed the total price of a personal computer. The method was clearly inappropriate for personal computers, but no large computer company was eager to explore new approaches and perhaps alienate its valuable sales force in pursuit of a chimerical market.

But the Apple proved that the market was very real indeed. It no longer took much vision to see that a company with a well-designed machine, some marketing skill, and the funds for promotion could reasonably expect to sell personal computers.

Of course, the Apple did not eliminate risks or obviate creativity. As 1980 wore on, Adam Osborne, who had started out in the industry selling his books at Homebrew, had a gleam in his eye and an idea that was clearly risky.

Easily the most quotable figure in microcomputing, Osborne had a tongue as glib as his pen. His commanding, distinctive voice, highlighted by a precise British accent, seemed to find the right word and delivery and to leave his listeners thinking that he had stated the matter in its final terms. But Osborne had gained more fame—or notoriety—for his writing, first for his books on microprocessors and then for his column that appeared first in *Interface Age* and later in *InfoWorld*.

The columns had begun as straightforward analyses of chip technology in the Silicon Valley. But Osborne quickly gravitated to other issues and soon was writing muckraking indictments of computer companies that manipulated their customers. He was particularly critical of the common policy of pre-announcing items and then bankrolling their development with money from the ensuing orders. Silicon Valley was the source of his information, and he called his column "From the Fountainhead." Osborne has never been accused of toe-scraping humility, and many readers innocently assumed he meant the title to refer to himself.

Osborne felt comfortable doing exposés about the industry since he was not directly involved in it. He was selling books. His Berkeley-based computer book publishing company, started a few years earlier as an offshoot of his microprocessor consultant work, had grown successful enough to attract the attention of McGraw-Hill. When he sold the book company, he began looking for something else to do.

For some time, he had been coming to believe in the need for computers that were portable. Portability would be the next product innovation, a fact he felt existing companies did not yet understand. During visits to computer shows, Osborne met industry pioneers like Bill Gates and Seymour Rubinstein and sought their reaction to this idea. "At first he was saying, 'Why doesn't someone do this?'" recalled Gates. "And the next thing I knew it was, 'It'll be called the Osborne 1.'"

But Osborne wasn't going to design it himself.

On a hot day in June of 1979 Lee Felsenstein found himself standing on the auditorium floor of the National Computer Conference in New York City. No one had told Felsenstein that the company for which he was consulting, Processor Technology, had folded. He waited, patient but sweating, with the prototype of his latest Proc Tech board in hand until it began to occur to him that Bob Marsh and Gary Ingram might *never* show up.

Shaking his head, Felsenstein returned to Berkeley, where he tried to drum up business to offset the lost Proc Tech royalties. He tried selling the design of the last Proc Tech board, an enhanced version of his VDM video board, to other companies but he had no luck. Felsenstein undertook various free-lance projects, on which he worked in his warehouse office. The jobs offered him a bare subsistence, since he was particular about the kinds of work he would accept. "I was running into the ground," he said. "I was just waiting for the opportunity to do what I wanted to do and closing my eyes to the monetary considerations."

Felsenstein recalled an evening in late 1979 when he sat wire-wrapping video boards late into the night while listening to alternative radio station KPFA. The disc jockey played the romantic ballad "The Very Thought of You" six times in a row. As it ended the first time, Felsenstein continued his work and wondered what song would be next. Up it came again and again and again. "That was the low point," he says. "It was as if I was trapped; the sun was never going to rise; I was just going to have to keep going and going and going. The rest of the world didn't exist and all I would do was listen to this song and keep working."

As 1980 began, things didn't improve much for Felsenstein. In February he moved into the Berkeley barn that housed the Community Memory project with an understanding that he wouldn't have to pay rent. But Community Memory was teetering financially, and Felsenstein found himself in a more and more precarious economic situation.

His luck took a turn at the West Coast Computer Faire in March 1980 when Adam Osborne approached Felsenstein with a bold idea. Osborne was going to start a hardware company and he was "going to do it right." Felsenstein told Osborne: "You took the words right out of my mouth."

Osborne and Felsenstein knew each other through the book company. Felsenstein had reviewed books Osborne's company had published and consulted on other technical projects. Their immediate problem involved the kind of hardware product to make. Felsenstein showed Osborne a batch of his unsold designs, including a controller that "would have been able to run a room full of joysticks and had a group space war game."

But Osborne summarily rejected them. He said he knew what he wanted. He had first considered a design similar to Clive Sinclair's bargain-basement ZX80, but he concluded that competing with Sinclair might be difficult and he rethought the matter.

Finally he decided to offer bundled software: applications software included with the machine. Until then, hardware and software companies served the same consumers but did not work together on purchases. Osborne knew that novice computer buyers often were confused about the software they needed. By offering the most common applications—word processing and spreadsheet—packaged with the computer, Osborne thought he could attract buyers. Of course, the device would be portable.

Osborne didn't want a box of state-of-the-art hardware. He wanted only those innovations necessary to make the computer a carry-along machine. It *had* to fit under an airplane seat. He asked for a 40-column display. The Sol had 64. Felsenstein split the difference and gave him 52. But Felsenstein had to minimize the number of characters because the screen had to be tiny—only five inches—to leave room inside for cushioning the tube. Since people would tote the machine around, they would inevitably drop it, so it had to be sturdy. The computer had to survive a drop test on the production line, and it had to have cushions. Felsenstein met the small screen requirement by storing a larger screen's worth of information in memory and giving the user keys with which to scroll the memory screen across the display. The user would see what seemed to be a sheet of paper sliding by behind the glass.

Serious microcomputers at that time had two disk drives, and Felsenstein put two in the Osborne 1. Unsure whether high-density drives could tolerate rough handling, he used relatively primitive drives that gave the machine adequate but unimpressive storage. "Adequacy," Osborne pronounced, "is sufficient." The machine had a Z80 microprocessor, 64K of memory, and standard interfaces to devices—typical fare for the time. But it was designed, from its overall dimensions down to the disk pockets Osborne insisted on, for portability. Osborne then set out to get the software. He needed a simple monitor program, a tool to facilitate software development. He called in Richard "The Surfer" Frank, a sandy-haired Silicon Valley software developer. Frank made a variety of contributions to the company and even provided space to work in his plant before Osborne had a building of his own.

For an operating system, Osborne turned to the industry champion: Gary Kildall's CP/M. He also needed a language, and BASIC was the obvious choice. Osborne had two widely used versions to choose from. Since the two BASICs had complementary virtues, he decided to offer them both and made deals with Gordon Eubanks for his CBASIC and Bill Gates for Microsoft BASIC.

Osborne also needed a word processor. In 1980 the man with the leading word processor was Seymour Rubinstein, president of MicroPro. Osborne gave

Rubinstein a part of his company and in return received WordStar at a bargain price. Osborne had offered Gates, Kildall, and Eubanks stock in the company also. Only Kildall refused, on principle, to avoid the appearance of favoring one customer over another. Gates turned down a position on Osborne Computer's board of directors but accepted the stock in exchange for a special deal on Microsoft BASIC. Osborne offered Rubinstein more: the presidency of the new company. Rubinstein turned it down and instead took the position of chairman of the board. He thought Osborne's idea so good he invested $20,000 of his own money in the company.

Unable to make a deal for VisiCalc, Osborne turned to Richard Frank and his company Sorcim to develop a spreadsheet program, which Frank called Super-Calc. The per-copy market value of Osborne's software now totaled almost $2000, and he planned to include it all in the basic price of the machine.

Until January 1981, when Osborne Computer incorporated and obtained office space in Hayward, most of the design was done in the Community Memory building, a big room with a black ceiling, white walls, and many sand-blasted wood beams, evidence of the "earthquake proof" architecture of the early 1900s.

Osborne introduced his Osborne 1 at the West Coast Computer Faire in April 1981, and it was the hit of the show. His booth was jammed with people. Osborne himself was there, his tall frame towering over others, and he seemed to be gloating. The machine was no technological marvel. But it was a bold step forward: the first commercially successful portable computer with all the software an average buyer needed. And the price — $1795 — was unheard of. Some people said he was selling software and had thrown the computer in for free.

There were sardonic comments from those — including irascible Bill Godbout — who remembered Osborne's tirades against manufacturers who took customers' money before making the products, and who now saw him doing the same thing himself. In September 1981, OCC had its first million dollar sales month. New companies quickly sprang up trying to duplicate or improve upon his design, and others seized upon his ideas of portability and included software in their system packages.

The $1795 price also became a target. The Kaypro portable had software similar to that of the Osborne 1, the same look, and the identical price. George Morrow also brought out a machine at $1795, and Harry Garland and Roger Melen of Cromemco introduced one for five dollars less. But whatever their merits, none of the portables, none of the machines with software included, none of the $1795 wonders had the impact of Adam Osborne's first venture into computer manufacturing. One of the industry's early participants had further advanced the development of the personal computer, and the Osborne 1 quickly became one of the new industry's top-selling personal computers, reaching a peak sales rate of about 10,000 a month. Since Osborne's initial business plan called for selling 10,000 total, OCC had certainly skyrocketed to success. Staying there was another matter.

&

One of the things HP learned is that closed architectures aren't going to work, that you really have to depend on third-party software suppliers.

Nelson Mills

The HP Way and the Xerox Worm

Osborne was among the last pioneers to open new territory before civilization arrived. After the Osborne 1 came out in 1981, the big companies began to enter and transform the market.

Hewlett-Packard hadn't rejected Steve Wozniak's Apple I design because it didn't believe in the *idea* of a personal computer. HP built large computers, but it also made calculators, so the company understood how to sell relatively inexpensive products. HP may have turned Wozniak down because, however good his machine, it did not lend itself to mass production. As Jobs later acknowledged, "It was designed to be built in a garage." Then, too, the Apple was not obviously a machine for engineers and scientists, HP's primary market. Woz was clearly told that the Apple was more appropriate for a start-up company than for HP. He may have been turned down because he had no degree. It would not have been surprising in any established computer company, and Woz did go back to school for his degree as soon as he finished propelling Apple into the Fortune 500. But HP had another reason to reject a personal computer design in 1976. The company was already working on one of its own.

In early 1976, a crew of engineers in HP's Cupertino, California, facility began to coalesce around a project with roots in HP's calculator technology. Chung Tung, the engineer in charge of Project Capricorn, brought in engineer Ernst Ernie along with Kent Stockwell to direct the hardware design and George Fichter to oversee software. There was no shortage of talent at HP, and Capricorn was a significant project.

Initially, Capricorn was intended as a computer-like calculator, more elaborate than any of HP's small machines. HP already made highly specialized calculators. The calculator market war that had driven Ed Roberts to create the Altair had not hurt HP as much as it had other calculator manufacturers because HP had concentrated on scientific calculators that did more and sold for more than the cheap commercial versions. Capricorn was at first intended to have a liquid crystal display, like a calculator, but with several lines instead of one. It would be a desktop, BASIC language calculator. By summer, the project had redefined itself and Capricorn was ornamented with a cathode ray tube, a significant change both in terms of manufacturing costs and of the potential market for the machine. Capricorn was turning into a computer.

HP was perhaps better suited to develop a personal computer than any other established computer company — with the possible exception of Xerox. HP was headquartered in Silicon Valley, near most of the semiconductor companies and in the midst of the growing micro mania. Some of the Capricorn engineers were actually hobbyists like Woz, working on their own homebrew systems. HP also had far more resources to create such computers than the garage start-ups. By the time they were actually designing a machine, the Capricorn staff had grown to over a dozen engineers and programmers.

The computer was soon becoming quite distinctive. It would have a small built-in printer and a cassette tape recorder for data storage, a keyboard, and a display, all in one desktop package smaller than the Sol (which had not appeared yet and would not include an integrated display or data storage when it did). Its chip was also ahead of its time — but this was not necessarily an advantage. In 1976, the only microprocessor that looked feasible was the Intel 8080, the Altair chip, but the Capricorn team wanted one better adapted to its purposes and turned the problem over to another HP division. Hence, Capricorn got its own HP-designed proprietary microprocessor. It was a decision some members of the team later regretted.

Another problem soon emerged. In the fall of 1976, the project was moved out of Silicon Valley to sleepy Corvallis, Oregon, a shift that played havoc with the schedule and damaged morale. Woz, who more than anything else wanted to design computers at HP, seriously considered joining the Capricorn team and moving to Corvallis. He thought he would like living in Oregon, and he wanted to get in on the project. But HP turned him down. Unlike Woz, many other Capricorn engineers felt that Corvallis was exile, that they were being asked to leave the center of the universe and move into the void. Some elected not to move and dropped out of Capricorn. When others made the move, they found the plant wasn't ready for them. At first, programmers had to commute 70 miles to do software development on the nearest large computer.

However, the Capricorn team was progressing. By November a prototype had been developed. It had no tape drive or printer or display yet, and the CPU chip and certain other microprocessors the engineers wanted to control periph- erals were still in the layout stage. In 1977 they solved the tricky problems of mixed technologies posed by building a printer into a computer. Also that year the chips began to appear. During a visit from corporate brass, one executive vice-president told the engineers that the machine needed more I/O ports on the back to connect it with other HP devices or to allow later capabilities. It was a little late to suggest significant design modifications, but the changes were made. The move and the modifications helped Capricorn slip a year behind schedule.

When project became product in January 1980 it was an attractive machine, solidly engineered and relatively expensive — even given its capabilities — at

$3250. It was called the HP-85 and had a 32-character line display, almost as wide as the 40 characters on Wozniak's Apple.

Although the HP-85 sold well enough for HP's purposes and led to a series of related machines, it did not set cash registers singing like the Apple II did. But it wasn't designed to. HP sold it not as a business machine but as a scientific and professional one. Nevertheless, HP's sluggish pace in completing and marketing the product unquestionably hurt sales. By the time this machine with its built-in cassette tape drive came out, the field was moving to floppy disks, which were more reliable and stored more information than tape cassettes. Yet the HP-85 cost more than some disk-based systems.

In the long run, the HP-85's greatest flaw may have been its closed system design that required HP software and HP peripherals. When the Apple II was announced in 1977, the Capricorn team believed its machine would compete with it. But by the time the HP-85 appeared, some Capricorn programmers were privately conceding the general and business market to Apple. There was real irony here, since the Apple II's 40-column, lowercase display was clearly inappropriate for basic applications like word processing and report generation, and since its 6502 was no number cruncher. Apple eventually got 80-column upper- and lowercase display capabilities, but only because Wozniak had left the architecture open and other people created the necessary boards and software. Third parties were continually improving the Apple II. They were shut out of the HP-85. HP soon concluded that the closed architecture had been a mistake. Still, HP had beaten the other established computer companies into the market by over a year, and the HP-85 and its successors carved out a solid market niche for themselves. The next big manufacturer to introduce a personal computer fared less well.

Xerox had made its name in copying machines, but the company had flirted with computers as well and maintained close ties with Silicon Valley. After acquiring Scientific Data Systems (SDS), a computer company in El Segundo, California, and renaming it Xerox Data Systems (XDS), Xerox became one of the Dwarfs—the seven mainframe computer companies living in Snow White's shadow. XDS, however, was a financial millstone and Xerox finally sold it, though retaining the El Segundo facility itself for some IC and electronics design and systems programming.

Xerox purchased Shugart, the disk drive manufacturer, in the winter of 1977-78. Don Massaro, president of Shugart through the early 1970s, recalled that in the days before Apple soared to the zenith, Steve Jobs was in his office nearly every week, nagging him to devise a disk drive that personal computer users could afford. Massaro and his colleague James Atkinson did, and it helped make Apple and Shugart leaders in their fields. When Xerox bought Shugart, it acquired that wedge into the personal computer market, and it also got Massaro, who proved instrumental in Xerox's foray into the market some years later.

But Xerox made its greatest contribution to the personal computer through PARC, the research center it opened in 1970. Xerox had separated the often-linked research and development, and PARC was strictly a cutting-edge institute with no commitment to develop commercial products. PARC was chartered to explore technological frontiers and it did. One Silicon Valley observer called PARC a national resource because of PARC's open sharing of technical knowledge with the outside world, an openness more akin to an academic institution or to the computer hobbyist movement than to the research wing of a large corporation. With both the freedom of a university and the financial backing of a large corporation, PARC was an exciting place for a computer engineer or programmer to work.

That combination attracted some talented people. Hungarian-born Charles Simonyi, who had learned his programming on a Russian vacuum tube computer and had degrees from Berkeley and Stanford, worked there. So did John Shoch, who finished his PhD at Stanford while helping get PARC started. The fiercely independent, farsighted Alan Kay was also there, and he adorned his desk with a cardboard model of his dream computer—a powerful machine Kay called Dynabook that would be small enough to fit in a bookbag. Larry Tesler brought the newest programming techniques to his PARC software. And David Liddle made a product of the research.

Over several years these engineers and programmers created an impressive workstation computer called the Alto. The Alto boasted an advanced language called Smalltalk, an input device borrowed from SRI called the mouse, and a technique called Ethernet for connecting individual Altos together for communication and cumulation of effort, as if they were one big computer. Xerox referred to the whole arrangement as the "office of the future," and it was both visionary and technically sound. Xerox marketed Altos to government agencies, placing them in the White House, the Executive Office Building, the National Bureau of Standards, the Senate, and the House of Representatives, where they were used to print the *Congressional Record*.

The Alto was 20 times more computer than the original Altair. It had impressive speed and display graphics and the Smalltalk language, a powerful step or two beyond BASIC. Since work was completed in 1974, some people, particularly those at Xerox, claim it was the first personal computer. But the Alto was never a commercial product. No more than 2000 were ever built, and its cost removed it from the category of a personal computer, even if it was a self-contained machine for one individual's use. It was priced as a minicomputer.

The Alto took two years to develop—from 1972 to 1974—and was used for three more years before Xerox decided to develop it further into a marketable product. In January 1977, David Liddle was placed in charge of this task, and Charles Simonyi came to work for him. But the project proceeded slowly. Many researchers at PARC, attracted by the freedom to design technologically dazzling innovations, were growing frustrated that their creations remained sequestered in the lab. They could see things happening in quickstep around them while Xerox dawdled. Before Xerox would get a personal computer product to market, several key people would have left. And afterwards others departed. Tesler went to Apple, Kay to Atari, and eventually, Simonyi to Microsoft.

Meanwhile, Xerox released its Ethernet network and began linking personal computers together. It took four years, but in June 1981, Xerox announced the 8010 Star information system. If was an impressive machine, using much of the advanced Alto technology Jobs had seen. But the Star cost $16,595 and was not really a personal computer either. Nor did Xerox try to convince people it was. For example, the company did not try to sell the machine in computer stores. If HP's laggardly development of the HP-86 had caused it to miss its commercial window, offering a tape-based machine in a disk-based world, the Xerox Star missed the whole commercial field. A month later, though, Xerox introduced a true personal computer.

The Xerox 820, announced in July 1981, was code-named The Worm during development, perhaps because Xerox had dreamed it would eat up Apple's market. Like many existing personal computers, the Xerox 820 used the Z80 chip. Xerox also offered Kildall's CP/M and the two BASICs written by Gates and Allen and by Eubanks.

Don Massaro had led the 820 project. The 820s would be cheap, individual workstations on Ethernet systems in Fortune 500 corporations, the same market the Star sought. Development took only four months, and the machine quickly went into manufacture. "All we wanted to do was reserve those desks for Stars later on," Massaro said. Given that target market, Xerox's next move didn't make much sense.

"It wasn't a low-cost, entry-level configuration," Massaro later explained. "It was designed to go after the end user market through our direct sales organization. Xerox has always sold through its own sales organization. Xerox had 15,000 salespeople worldwide and that was one of the real strengths of Xerox." But ComputerLand waved huge purchase orders before Xerox corporate eyes, and "in a moment of weakness we went to that channel."

Mass marketing was a mistake. Xerox fared poorly in the developing shelf-space war in ComputerLand stores. Perhaps it was the paucity of technological innovation in the 820, Xerox's failure to learn from the lesson of open architecture. Or perhaps the competition was simply getting too heavy even for Xerox by that point. In Bill Gates's view, the company misunderstood the market. "Xerox was aiming a little too high and trying to do something very difficult and didn't see the opportunity," said Gates. "When they did, they threw something together in a couple of months and it was too little too late. "We got creamed," Massaro admits. And it was IBM that did it.

&

IBM is a big company.

Bill Gates

IBM

HP and Xerox had made less than spectacular entries into the personal computer market, and there was intense curiosity within that industry about how IBM would fare. The megafirm was considered successful in almost everything it had tried. Its resplendent reputation had existed at least since the mid-1960s, when IBM owned two-thirds of the computer market. And when IBM chief Tom Watson, Jr., had bet the company on a new semiconductor-based computer line that instantly made IBM's most profitable machines obsolete and the bet paid off, IBM only appeared all the more infallible. T. Vincent Learson, who had directed development of that computer, the 360, succeeded Watson as CEO in 1971. Two years later, he was succeeded by Frank Cary, a man willing to risk, if not the company, at least some of its pristine reputation on a very un-IBM venture.

Size alone did not define success in the personal computer business. In Bellevue, Washington, Microsoft was a little company compared with Apple, and nonexistent next to the multinational IBM. But though it had only a few dozen employees, mostly programmers who came to work in T-shirts if they wanted to, Microsoft was clearly a success. It had even made money with hardware.

The hardware story was clearly one of a tailgate success. Paul Allen and Bill Gates were sitting in the back of a pickup truck in the Microsoft parking lot discussing the Apple problem. Microsoft by then had written a quarter million bytes of software, and none of it would run on the leading personal computer. Gates shook his head at the thought of converting it all to Apple's 6502 code, and Allen suggested, "Maybe there's a way to do it in hardware."

They brought in Tim Patterson of Seattle Computer Products, located across Lake Washington, to try to build a card for the Apple that would let it run Microsoft's 8080 and Z80 software. Patterson did a series of prototypes before Don Burdis took over the project. One afternoon Allen, Gates, and another Microsoft employee sat discussing the project's potential. They agreed that if Burdis could make the SoftCard work, they might sell about 5000 of them. Burdis did. They sold that many in three months and many more thereafter.

In the summer of 1980 Microsoft decided to end its translation nemesis for good. Microsoft approached it by first rewriting all its software into a "neutral" language on a large DEC minicomputer and then writing the chip-specific translator programs that would automatically convert their "neutral" software to the form needed by the 6502 or any other particular processor. The task was massive, but cost-effective if the company intended to supply software to all microcomputer manufacturers and to establish its products as industry standards. That was the idea.

In June, Paul Allen was working on enhancements to a BASIC for machines built around Intel's new 8088 and 8086 chips. The 8086 was one of a fresh generation of microprocessors created explicitly for small computers; it had a more logically designed instruction set and more capabilities for the systems programmer to use. It also possessed a 16-bit architecture; that is, the 8086 could handle information in chunks twice as large as those the 8080, the Z80, the 6502, or any other common microprocessors on the market could handle. In some ways, the new chip affected a machine's performance exponentially. For instance, its memory capacity jumped by a factor of thousands. The 8088 was a compromise version of the 8086 with some 8-bit characteristics but the same instruction set. Zilog and Motorola also had 16-bit microprocessors, and Microsoft did not intend to ignore the innovation.

Also that July, Bill Gates, busily developing a BASIC for Atari, received a phone call from a representative of IBM. He was surprised, but at first not greatly surprised. IBM had called once before about buying a Microsoft product, but the deal had fallen through. However, this communication was more tantalizing. IBM wanted to send some researchers from its Boca Raton, Florida, facility to chat with Gates about Microsoft. Gates agreed without hesitation. "How about next week?" he asked. "We'll be on a plane in two hours," said the IBM man.

Gates swallowed and agreed, knowing he would have to cancel his next day's appointment with Atari chairman Ray Kassar. "IBM is a pretty big company," he explained sheepishly.

Since IBM *is* a big company, he decided to turn to his colleague Steve Ballmer. Ballmer embodied Gates and Allen's business acumen. Gates had met Ballmer at Harvard in 1974, and when, in 1979, Gates decided that Microsoft was getting difficult to manage, he called Ballmer, who had since gained marketing experience with Proctor and Gamble. Ballmer was brash and ambitious. After Harvard, he had entered Stanford University's MBA program but had quit, deciding he could make more money out of school than in it.

Ballmer had been glad to join Microsoft. He was enthusiastic about the little software company, and he liked Bill Gates. He reminded Gates how, at Harvard, he had convinced Gates to join his men's club. As an initiation rite he dressed his friend in a tuxedo, blindfolded him, brought him to the student cafeteria, and made him talk to other students about computers. Gates's dealings with IBM would remind him of this experience.

Gates liked Ballmer too. Gates had played poker during the evenings in the Harvard dorms and after being cleaned out, he often went to Ballmer to describe the game. As they started working together at Microsoft in 1980, Gates found he still enjoyed discussing things with his friend, who quickly became one of his closest business confidants. He particularly wanted to talk with him on the day of IBM's call. "Look, Steve," Gates said, "IBM is coming tomorrow and IBM is a *big* company. We better show those guys a little depth. Why don't we both sit in on the meeting?"

Neither of them could be sure that the call warranted a high adrenaline level, but Gates couldn't help getting worked up over it. "Bill was super-excited," Allen later recalled. "He hoped they'd use our BASIC." Thus, Ballmer said, he and Gates "did the thing up right," meaning suit and tie, unusual attire at Microsoft.

Before the meeting began, IBM asked Gates and Ballmer to sign an agreement promising not to tell IBM anything confidential. Big Blue used this device to protect itself from future lawsuits. Hence, if Gates revealed a valuable idea to the company, he could not sue later on if IBM exploited the concept. IBM was familiar with lawsuits. Adroit use of the legal system had played an important part in its long control of the mainframe computer business. It all seemed rather pointless to Gates, but he agreed.

The meeting seemed basically an introductory social session. Two IBM representatives asked Gates and Ballmer "a lot of crazy questions," Gates recalls, about what Microsoft did and about what features mattered in a home computer. The next day, Ballmer typed up a letter to the IBM visitors thanking them for the visit, and he had Gates sign it.

Then nothing happened for a month. In late August, IBM phoned again to schedule a second meeting. "What you said was real interesting," the IBM representative told Gates. This time IBM would send five people including a lawyer. Not to be outdone, Gates and Ballmer decided to front five people themselves. They asked their own counsel—a Seattle attorney whose services Microsoft had used—to attend the meeting along with two other Microsoft employees. Allen, as usual, stayed in the background. "We got five people in the room," said Ballmer. "That was a key thing."

At the outset IBM's head of corporate relations explained why he had come along. It was because "this is the most unusual thing the corporation has ever done." Gates thought it was about the weirdest thing Microsoft had ever been through too. Once again, Gates, Ballmer, and the other Microsoft attendees had to sign a legal document, this time stipulating that they would protect in confidence anything they viewed at the meeting. Then they saw the plans for Project Chess. IBM was going to build a personal computer.

Gates looked at the design and began to question the IBM people across the table. It bothered him that the plans made no mention of using a 16-bit processor. He explained that a 16-bit design would enable him to give them superior software—assuming they wanted Microsoft's. He was emphatic and enthusiastic and probably didn't express himself with the reserve they were used to. But IBM listened.

IBM did want Microsoft's languages. On that August day in 1980, Gates signed a consulting agreement with IBM to write a report explaining how Microsoft could work with IBM. The report was also to suggest hardware and

Gates's proposed use of it.

The IBM representatives added that they had heard about a popular operating system, CP/M. Could Gates sell that to them as well? Gates patiently explained that he didn't own CP/M, but that he would be happy to phone Gary Kildall and help arrange a meeting. Gates later said that he called Kildall and told him that these were "important customers" and to "treat them right." He handed the phone over to the IBM representative, who made an appointment to visit Digital Research the next day.

Dorothy McEwen handled Digital Research's accounts with hardware distributors. She didn't like to talk about how IBM came to town and left dissatisfied, ultimately to buy a different operating system for its first personal computer. But Kildall explained that IBM's call caught his company by surprise. The nondisclosure agreement IBM asked McEwen to sign troubled her because she felt that it jeopardized Digital Research's control of its software. Company lawyer Jerry Davis agreed that the agreement should have been modified. Apparently the IBM representatives weren't used to being second-guessed; instead of pursuing a contract with Digital Research, they flew back to Seattle and Microsoft to contract for an operating system.

In retrospect, and not without a certain competitive delight, Gates faulted Kildall for failing to negotiate a deal with IBM. Instead of meeting the IBM representatives, "Gary went flying," said Gates, a story that became well known in the industry.

Kildall disputed Gates's recollection. He denied that he was out flying for fun while the IBM representatives cooled their heels. "I was out doing business. I used to fly a lot for pleasure, but after a while you get tired of boring holes in the sky."

Gates required no prodding. Once IBM agreed to use a 16-bit processor, he realized that CP/M was not critical for the new machine, since applications programs written for CP/M were not designed to take advantage of the power of 16 bits. Kildall had seen the new processors too and was planning an 8086 CP/M called CP/M-86. But it made just as much sense, Gates told IBM, to get a different operating system.

IBM was uncertain until Paul Allen talked to Tim Patterson at Seattle Computer Products. Patterson's company had already developed an operating system, SCP-DOS, for the 8086, and Allen told him that Microsoft wanted it.

At the end of September, Gates, Ballmer, and a colleague took a red-eye flight to deliver the report. They assumed it would determine whether or not they got the IBM personal computer project. They nervously finished collating, proofreading, and revising the document on the plane. Kay Nishi, a globe-trotting Japanese entrepreneur and magazine publisher who also worked for Microsoft, had written part of the report in "Nishi English," which, according to Ballmer, "always needs editing." The report proposed that Microsoft convert SCP-DOS to run on IBM's machine. After the sleepless flight, Gates and

Ballmer were running on adrenaline and ambition alone. As they drove from the Miami airport to Boca Raton, Gates suddenly panicked. He had forgotten a tie. Already late, they swung their rental car into the parking lot of a department store and waited for it to open. Gates rushed in and bought a tie.

IBM wanted to finish the personal computer project in a hurry—within a year. It had created a small team of 12 to avoid the kind of corporate bottlenecks that can drag a project on for years—three and one-half for the Xerox Star, and four for the HP-85. A source close to IBM said that IBM's president Frank Cary dealt roughly with all internal politics conducing to delay. During the day, Gates answered dozens of queries from members of IBM's project team. "They pelted us with questions," says Ballmer. "Bill was on the firing line."

By lunchtime Gates was fairly confident Microsoft would get the contract. Philip Estridge, the head of the project, an IBM vice-president and owner of an Apple II, told Gates that when John Opel, IBM's new chairman, heard that Microsoft might be involved in the effort he said, "Oh, is that Mary Gates's boy's company?" Opel had served with Gates's mother on the board of directors of the United Way. Gates believed that connection helped him get the contract with IBM, which was finally signed in November 1980.

Microsoft first had to set up a work place for the project, a more difficult task than might be imagined. IBM wasn't just any company. It treasured secrecy and imposed the strictest security requirements. Gates and Ballmer decided on a small room in the middle of their offices in the old National Bank building in downtown Seattle. IBM sent its own file locks, and when Gates had trouble installing them IBM sent its own installer. The room had no windows and no ventilation, and IBM required that the door be kept constantly closed. Sometimes the temperature inside exceeded 100 degrees. IBM conducted several security checks to make sure Microsoft followed orders. Once Microsoft was caught taking a breath, and the IBM operative found the secret room wide open and a chassis from a prototype machine standing outside it. Microsoft wasn't used to dealing with this kind of organization.

But Microsoft learned. To speed communication the two firms set up an electronic mail system, which sent messages instantly back and forth between a computer in Boca Raton and one in Seattle. Gates also made frequent trips to Boca Raton.

The schedule was grueling. The software had to be completed by March 1981. IBM's project managers showed Gates timetables and more timetables, all of which "basically proved we were three months behind schedule before we started," Gates said.

The first order of business was the operating system. Since all the languages were going to run with the operating system, the programmers had to know its technical details to do their work. Gates hired Tim Patterson to help him with the operating system.

Gates took charge of converting Microsoft BASIC, written for the old Altair, to the IBM computer. He worked on it with Paul Allen and another Microsoft employee. Six years before, Allen, as MITS software director, had nagged Gates to do the Altair disk code and teenaged Gates had procrastinated. This time Gates was supervising and Allen did most of the work. Other Microsoft programmers labored on the various language conversion projects.

Gates was feeling the pressure from IBM, and he passed it on to his own employees. Some of them were used to spending winter weekends as ski instructors. But not that winter. "Nobody went skiing," said Gates. When some wanted to fly to Florida to watch the launch of the space shuttle, Gates was unsympathetic. But when they insisted, he said that if they completed a set amount of work beforehand, they could go. The programmers spent five days straight at Microsoft, even sleeping there, in order to meet his demands. Allen remembers being up until 4 A.M. programming when Charles Simonyi, formerly of PARC, walked in and declared that they were flying down to Florida for the launch that morning. Allen protested. He wanted to continue his work. Simonyi dissuaded the exhausted programmer and they were on the plane a few hours later.

Gates discussed the design of the new machine with IBM continually, usually with Estridge. He pointed out that the open architecture of the Apple computer had contributed immeasurably to its success. Gates had reason to appreciate openness since the SoftCard, Microsoft's only hardware product, was a cornerstone of the corporation. Since Estridge owned an Apple II, he was leaning toward an open architecture at the outset. With Gates's encouragement, IBM defied its tradition of secret design specifications and turned its first personal computer into an open system.

This was an extraordinary move for IBM, the most aloof and proprietary of all computer companies. It was deliberately inviting the "parasites" Ed Roberts had condemned. IBM would use standard parts and design considerations created by kids in garages, and it would encourage more contributions from them. It was shrugging off the tailored tux to don the ready-to-wear clothes of the hobbyists and hackers.

Gates understood the open-system issue from MITS's experience. Ed Roberts had accidentally created an open system in 1974 by making the Altair a bus-based machine. Other manufacturers could and did produce circuit boards for the Altair, and an entire S-100 industry developed to Roberts's dismay. When Roberts tried to hide the bus's details, the industry effectively took the bus away from him, redefining it to standard specifications.

Gates was intent on making MS-DOS the industry's operating system now that he had abandoned the symbiotic relationship Microsoft had once enjoyed with Digital Research. He made a strong and convincing case for an open operating system too. If people knew the details of the operating system, they could develop software for it more easily. Gates may have had additional considerations in mind however. Having broken into mainframe operating systems when he was 14, having seen his original Altair BASIC become an industry standard through theft, he may simply have found it wiser to give away what would otherwise be preempted.

Although pressure to finish the software was extreme, Gates was confident in his ability and that of his company, which was glittering with programming talent. But he had one fear that he could not overcome. It concerned him even more than the deadline, and it haunted him right up to the announcement of the IBM computer: Would IBM *cancel* the project? Gates realized that IBM was a goliath with many, many projects. Only a small percentage of the research and development work done at IBM ever appeared as finished projects. What other secret IBM personal computer projects might be proceeding in parallel with Chess he didn't know and would probably never know. "They seriously talked about canceling the project up until the last minute," said Gates, "and we had put so many of the company's resources into the thing."

Gates was under strain, and the talk of cancellation upset him. He also worried about the stories appearing in the press about an IBM personal computer. Some were quite precise. Would IBM question his company's compliance with its security requirements? When an article in the June 8 issue of *InfoWorld* accurately described four months early the details of the IBM machine, including the decision to develop a new operating system, Gates panicked. He called the newspaper's editor to protest the publication of rumors.

IBM Discovers the Woz Principle

On August 12, 1981, International Business Machines announced its first personal computer. It was called the IBM Personal Computer, and it radically and irrevocably changed the world for microcomputer makers, software developers, retailers, and the rapidly growing market of microcomputer buyers.

In the 1960s there was a saying among mainframe computer companies that IBM was not The Competition, it was The Environment. Whole segments of the industry, known collectively as the plug-compatibles, grew up around IBM products, and their prosperity depended on IBM's. To the plug-compatibles, the cryptic numbers by which IBM identified its products were not the trademarks of a competitor, but familiar features of the terrain, like mountains and seas.

When IBM brought out a personal computer, it too had one of those product numbers. But the IBM marketing people knew they were dealing with a new kind of customer and that a number might not convey the right message. It isn't hard to guess what IBM thought the right message was. By naming its machine the Personal Computer, it suggested this device was the only personal computer. The machine quickly became called the IBM PC, or simply the PC. The operating system, originally SCP-DOS (for Seattle Computer Products), became MS-DOS under Microsoft, but IBM referred to it as PC-DOS on its machine, and some users slipped into the habit of calling it just DOS.

The PC announcement brought one more worry for Bill Gates. At the last minute, IBM had gone back to Pacific Grove and reached an agreement with Gary Kildall for CP/M-86. But IBM reassured Gates that the Microsoft DOS was its "strategic operating system." Besides, CP/M-86, the 16-bit CP/M, wasn't available yet. Gates was relieved.

As for Gary Kildall, he had been disturbed when he found out how like CP/M the IBM operating system was. He said he spoke to IBM officials: "I told them that they wouldn't have proceeded down that path if they knew [the IBM operating system] was that closely patterned after mine. They didn't realize that CP/M was something owned by people." In fact, MS-DOS resembles CP/M closely in terms of its functions and appearance to the user.

The IBM PC itself was almost conventional from the standpoint of the industry at the time. Lee Felsenstein got his hands on one of the first delivered and opened it up at a Homebrew meeting. "I was surprised to find chips in there that I recognized. There weren't any chips that I *didn't* recognize. My experience with IBM so far was, when you find IBM parts in a junk box you forget about them because they're all little custom jobs and you can't find any data about them. IBM is off in a world of its own. But in this case they were building with parts that mortals could get." The machine used an 8088 processor, a novelty in a commercial product, but a chip many people found interesting and suitable for a personal computer. It wasn't the premier chip available, but it did put the IBM PC a notch above any other machine then sold. The PC did impress Felsenstein — not technologically, but politically. He liked to see IBM admitting that it needed other people. The open bus structure and thorough, readable documentation said as much. "But the major surprise was that they were using chips from Earth and not from IBM. I thought, 'They're doing things our way.'"

In addition to operating systems and languages, IBM offered a number of applications programs for the PC that were sold separately. Surprisingly, IBM had developed none of them. Showing that it had learned from Apple, IBM offered the ubiquitous VisiCalc spreadsheet, the well-known series of business programs from Peachtree Software, and a word processor called EasyWriter from Information Unlimited Software (IUS).

The EasyWriter deal may have involved the ultimate in culture shock for the IBM people. They had designed their machine with non-IBM components. They had released to the general public the sort of information they had always kept secret. They had bought an operating system instead of writing it, had done and dealt with things that had always been utterly beyond IBM's pale. But they hadn't bargained for John Draper.

IBM had approached IUS about EasyWriter, and Larry Weiss of IUS contacted EasyWriter's author, John Draper, alias Captain Crunch, avowed enemy of bureaucracy and the king of the phone phreaks. Draper recalled, "Eaglebeak [Weiss] comes to me and he says, 'John, I got this deal that you're not going to believe, but I can't tell you anything about it.' And then we had this meeting at IUS. There were these people in pinstripes and me looking like me. This was the time that I realized we were dealing with IBM. I had to sign these things saying that I wasn't going to be discussing any technical information, I wasn't even supposed to disclose that I was dealing with IBM. They were coming out with a home computer and Eaglebeak said something to me about putting EasyWriter on it."

Draper had written EasyWriter out of frustration years before because the Apple then had no satisfactory word processor and he couldn't afford an S-100 system on which he could run Michael Shrayer's Electric Pencil. Draper liked Electric Pencil, the only word processor he'd seen, so he fashioned his own after it. Demonstrating it at the Fourth West Coast Computer Faire, he ran into Bill Baker, a transplanted Midwesterner who had started IUS, and Baker agreed to sell EasyWriter for him. And it had led to this, to Captain Crunch sitting down with IBM.

IBM gave IUS and Draper six months to convert EasyWriter to run on the PC, and Draper went right to work. "In order to keep from slipping and talking about IBM, we called it Project Commodore," Draper recalled. Soon, Baker was irritating Draper. "Baker comes down on me for not working 8 to 5 and that's bullshit. Look, man, I don't operate in that style. I operate in a creative environment. I don't go by the clock. I go by the way my mind works." Then IBM made changes in the hardware that Draper had to incorporate. The six months passed and the release program wasn't done. Draper found himself pressured to say that an earlier but completed version was adequate and that it could be released with the machine. With grave reservations he finally agreed, and IBM's machine was sold with Captain Crunch's word processor. IBM later offered free updates to the program.

A word processor was sober software, no matter who wrote it, but at the last minute IBM decided to add a computer game to its series of optional programs. Toward the end of the press release announcing the PC, the company declared, "*Microsoft Adventure* brings players into a fantasy world of caves and treasures." Corporate data processing managers around the country read the ad and thought, "This is IBM?"

The unveiling of the PC received wide play in the national press. It was by far the least expensive machine IBM had ever sold. IBM realized that the personal computer was a retail item that consumers were buying in retail computer stores and could not, therefore, be marketed by its sales force. The company again departed from tradition and arranged to sell its PC through the largest and most popular computer retail chain, the IMSAI spin-off ComputerLand. This was a much bigger departure for IBM than it had been for Xerox. IBM didn't stop there, but also announced plans to sell the PC in department stores just like any appliance.

Although the non-CP/M operating system took many by surprise, software companies quickly began writing programs for it. Hardware firms also developed products for the PC. Since PC sales started fast and increased steadily, these companies were easily convinced that PC-based products would find a market. In turn, the add-on products themselves spurred PC sales, since they increased the utility of the machine. IBM's open system decision was now paying dividends.

Apple Computer could not have been surprised by the IBM announcement, as it had predicted an IBM micro several years earlier. Steve Jobs claimed that Apple's only worry was that IBM might offer a machine with highly advanced technology. Like Felsenstein, he was relieved that IBM was using a nonproprietary processor and an accessible architecture. Apple responded publicly to the PC announcement by asserting that it would actually help Apple because IBM publicity would cause more people to buy personal computers.

Clearly the world's largest computer company had endorsed, in the PC, the personal computer as a viable commercial product. Although the industry had been founded by innovative hobbyists and small companies, only IBM could bring the product fully into the public eye. "Welcome IBM," Apple said in a full-page advertisement in the *Wall Street Journal*. "Welcome to the most exciting and important marketplace since the computer revolution began 35 years ago....We look forward to responsible competition in the massive effort to distribute this American technology to the world."

IBM's endorsement did increase demand for personal computers. Many businesses, small and large, had still balked at the idea of buying a personal computer. Many had seriously wondered why IBM wasn't doing it. Now the question vanished. The personal computer had arrived to stay. Between August and December, IBM shipped 13,000 PCs. Over the next two years, it would sell 40 times that number.

The early microcomputers had been designed in the absence of software. When CP/M and its overlayer of applications software became popular, hardware designers built machines that would run those programs. Similarly, the success of the IBM Personal Computer caused programmers to write an array of software for its operating system, MS-DOS. New hardware manufacturers sprang up to introduce computers that could run the same programs as the IBM PC. Many of these machines have been called IBM look-alikes or work-alikes. Some offered different capabilities than those of the IBM machine, such as portability, additional memory, or superior graphics, and many were less expensive than the PC. But all served to ratify the PC operating system. MS-DOS quickly became the standard operating system for 16-bit machines.

Even DEC acknowledged it. DEC finally entered the fray a year later with a dual-processor computer called the Rainbow that could run both 8-bit Z80 software under CP/M and 16-bit 8088 software under CP/M-86 or MS-DOS.

All the companies in the industry had to cope with the imposing presence of IBM. ComputerLand was dropping the smaller manufacturers for IBM, and even Apple found that it had to respond to IBM's incursion into the ComputerLand stores. Apple terminated its contract with ComputerLand central and started dealing directly with the outlets. It was the end of the beginning.

A shakeout that had been only foreshadowed in the failures of MITS, IMSAI, and Processor Technology began to loom real in the eyes of the pioneering companies, and with over 300 personal computer companies in existence, many hobbyist-originated companies began to wonder if they would still be in business two years hence. IBM had forced even the big companies now in the market to reappraise their situations.

Xerox, Don Massaro said, had carefully considered the possibility that IBM might produce a personal computer. "We did a worst-case scenario in getting approval for the [Xerox 820] program. We said, 'What could IBM do? How could we not be successful in this marketplace?' The scenario was that IBM would enter with a product that would make ours technically obsolete, they would sell it through dealers, and it would have an open operating system." It seemed an unlikely prospect. "You see, IBM had *never* done that, had never sold through dealers, and had certainly never had an open operating system. I thought IBM would have their own proprietary operating system for which they would write their own software, and that they would sell through their own stores." Instead, Xerox's worst fear came to life in painful detail, and "the whole world ran off in that direction. IBM just killed everybody."

Not everybody. But the circle of attention had narrowed. There were now two personal computer companies that everyone was watching: Apple and an IBM nobody knew, an IBM that had, in John Draper's words, "discovered the Woz Principle" of the open system.

The presence of IBM and the other big companies shook the industry to its hobbyist roots. Tandy, with its own distribution channels, was only modestly affected. Commodore was concentrating on European sales and sales of low-cost home computers.

The companies that had pioneered the personal computer began dropping out of the picture. The shakeout began in earnest. The resurrected IMSAI was one of the first to go. Todd Fisher and Nancy Freitas supplied the IMSAI computer that figured prominently in the popular movie *War Games*, and it was effectively the company's last act. Shortly thereafter, Fisher and Freitas gave the pioneering microcomputer company a decent burial.

By late 1983, even some of the most successful of the personal computer and software companies to spring up out of the hobbyist movement were hurt. North Star, Vector Graphic, and Cromemco all felt the pinch. There were massive layoffs, and some companies turned to offshore manufacturing to stop up leaking profits. Chuck Peddle, who had been responsible for the PET computer and had been active throughout the industry, in semiconductor design at MOS Technologies and in computers at Commodore and briefly at Apple, was now running his own company, Victor, with a computer similar to IBM's. In the face of the IBM challenge, Victor soon had to cut back its work force severely in the face of softening sales. George Morrow's company considered a stock offering, but then withdrew the idea in response to IBM's growing influence in the market.

On September 13, 1983, Osborne Computer Corporation declared bankruptcy amid a mountain of debt accumulated trying to catch up with Apple and IBM. Of all the company failures in the history of the personal computer industry, none was more thoroughly analyzed. OCC had flown high and fast, and its fall was startling. At the height of their success, Osborne executives appeared on the television program *60 Minutes*, predicting that they would soon be millionaires. They were, on paper, but the company's financial controls were so lax that the figures were meaningless. The media coverage of the company's failure was intense, but the analyses were conflicting. Certainly there were problems with the hardware, but most companies have them, and Osborne dealt with them. Osborne executives made serious mistakes in the timing of product announcements. But what seems clear is that the company grew so fast in its attempt to be one of the three major companies that Adam Osborne had predicted would dominate personal computing in a year or so that its managers were unable to control it. As industry analyst John Dvorak put it, "The company grew from zilch to $100 million in less than two years. Who do you hire who has experience with growth like that? Nobody exists." Osborne was just too successful.

Others fell under IBM's shadow. Small software companies like EduWare and Lightning Software allowed themselves to be bought by larger ones, and all software companies learned to think of first doing "the IBM version" of any new software product. Even major corporations adjusted their behavior. Atari and Texas Instruments swallowed millions in losses in their attempts to win their way into the personal computer market through low-cost home machines. Atari suffered deep wounds. And although TI had more of its low-cost TI-99/4 computers in homes than almost any other computer, it announced in the fall of 1983 that it was cutting its losses and getting out of personal computer manufacturing.

IBM's entry also affected the magazines, shows, and stores. David Bunnell, who had gone from MITS to start *Personal Computing* magazine, responded to IBM's arrival by coming out with a thick magazine directed at users of the IBM machine. Soon major publishers were fighting over Bunnell's magazine. Wayne Green, having built *Kilobaud* into an empire of computer magazines by 1983, sold the lot to an East Coast conglomerate. Art Salsberg and Les Solomon rode out *Popular Electronics*'s transformation into *Computers and Electronics*. Jim Warren started an IBM PC Faire in late 1983 and then sold his show-sponsoring company Computer Faire to publishing house Prentice-Hall, claiming that the business was too big for him to manage. ComputerLand and the independent computer stores found themselves competing with Sears and Macy's as IBM opened new channels of distribution for personal computers.

Late in 1983 IBM announced its second personal computer. Dubbed the PCjr, the machine offered little technological innovation. Perhaps to prevent business users from buying the new and less expensive machine in place of the PC, IBM equipped the PCjr with a "chicklet" keyboard, a style of keyboard unsuited to serious, prolonged use. Despite the PCjr's unimpressive technological design, by announcing a second personal computer, IBM demonstrated that it recognized a broad, largely untapped market for personal computers. IBM intended to be a dominant force in that market.

Apple, in preparation for its inevitable head-to-toe battle with IBM, made several significant moves. In 1983, the firm hired a new president, former Pepsi Cola executive John Sculley, to manage its underdog campaign against IBM. In January 1984, Apple introduced its Macintosh computer.

The Macintosh had been under development for years. Jef Raskin, who had left his editorial position with the hobbyist magazine *Dr. Dobb's* in 1977 to head Apple's documentation team, first toyed with the notion of a special-purpose computer that would employ some technological tricks Steve Wozniak had in mind. He had named the machine Macintosh, after a variety of apple.

In time, Steve Jobs took an active hand in directing the Macintosh development, and turned the project into one of squeezing into a widely-affordable computer all the technological innovations that had impressed him during his visit to Xerox PARC. Jobs put together a small team of dedicated programmers, designers, and writers to produce the machine. Randy Wigginton set to work on the machine's word processor, and Chris Espinosa, who had written the "red book" that explained the Apple II, took over the documentation effort. Bill Atkinson, who had gone to PARC with Jobs, worked on programs to exploit the graphics capabilities of the machine, and new designers and programmers were brought on and encouraged to do state-of-the-art work.

IBM had chosen to emphasize its name — the best-known three letters in the computer industry. Apple decided to provide state-of-the-market technology. The Macintosh immediately received accolades for its impressive design — highly developed software technology that used a mouse interface and a powerful 32-bit microprocessor in a lightweight, portable package.

Nearly three years after his plane crash, Apple co-founder Steve Wozniak returned to Apple to work as an engineer. He found an atmosphere that had changed significantly since he had left. Security was tighter, channels of communication were more formal, and his former garage-shop buddy had become one of the most famous, most successful, and richest executives in the country. Everyone wore shoes. Apple had become a big company. Woz, ever loyal to the Apple II users, set to work devising a circuit board that would give existing Apple IIs many of the capabilities of the new Lisa and Macintosh machines.

Some of the architects of the personal computer revolution dropped out of the action, like Ed Roberts who took his MITS profits and bought a farm and began studying medicine. Many others stayed in the thick of things. Bill Gates and Paul Allen's Microsoft had developed the system software for IBM's machines, and was one of the first companies to offer software for the Macintosh. Gary Kildall's Digital Research remained an important software company, while Kildall himself went into the back room and wrote a new programming language (LOGO) he thought his kids would enjoy. Adam Osborne contemplated starting a software publishing company. Lee Felsenstein continued work with the Community Memory project, never far from his and the industry's computer-power-to-the-people roots.

Inevitably the money dealers had come to where the money was, and the financial success of the industry rooted in hobbydom severed the industry from its roots. But the computer-power-to-the-people spirit Lee Felsenstein and others had sought to foster had by no means disappeared. Even staunchly conservative IBM had bent to it in adopting an open architecture and an open operating system. IBM's corporate policy in the 1950s and 1960s had often been to lease computers and to discourage sales. For the computers made then, this was appropriate. With proprietary architectures and software, the power of the machines really belonged not to the people who used them, but to the companies that had built them.

The personal computer and all the growing power it harnessed belonged to the people.

&

I was sitting like a spider in the middle of a web. This magazine was the only outlet these guys had. There was nothing else. And I was crazy enough to talk to them.

Les Solomon

I knew the Altair was an exciting project and it really turned me on. But it was much more a labor of love.

Ed Roberts

We were called computer nerds. Anyone who spends their life on a computer is pretty unusual.

Bill Gates

We didn't do three years of research and come up with this concept. What we did was follow our own instincts and construct a computer that was what we wanted.

Steve Jobs

Starting a company didn't mean that much to me. I can design computers. I know I can.

Steve Wozniak

You were dealing with entrepreneurs mostly. Egos, a lot of egos.

Ed Faber

Apple legitimized the product. IBM has consolidated the legitimization.

George Morrow

IBM came into the micro industry and changed the rules entirely. It's the giant and the dwarfs all over again.

Adam Osborne

A year was a lifetime in those days.

Lee Felsenstein

Epilogue

Index